CENTRAL MISSOURI AT WAR: 1861-1975

JEREMY P. AMICK

YorkshirePublishing
www.yorkshirepublishing.com
Write Now.

ISBN: 978-1-950034-23-9
Central Missouri at War: 1861-1975
Copyright © Jeremy P. Ämick

Yorkshire Publishing
4613 E. 91st St,
Tulsa, OK 74137
www.YorkshirePublishing.com
918.394.2665

Contents

Acknowledgements

This book would not have come to fruition without the scores of veterans who have been willing to share with me their humble accounts of military service, ensuring their legacy is perpetuated through firsthand recollection. First, I would like to thank Emily Crawford for providing the upper photo on the cover of the book picturing Marcellus Markway (left), and his friend Carl DeBroeck, when the two soldiers met overseas during World War II. The lower photo on the cover of the book was provided by Veterans of Foreign Wars Post 1003 and features the parade held in Jefferson City on October 7, 1919 as a homecoming for returning World War I veterans. I would also be remiss if I failed to acknowledge the friends and families of many of the deceased veterans featured in this book. Your dedication has preserved a treasure trove of records and photographs of scores of Central Missouri's military members who are no longer with us. You have helped ensure the travesty of forgotten sacrifice never becomes a reality in our community through your efforts to memorialize our fallen and deceased. These actions serve as an inspiration to later generations who choose to continue to fight for our freedoms by donning the uniform of our nation's armed forces. The willingness to volunteer of oneself is what has made our country the greatest and most powerful in our world's history and it is our job to ensure that the stories of sacrifice buried beneath our feet are never silenced.

Dedication

As always, I would like to thank my wife, Tina, who is humbled by the service and sacrifices of all our nation's veterans and has been supportive and understanding of the time I have invested in this endeavor. Thank you, my eternal love.

Central Missouri at War

1861-1975

Central Missouri has always been a region of our nation that has never wavered in its support of our military members and veterans. Since 2010, I have been provided the honor of visiting with scores of veterans throughout the region for newspaper articles and military history compilations, documenting, in writing, first-hand accounts of the impact of their military service. Additionally, it has been quite an inspiring and eye-opening experience to meet the families of our deceased veterans who simply wish to gain insight into the military service performed by a loved one who is no longer with us, seeking to ensure their stories are never diminished by the passage of years.

Sometimes, the story unfolds through the memories and reflections of a sibling or descendant of a veteran who was killed in action in a combat zone. For this person, having the opportunity to gather a little bit of information about the circumstances surrounding the death of a loved one brings a bit of closure while also reaffirming their appreciation for the ultimate sacrifice they made on behalf of their country. Other times, it has been the son or daughter of a World War II veteran, who grew up never hearing any details of their parent's military experiences. The children then wish to discover where their parent may have trained or what overseas challenges they faced during a combat deployment. The most in-depth of these interviews, of course, have been with veterans still among us. Those who are able to share in great detail a number of accounts regarding their journey from childhood to military uniform.

Why did you choose to serve? Were you drafted or did you instead choose to enlist? Why did you choose a specific branch of service over another? For what reasons would you recommend military service to the younger generation? These are all questions that I have been known to ask during these interviews and I enjoy hearing the responses.

This extensive compilation of veterans' stories signifies a collection of interviews and articles about veterans and military events from Central Missouri spanning the Civil War to the Cold War. Although it represents several years of interviews and research, I would never make the auspicious claim that this work reflects the unique experiences of all veterans from throughout the region. Instead, I believe it serves as a snapshot of the scores of venerable individuals who have donned a uniform of our nation's armed forces. My wish is that this book not only helps preserve at least a morsel of the legacy of those who have spent a portion of their lives in military service, but that you will enjoy reading these accounts as much as I have enjoyed writing them.

It is also my wish that these stories might serve as a challenge to the reader to speak with veterans, wherever you may encounter them, acknowledging those who have either been drafted or volunteered to perform a service that too many Americans are either unwilling or unable to perform. They all have stories that deserve to be shared and passed down through generations in to ensure that subsequent generations might catch a glimpse into the payment of blood, toil and tears that others have made on their behalf, leading to a personal understanding as to what drove these individuals into such an honorable profession as the military.

These stories represent a living history that continues to be shaped—the stories of our human experience. They are the stories of America, and more specifically, the stories of Central Missouri. Ladies and gentlemen, it is my sublime pleasure to introduce you to some of the heroes among us.

Jeremy P. Ämick
Russellville, Missouri
May 2019

CHAPTER 1

CIVIL WAR & SPANISH-AMERICAN WAR

Wyatt Zimmerman

California

As noted in the book *Germans in the Civil War,*[1] German Americans were one of the largest immigrant groups to serve during the period of the Civil War, accounting "for about one-tenth of the Union army, about 200,000 of some 2 million troops." In the years from 1850 to 1860, the authors note that the United States experienced an "influx of over a million Germans…"

Many of these men pulled up their well-established roots to flee the turmoil and unrest fomenting in Europe, which would eventually lead to the establishment of a German nation, seeking to deliver the promise of a better life for their families in America. Few could ever realize, however, that even greater strife awaited them in the United States when the Civil War broke out in 1861. Now, several decades following the death of one of these immigrants turned Union soldier, a descendant wishes to preserve the memory of her departed relative's service by adorning his final resting spot with a military headstone.

"Wyatt Zimmerman was one of my great-great-grandfathers," said Delores "Dee" Wolfe of Holden, Missouri. "He was buried in Strickfadden Cemetery[2] (north of the mid-Missouri community of

---

[1] Kamphoefner & Helbich, *Germans in the Civil War: The Letters They Wrote Home*, xi.

[2] The Strickfadden Cemetery is located in Cooper County, Missouri, near the Moniteau County line. According to the Cooper County Genealogical Society website, he earliest recorded burial is 1837 with a total of ninety-seven burials in the cemetery. Cooper County Genealogical Society, http://cooper.mogenweb.org/.

California, Missouri) and all that identified his gravesite was a plain mortar block [without any lettering]," she added.

During the last several decades, Wolfe's interest in history has matured due to her genealogical research, helping to guide her discovery of Zimmerman's military background and providing her with the necessary credentials to join an organization dedicated to preserving Civil War history.

"Because of my relation [to Zimmerman], I was able to join the Daughters of Union Veterans of the Civil War [DUVCW]," Wolfe said.

During her research, Wolfe discovered that Zimmerman—who was born in Mombach, Germany in 1824—immigrated to the United States with his parents and siblings in 1840. He eventually became a citizen in Boonville, Missouri, on July 11, 1856 and went on to serve as a private in Company F of the 52nd Regiment of the Enrolled Missouri Militia.[3] Following his discharge in 1863, the veteran engaged in farming near California, Missouri, until his passing in 1874 at the age of fifty, leaving behind a wife and seven children.

In researching Zimmerman's background while preparing her application for membership in the DUVCW, Wolfe visited Strickfadden Cemetery, at which point she discovered the veteran's poorly-marked gravesite.

"I was able to use a map of the cemetery layout to identify his grave," Wolfe said, and with a hint of melancholy, added, "that's when I discovered the simple, unmarked block was the only tribute to his life."

When she returned home, Wolfe—who has in the past acquired military memorial markers for the graves of her father and uncles—researched some of her previous paperwork from the Department of Veterans Affairs and found that Private Zimmerman might also be eligible for such an enduring legacy.

---

[3] The Enrolled Missouri Militia was similar to the Home Guard in that they were organized in their local communities and ordered into service when needed in their local areas. They often had to provide their own clothing, arms and ammunition.

"I applied for a Civil War marker and it was approved," she beamed.

During a ceremony in 2015—attended by several dozen community members, descendants of Zimmerman and organizations such as the Daughters of 1812, Sons of Union Veterans of the Civil War and the DUVCW—Zimmerman's new headstone was unveiled, 141 years after the Union veteran was laid to rest.

"In performing my research on [Zimmerman] and honoring him with this marker, it has really generated a lot of interest among my family as to our history," Wolfe said. "It has also helped connect me with distant cousins and other relatives that I have never had contact with before."

Most importantly, Wolfe stressed, is not only the opportunity to share with others information about the availability of military markers for deceased veterans, but being able to return a favor to a relative she never met in person and whom she has only come to know through hours of investigation.

"I can't begin to imagine the rough life he had to live—leaving the hardships of Germany only to come into the turmoil of the Civil War," she said. "It's simply unimaginable." She added: "In a sense, it was as if I felt getting his memorial marker was something that I had to do, because of our relationship... my connection to him. I was able to join the DUVCW because of him and this was something that I felt I could do for him out of respect and appreciation for his service."

For more information regarding the eligibility for headstones, markers or medallions through the Department of Veterans Affairs, please visit the National Cemetery Administration website at http://www.cem.va.gov/cem/index.asp. *(Photograph courtesy of Delores Wolfe)*

Prairie Grove Cemetery

Tipton

Peacefully situated on a small wooded lot between the Tipton Correctional Center and a gravel road on the northern end of the community of Tipton, Missouri, the Prairie Grove Cemetery draws little notice. But within the confines of this hallowed piece of ground are buried the stories of former slaves who donned the uniforms of Union soldiers during the Civil War and went on to fight for freedoms they had themselves been denied. The Moniteau County Historical Society notes that the cemetery was formerly listed as the Tipton Colored Cemetery in the *Moniteau County Cemetery Book*,[4] and, of the estimated two hundred fifty burials that have taken place, many of the graves remain unmarked.

"I was the caretaker there for several years," said James Shipley, a lifelong resident of Tipton. "Years ago, me and my brother worked to clear off a bunch of trees and brush that had basically taken over most of the cemetery."

Of the various headstones still standing—some marked and others whose lettering time has worn away—one may notice the many near-faded inscriptions of a name and the "U.S.C.I." designation, representing the Civil War service in the United States Colored Infantry of the person buried beneath. According to the 2000 edi-

---

[4] The *Moniteau County Cemetery Book* is a project that continues to be updated through the voluntary efforts of members of the Moniteau County Historical Society. According to the society's website, there are 179 known cemeteries in Moniteau County and more than 28, 300 recorded burials. For more information, visit www.moniteau.net.

tion of the book *Moniteau County Missouri History*,[5] at the beginning of the Civil War in 1861, of the county's "population of 9,370 there were 720 slaves and 2 Freedmen." The lives of many of these Missouri slaves were forever changed in mid-November 1863 when General John M. Scholfield, commander of the Union forces of the Department of Missouri, issued General Order 135.

The order provided the authorization for the "immediate enlistment of slaves, regardless of owners' loyalty or consent (with promise of compensation to loyal masters)," as written in the book *Freedom: A Documentary History of Emancipation, 1861-1867*[6]. Many of these slaves were then placed in regiments of the colored infantry and sent to fight a war often far from their Mid-Missouri homes. The enduring impact of this military recruiting initiative is still evident through the names of the soldiers interred in Prairie Grove Cemetery, such as that of Samuel Craig, listed as having served with Company B, 68th U.S.C.I.

In viewing the *Descriptive Recruitment Lists of Volunteers for the United States Colored Troops for the State of Missouri, 1863-1865*, we discover that his former master, Joseph Craig, signed his twenty-six-year-old slave into Union service at Tipton on February 26, 1864. Details of his military experience gain clarity through his muster roll (accessible through the Missouri State Archives), which notes he was sent to St. Louis and entered service on March 8, 1864 at Benton Barracks[7]—a former military encampment where soldiers battled the deadly enemy of diseases such as small pox, measles and meningitis.

Initially designated the 4th Missouri Colored Infantry, Craig's regiment became the 68th U.S.C.I. on March 11, 1864, thus commencing a history of service that has been well-chronicled by historians. Beginning with several months in defense of Memphis, Tennessee, and moving forth to the siege and capture of Fort Blakely, Alabama, in the spring of 1865. The battle-hardened soldiers of the regiment spent the latter part of their enlistment at various points in

---

[5] Moniteau County Missouri History (2000), *African-American History in Moniteau County*, 148.

[6] Berlin, Reidy & Rowland, *Freedom*, 188.

[7] There is no longer any evidence of Benton Barracks' existence. However, it was located on the site of the present Fairground Park in St. Louis.

Texas, unit mustering out of the service at Camp Parapet in Louisiana on February 5, 1866.

Records pertaining to Craig's life after the war are rather scant, but census records indicate that the veteran chose to remain in the Tipton area and went on to enjoy life as a free man—later marrying, raising several children and working as a laborer.

In 1916, the Industrial Home for Negro Girls was opened adjacent to the cemetery on the site of what has since become the Tipton Correctional Center. During its forty years of operation, Shipley noted, many of the girls who died while at the home were buried in unmarked graves in the northeast corner of the cemetery.

"When my brother and I started taking care of the cemetery, that was one of the areas that was all grown over with brush and weeds," said Shipley, discussing where the young girls are buried. "I don't recall there ever being any stones in that section (to mark the graves)," he added.

Though many unadorned granite markers mark the final resting spot of other black Civil War veterans such as George Washington of the 65th U.S.C.I.—one of the regiments that raised the funds to establish what is Lincoln University—steps have been taken in recent years to ensure the preservation of the memory of these soldiers' sacrifices.

"Many years ago, Prairie Grove (Baptist) Church took over the cemetery," said Shipley, describing a local congregation that was founded by former slaves after the Civil War. "The congregation wanted to be sure that it was in the church's name so that there would always be someone around to take care of it."

Shipley, who served as a mechanic with the famed Tuskegee Airmen during WWII, added, "I don't know much about the Civil War veterans that are buried in this cemetery because they have all been gone for such a long time."

He added, "But I do think it's important that cemeteries like this are taken care of because they are a part of the community's history and these veterans—regardless of their color—are men who wore the uniform and fought for their country...and that should never be forgotten." (*Photograph courtesy of Jeremy P. Amick*)

Charles Gustav Loesch

Jefferson City

With an estimated 2.75 million soldiers fighting in the Civil War, there was little that could have distinguished Jefferson City, Missouri, veteran Charles Gustav "Gus" Loesch from his brothers in arms. However, his mere endurance to nearly one hundred and one years of age would ensure that his story of service in the Union Army would be preserved for generations to come.

A first-generation American, Loesch's father, Gustav Wilhelm, immigrated to the United States in 1838 after having served six years in a cavalry regiment of the German military under Prince John VIII. He later chose to lay down roots in Cole County, Missouri, and embarked upon a career as a farmer.

"Gustav was especially anxious (to immigrate) as he did not wish to be called into the military services again," wrote the late Alvina Erhardt Gottschamer in the privately published book *The Loesch Family in America: 1838-1910*. As troubles continued to develop in their home country, the recently married Gustav Wilhelm also sought a better life in America for his children yet to be born.

Born March 26, 1843, Charles "Gus" Loesch was raised on a farm south of Jefferson City near the Zion community and soon followed in the military tradition of his father. Family records show he became a member of the Union Army on August 12, 1862, while the March 26, 1933 edition of the *Daily Capital News* noted he "joined up under Major W.H. Lusk, also a Jefferson City man."

In later years, as Loesch reached the age of ninety years and beyond, several Mid-Missouri newspapers began to chronicle his military service as one of the few, if only, surviving veterans of the Civil War in the community.

His military career began with training in St. Louis and assignment to Company G, 10th Missouri Cavalry under the command of Captain Henry G. Bruns of Jefferson City. (Bruns was later wounded during the Battle of Iuka, Mississippi, and died from his injuries on July 9, 1863, thus earning him the unfortunate distinction as being the first Jefferson City resident killed in the war.) Private Loesch remained with the regiment and preceded General William T. Sherman in his drive through the South during the war, participating in several major campaigns that he modestly described in the March 21, 1943 edition of *Jefferson City Post-Tribune* as, "We just started things and let the infantry finish them up."

"[On] February 26, 1864, Rebels captured Gus in Canton, Mississippi, and imprisoned him in Andersonville, Georgia,[8]" wrote Gottschamer, describing the service of her great uncle. "He was released one year, to the day, later, February 26, 1965, and admitted to Hospital Division One in Maryland," she added.

Mustered out of the service on June 24, 1865, Loesch married Sophia Kingery three years later and the couple went on to raise six children while living on a farm near the rural Cole County community of Hickory Hill. On his 90th birthday on March 26, 1933, the *Daily Capital News* printed an interview with Loesch in which he described walking as his "life and health." In the same article, he also noted that in the previous month he had traveled more than one

---

[8] James Madison Page, who served as a second lieutenant with Company A, Sixth Michigan Cavalry, was confined at Andersonville Prison during the Civil war, explained that many of his fellow Union soldiers wrote books teeming "with accounts of the brutality, insults and suffering heaped upon them by rebel officers and guards, seemingly for cruelty's sake." However, Page goes on to note that he "cannot recall a solitary instance, during the fourteen months that I was a prisoner of being insulted, browbeaten, robbed, or maltreated in any manner by a Confederate officer or soldier." Page and Haley, The *True Story of Andersonville Prison*, 56. Regardless of any disparate accounts, the National Park Service notes that 45,000 Union soldiers were imprisoned at Andersonville and nearly 13,000 died during their captivity. National Park Service, *Andersonville*, www.nps.gov.

hundred and thirty-seven miles by foot and that he "would pine away in a week" if he were unable to continue with his beloved exercise.

The Civil War veteran remained a prominent fixture in Cole County for many years following his ninetieth birthday, participating in Memorial Day services at the Jefferson City National Cemetery and frequently a distinguished guest at local events in the community. During a meeting of the Brazito Republicans in the summer of 1940, when Loesch was ninety-seven years old, he told candidate Forrest Donnell that if he were elected as the state's governor in the upcoming election, he wished to be present for his inauguration. Early the next year, Governor Donnell followed through on his promise by reserving a special spot for the Civil War veteran in his inaugural parade.

Weeks later, Loesch's family held a birthday party for the ninety-eight-year-old veteran near the community of Brazito with three hundred guests in attendance, including the new governor. *The Sedalia Democrat* reported on November 3, 1942, that the ninety-nine-year-old Loesch, "perhaps Missouri's oldest voter," had traveled "to the polls at nearby Brazito early this morning to keep intact his record of voting in every election since he cast his first ballot for U.S. Grant for President in 1868."

The veteran clarified his voting history by explaining that he "would have voted for Lincoln when he ran for re-election, but I was in a Confederate war prison at the time."

With all the accolades and notoriety afforded a local hero, Loesch lived to witness more than eight hundred persons in attendance at his one hundredth birthday party held in Brazito on March 29, 1943. Sadly, on March 22, 1944, just four days before his one hundredth and first birthday, the veteran passed away, two weeks following the death of his son-in-law, Ira Mulvaney.

Maintaining a vivid recollection of the man she enjoyed visiting as a young girl, Loesch's great niece stated, "While my grandmother was still living (Loesch's sister), she would take me to go and visit Uncle Gus," recalled Gottschamer. "I can remember, as a little girl, attending his one hundredth birthday party when the governor came." Softly, she added, "He was always such a gentle person who never got too worked up about anything…which I always attributed to everything he saw and experienced during the war." *(Photograph courtesy of Phyllis Erhart)*

Massacre on Curtman Island

Henley and Olean

Prior to Confederate General Sterling Price's raid of Missouri during the fall of 1864, many parts of the state experienced a "huge Southern guerilla and Confederate recruiting effort behind Union lines...," wrote Bruce Nichols in his book *Guerilla Warfare in Civil War Missouri, Volume III, January – August 1864*[9]. These preparations resulted in small, yet often bloody, engagements that impacted many of our local communities and resulted in the deaths of scores of citizens, regardless of their loyalties to either the North or South. Evidence of the consequences of the guerilla activities that permeated the countryside can be found in Allen Cemetery near Olean, Missouri, where lies several Union soldiers who were ambushed by a ruthless, self-proclaimed Confederate general.

"Using stealth and cunning, (General) Crabtree could terrorize parts of Cole and Miller Counties with impunity," wrote Lohman resident Don Buchta in his self-published book *Guerilla Terrorism Along the Osage*. He continued, "The best efforts of the local militias and authorities to seize him were in vain. His hit and run tactics were legendary and his knowledge of the terrain in the Teal Bottoms enabled him to frustrate the best efforts to capture him."

Buchta noted that little is known of the background of Crabtree and only speculation exists as to his actual first name. However, his research and past interviews with a now-deceased historian from the

---

[9] Nichols, *Guerilla Warfare in Civil War Missouri,*

Miller County community of Tuscumbia have led Buchta to believe the "general" may have been from the West Plains area.

"Clyde Jenkins did a lot of research on the history of Miller County and was essentially the local expert on Crabtree and his activities," recalled Buchta. "I went down and met with him before he passed away (in 1997) and his research indicated that Crabtree was sent up to Central Missouri to acquire as many horses as he could for the Southern cause."

A Navy veteran of World War II, former state representative, county commissioner and clerk for Miller County, Jenkins' self-published in 1971 the book *Judge Jenkins' History of Miller County*, in which he described one guerrilla attack that shocked the local population. As Jenkins explained, Crabtree and his men began their raids in Cole County and the surrounding areas as early as the fall of 1861, when he "ordered out in every direction small squads of men to hit every place opposed to the South, appropriating provisions..."

In response to the guerilla general's unyielding depredations, an order was issued by the Military District of Central Missouri in July 1864 to execute a captured associate of Crabtree by the name John P. Wilcox. This execution, records note, was carried out in Jefferson City on August 12, 1864. Outraged by the murder of one of his associates, Crabtree sought revenge for the death by stepping up his attacks while at the same time being pursued by Captain Thomas Babcoke, commander of a company of Union soldiers enlisted from the Mt. Pleasant area in Miller County.

Lt. John P. Starling, a Miller County resident enrolled in Capt. Babcoke's company on August 13, 1864 and entered into active service ten days later. However, Starling and the handful of men he commanded soon became unexpected recipients of Crabtree's vengeance. On August 30, 1864, "16 men under (the command of) First Lieutenant John Starling, were on Curtman Island, in the Osage River, scouting the dense willow thickets on information that Crabtree was hiding there," wrote Jenkins. He continued, "At the noon hour, the men stacked their arms, to rest and enjoy their provisions, but this was a fatal mistake. Suddenly, without any warning, on all sides, the Militiamen were surrounded by Crabtree's men. At gunpoint, their stacked firearms were taken away."

Jenkins goes on to explain that the sixteen prisoners were then lined up and, after being reviewed by Crabtreee, seven were pulled from the group and shot by a firing squad. Those not executed were given warnings against pursuing Crabtree and his men.

"The bodies of six of the men shot on Curtman Island were taken to Allen Cemetery (near Olean) for burial," said Don Buchta. "In my research, I found that one of the men shot was not instantly killed and crawled off into the brush. He later died and after being found by locals, was buried somewhere in the vicinity of Curtman Island, I believe."

Crabtree's reign of terror soon came to a close "some months later," when, according to the book "The Heritage of St. Thomas Community – City – Parish," by Daniel Schmidt, the general was shot by St. Thomas resident Adolph Loethen while being pursued for raiding farms in the southern Cole County area. Though shot, Crabtree was able to evade his captors but later died from his wound and was secretly buried by his men. Herman Scheuler, another resident of St. Thomas who accompanied Loethen in pursuit of Crabtree, was reportedly able to locate the bushwhacker's grave and found him buried in the wedding suit that Crabtree had stolen from him days earlier.

"Crabtree killed more people, burned more buildings, stole and destroyed more property, than any man in Cole, Miller, and Osage County before or since the Civil War," Schmidt noted.

Decades later, Allen Cemetery continues to serve as a poignant reminder of the atrocities that unfolded in our own backyard during the Civil War. It is a story that contains all the ingredients of a blockbuster Hollywood production—theft, pursuit, vengeance, murder—yet has been essentially erased from the collective memory of our communities.

This is one of hundreds of fascinating stories lying in wait in the countless cemeteries scattered across Mid-Missouri—tales waiting to be shared with those simply willing to take a moment to pause and listen to the soft whispers of history from beneath the faded lettering on a worn tombstone. (*Photographs courtesy of Jeremy P. Ämick*)

The Battle of Cole Camp

Cole Camp

In years past, admits Cole Camp, Missouri, area historian Jeffrey Lutjen, he was not one to express an avid interest in history. In more recent years, as he has gained in both age and experience, he developed an appreciation for the preservation of local history—specifically that related to a Civil War battle that occurred near the community of Cole Camp, which has since inspired him to honor the memory of the first area casualty of the war.

"John Tyree is really an interesting character in our local Civil War story and quite possibly could have saved many lives of the Home Guards if they had only listened to his warning," said Lutjen.

Online geneaology records indicate that John Claiborne Tyree was born in Virginia in 1795, married in 1821 and moved to the Cole Camp area sometime in the 1830s. He was reputed to have been a fairly successful farmer and a prominent member of the community. Though he owned slaves at the outbreak of the Civil War in 1861, Tyree was considered an ardent unionist.

"As the story goes, Tyree traveled to Warsaw on June 18, 1861," said Lutjen. "While he was there, he overheard some of the Confederates discussing plans to attack the German Home Guard unit at Cole Camp the next day." (They were referred to as "German" Home Guard since Cole Camp was at the time largely populated by German immigrants.) Lutjen continued, "Tyree then returned home later that evening and traveled to a barn where the German Home Guard was staying and tried to warn their commander, Captain (Abel) Cook, about the planned attack. At the time, Tyree was 66 years old and I don't know if it was his age or what the reason was, but they didn't listen to his warning and made no preparations whatsoever."

As Lutjen went on to explain, Tyree was making his way back to his home a few miles west of Cole Camp when he encountered member of the Missouri State Guard from Warsaw making their approach in the late evening. After they stopped Tyree, a lantern was brought forth to illuminate his face, at which time a couple of the Confederates recognized him as having been in Warsaw earlier that day.

"He was declared a spy, they tied him to a tree and shot him right there," Lutjen flatly noted.

The Missouri State Guard continued east along the Butterfield Overland Mail Route—a stagecoach line— eventually reaching the site a couple of miles beyond Cole Camp where a "half-organized regiment of unionists, under Capt. Cook, was asleep in two barns, with no pickets out save northward…" wrote Horace Greeley in *The American Conflict: A History of the Great Rebellion in the United States of America*. The author went on to explain that the Unionists (Home Guard) were surprised by the Missouri State Guard force "and utterly routed—being unable to offer any serious resistance." Greeley further noted, "Capt. Cook and a portion of his followers barely escaped with their lives." [10]

Lutjen, in researching the consequences of the Home Guard's refusal to heed Tyree's warnings, has concluded that the ultimate reason for failure rests on the shoulders of the of the leadership of the Union force.

"From the first of June until the battle, Captain Cook did nothing to discipline and train the troops in combat techniques of the day," he wrote in his self-published 2012 publication, *Trail of the Cole Camp German Home Guard Units*. He further wrote, "Discipline was non-existent and alcohol was allowed in the camp. If he would have been any kind of commander at all, he would have put a stop to this…," adding that his actions (and failures) represented "a total lack of leadership from the high command."

---

[10] Greeley, *The American Conflict*, 575.

Some historians claim that the German Home Guard suffered around 36 casualties while other estimates place this number as high as 200. The Union Cemetery west of Cole Camp contains plaques denoting the burial of 180 Union soldiers along two trenches. The nearby Monsees Cemetery contains a plaque denoting the mass burial of seventeen Home Guard members.

"I would like to someday see if we can get (ground penetrating) radar to go over those trenches to see if there are actually that many people buried at Union," said Lutjen, "because all of the records I can find only list 36 Union casualties from the Battle of Cole Camp. I believe the bodies in Union Cemetery might be from a later (Civil War) battle."

In recent years, Lutjen has grown to embrace the rich history of the Cole Camp community and devoted his efforts to researching local Civil War engagements. However, it was seeing the shabby condition of a local cemetery that has recently inspired him to be more ardent in preserving local history.

"When I first saw the Tyree Cemetery several years ago, the wooden fence had fallen down around it and grazing cattle had knocked over the headstones," said Lutjen. "That's when I decided that it was time to help properly memorialize the man who became our first local casualty of the war." He added, "Through help in the community, the fence has been replaced and the tombstones repaired and we are dedicating a plaque to John Tyree's memory that will be affixed to the gate of the cemetery." Pausing, he concluded, "With the age of the graves, I knew there was probably none of his family still around to care for the cemetery but I see it as our way to honor his memory and the fact that he gave his life to try and warn the community during the Civil War."

Colonel Thomas A. Johnston

Boonville

Born on a small farm south of Boonville on November 13, 1848, Thomas Alexander Johnston was for several decades associated with one of the premier military schools in the United States. During his tenure, he was both a role model and inspiration for many young cadets, one of whom would become a famous humorist and actor.

When only sixteen years old, Johnston enlisted with the Confederate forces during the Civil War, serving alongside both his father and brother. During his nine months of service as a private with the army of General Sterling Price, he participated in expeditions in Arkansas, Kansas and Missouri. Following the surrender of the Confederate forces at Shreveport, Louisiana, in June 1865, he returned to his studies at a small Cooper County academy before enrolling at Kemper Military School in 1867, from where he graduated in 1871.

As noted in the *Sedalia Weekly Democrat* on February 9, 1934, Johnston went on to attend "the University of Missouri, where he studied the classics, Latin and Greek, and later served as an assistant instructor of Latin there." The article goes on to report that the former Confederate cavalryman was "valedictorian of his university graduating class" and returned to Boonville to join the faculty of the Kemper Military School, where he was employed "as a teacher of the classics and mathematics" for nine years.

Founded in 1844, by Frederick T. Kemper, the Kemper Military School was once the oldest military school west of the Mississippi. The session catalog for Kemper's 1923-1924 school year notes that

Kemper himself "conducted the school for thirty-seven years till his death in 1881."[11]

Upon the death of the school's founder, Johnston was chosen to serve as the school's president—a position that in a few years brought him into contact with arguably the most notable of cadets to set foot on campus.

"Will Rogers entered Kemper on January 13, 1897, coming from his father's ranch near Oologah, Indian Territory (Oklahoma)," wrote the late Lt. Col. A.M. Hitch, a former Kemper superintendent, in his book *Cadet Days of Will Rogers*.[12]

Lt. Col. Hitch further explained that the young Rogers left quite "a lasting impression on one cadet," showing up to campus "dressed up in a ten-gallon hat, with a braided horse-hair cord, flannel shirt with a red bandana handkerchief, highly colored vest, and high heeled red top boots with spurs and with his trouser legs in his boot tops."

Years before Rogers became a much celebrated cowboy humorist, he failed to endear himself to Col. Johnston and the staff of Kemper as many of his fellow cadets viewed him as the class clown, "continually setting his crowd or his table or the class in an uproar," Lt. Col. Hitch wrote.

Ironically, Hitch explained, one of Rogers' former teachers at Kemper reportedly exclaimed, while listening to the former cadet years later on a radio show, "Just think of it! There's Will Rogers getting big money for saying the same things over the radio he got demerits for saying in the mess hall at Kemper."

Despite the utterance of any unwelcome witticisms and remarks from Rogers, the brief time he spent at Kemper as a cadet would serve as a joyful point of reflection for the comedian in the years to come. Following Rogers' departure from the Kemper in 1899, Johnston went on to become superintendent of the school and helped grow the student body to an annual enrollment of more than three hundred in addition to a faculty of thirty-five officers, likely never realizing the greatness for which one of his former "problem" students was destined.

---

[11] Kemper Military School 1923-1924 Catalog, *The School*, 29.
[12] Hitch, *Cadet Days of Will Rogers*, 4.

In 1930, Johnston was visiting California when several former Kemper students hosted a big dinner in the superintendent's honor. While on the trip, Rogers, who was by then a major star, showed Johnston through one of the studios where he worked and introduced him as such: "Boys, this is my old school teacher. He and I couldn't agree on how to run the school so I quit."

Colonel Johnston returned to his native community of Callaway County following his brief trip to the West Coast and continued as superintendent at Kemper until his death on February 5, 1934, nearly six months after the death of his beloved wife, Caroline.

The *Sedalia Weekly Democrat* reported on February 7, 1934 that a "beautiful floral wreath, immense in size and on an easel" was delivered to Johnston's funeral. The newspaper further noted that the elaborate tribute, comprised of "roses, Garza chrysanthemums, sweet peas and greenery," was sent by Will Rogers, who was "very fond of Col. Johnston."

Sadly, Will Rogers perished in an airplane crash in Alaska the year after the Kemper superintendent's death. However, Johnston's influence in shaping his life and that of scores of other students was widely recognized and lauded even in the years prior to his passing.

"Colonel Johnston has endeavored to fit the youths under his guidance, physically, mentally and morally, to meet life's responsibilities," wrote Walter B. Stevens in 1915, adding, "and the spark of latent manhood has been aroused in many an individual through his teaching..."

In the days following his death, the *Sedalia Weekly Democrat* in their February 9, 1934 edition summarized the late school superintendent's impact through the simple reflection, "He was an inspiration, and long after young cadets left Boonville his influence remained with them."

Kemper Military School filed for bankruptcy and closed in 2002 after one hundred fifty-eight years of educating students. Although the Administration Building was recently demolished, some of the buildings on campus have been repurposed for use by organizations such as State Fair Community College and Boonslick Heartland YMCA. *(Photograph courtesy of Jeremy P. Amick)*

Battle of Bode Ferry

Taos

Edward "Ed" Lynn Bode has enjoyed collecting historical tidbits related to a distant relative who owned a ferry crossing during the Civil War, which resulted in an interesting encounter with a famed Confederate general. His research has not only been enlightening with regard to his relative, but has shed light upon a skirmish that occurred within the larger context of General Sterling Price's Missouri Expedition in the fall of 1864.

"There were two Bode brothers and a nephew who emigrated from Germany and arrived Missouri in the 1850s," said Ed Bode, while flipping through documents chronicling much of his research on the family. "The nephew, Frederich "William" Bode, operated the Bode Ferry near Taos for many years."

William Bode would go on to marry the former Katharina Winklemann on November 27, 1861 and the couple soon established their home on the south side of the Osage River in Osage County, from where they could oversee the ferry operations. The eruption of the Civil War soon led to divided loyalties as citizens were torn between separate ideologies. In his book *Man of Two Worlds*, Ray Grothoff explained that "many German immigrants were pro-Union and against secession."[13] He also wrote that while some objected to slavery on moral grounds, others "had no experience with slavery in their native land and tended to own smaller farms, which they could more easily work with their own families or hired help."

---

[13] Grothoff, *Man of Two Worlds*, 7.

With Osage County being predominantly German, William Bode aligned with the pro-Union forces and records available from the Missouri State Archives indicate he enrolled with the 28th Enrolled Missouri Militia, composed of men primarily from Osage County. He was ordered into active service on September 12, 1862 and relieved from duty one month later. The Enrolled Missouri Militia (E.M.M.) was established in 1862 as a part-time force to augment the Missouri State Militia and were not supposed to serve more than 30 days of active duty at a time, although many soldiers in the E.M.M. would serve longer stints. The E.M.M. often performed garrison assignments that included guarding supply depots, railroad bridges, etc.

Following Bode's brief duty with the E.M.M., he focused his efforts on business ventures such as the oversight and operation of his ferry. However, the war continued despite his lack of involvement and, in the fall of 1864, would result in a fascinating encounter with troops under the command of a famed Confederate general.

"In early days of October 1864, (Confederate) General 'Jo' Shelby moved west toward Jefferson City to meet up with General Sterling Price, who intended on capturing Jefferson City," said Ed Bode. "When they got to the William Bode's ferry across from Taos on the Osage County side of the river, they captured William Bode and tied him up."

Joseph Shelby lived in Missouri for a large part of his life and was a veteran of the Battles of Wilson Creek and Pea Ridge. He later gained a level of notoriety for his command of the "Iron Brigade"—a cavalry brigade that was recognized for its toughness and resiliency in operations in the Trans-Mississippi Theater of the Civil War. The Confederate soldiers, stated Ed Bode, were so famished from the feverish pace of their travels in support of General Price's Missouri Expedition that by the time they reached Osage County, they remained near Bode's home for several hours and had his wife fry chickens for breakfast and lunch.

"There were militia soldiers on the north side of the Osage River—on the Cole County side—and Shelby's troops began firing cannons down upon them," said Ed Bode. "Shelby's troops then began to wade across shoals of the Osage and once across, the Union troops retreated up the hill." He added, "That's when Shelby's troops began to bring their cannons across on the ferry and the Bode's were released."

During the skirmish, Bode said, a house once located at the ferry landing area on the north side of the river incurred slight damage when a cannon ball went through a window on the second floor. Bode noted that the story, that has been passed down through generations, was shared by older local residents. Bode further explained that segments of Shelby's division crossed the Osage River at two other locations south of Wardsville. Once across, they spent the night and, the next day, moved through Wardsville to eventually connect with General Sterling Price at site overlooking Jefferson City, the result of which has been the subject of scores of articles and books.

In the book An *Osage County Civil War Patchwork*," Roberta Schwinkle recites an article that appeared in the March 17, 1982 edition of the Unterrified Democrat, which described the recovery of an artifact of the skirmish at Bode Ferry. As the article explained, a cannon ball was uncovered on a farm in the area while a local resident was digging a foundation for a new outbuilding.

While sifting through stacks of paperwork pertaining to the events that unfolded at Bode Ferry in the fall of 1864, Ed Bode explained that two Confederate and two Union soldiers were killed during the skirmish and buried nearby. He then acknowledged the reason behind his efforts to research and preserve this small segment of local Civil War history.

"A lot of people have heard about Bode Ferry but few are aware of the skirmish that occurred there," he said. "General Sterling Price was waiting for Shelby to reach the Jefferson City so that they could attempt to take the capital...and William Bode's ferry is how he got there." He added, "Besides it being the location where many Confederate soldiers entered Cole County, it is nice to know that your family name has a place in Cole and Osage County history." *(Photograph courtesy of Ed Bode)*

Colonel Frederick Wilhelm Victor Blees

Macon

When traveling north along U.S. 63, motorists pass by a massive complex just south of Macon, Missouri, that was constructed more than a century ago and is described in the inventory of the National Register of Historic Places as a "variant of the Romanesque Revival style."[14] Once home to a renowned military academy, the remaining structures on the property serve as an enduring testament to the lofty dreams of its namesake, Frederick Wilhelm Victor Blees.

"Colonel Blees was born in Prussia (now Germany) in 1860," said Mardine White, one of several dedicated volunteers with the Macon County Historical Society.

As White explained, Blees was well educated and became a second lieutenant in the Prussian Army but then moved to the United States in 1881, becoming a naturalized citizen later the same year. While working as a teacher, he met and married Mary Virginia Staples in 1886. The former German officer received his first exposure to the structure of American military academies when he was appointed as commandant of cadets at Griswold College in Davenport, Iowa, in 1890. While in Iowa, Blees progressed through the military ranks after joining the Iowa National Guard, and, as noted in the 1891

---

[14] U.S. Department of the Interior, *Blees Military Academy*, www.dnr.mo.gov.

Report of the Adjutant-General to the Governor of Iowa, was appointed a lieutenant colonel by Gov. Horace Boies.[15]

Attaining the rank of colonel, in 1892 he accepted headmastership of St. James Military Academy at Macon, which, as his obituary shows, "he conducted with marked success, making it one of the flourishing institutions in the state."

An article in the September 15, 1906 edition of *The Macon Republican* explained that following the death of his father in 1896, Blees closed the St. James Military Academy and returned to Germany, promising the citizens of Macon, "When matters across the water are straightened out, I'll return and build you the finest military academy in the west."

Blees inherited an estate estimated to be worth millions from his father and returned to Macon, quickly using his new-found fortunes to not only fulfill a promise, but to help advance the community he now called home.

"Colonel Blees helped fund several public projects such as the construction of sewer systems and paving of streets in Macon," said White, recalling some of the research conducted on Blees' life by members of the local historical society.

At a well-attended ceremony held on June 17, 1899, the cornerstone was laid for the new Blees Military Academy. During the ceremony, a copper box was placed inside the cornerstone containing a copy of the program for the exercises, copies of local newspapers, an old St. James Bible and prayer book in addition to photographs of Blees, his family and those associated with the dedication and construction of the academy.

The academy initially consisted of a large brick academic hall (measuring 224 feet long by 88 feet wide) and an adjacent heating facility. A smaller annex building situated to the right of the academic hall was built in 1900, serving as the school's gymnasium and containing an indoor running track, shooting gallery and swimming pool.

---

[15] Report of the Adjutant-General, *General Orders No. 21*, 182.

"I've heard claims that the building (academic hall) went up in seven months. It was worked on twenty-four hours a day, seven days a week," said White. "Another interesting thing about the building," she added, "is that it was essentially fireproof...even [Blees'] desk was made out of metal."

Newspaper and historical accounts paint a picture of a school that soon acquired a superb reputation throughout the Midwest. However, the training of young men in academics and a military lifestyle did not remain the sole focus of Blees' efforts since he also chose to pursue certain entrepreneurial endeavors. According to the Macon County Historical Society, Blees helped establish many enterprises such as the Macon Shear Company, Macon Citizen Printing Company, Jefferson Hotel, Blees Theater and the Blees-McVicker Carriage Company. He also purchased the first electric automobile made by Studebaker in 1902. (The second such vehicle was purchased by inventor Thomas Edison.)

Despite any appearances of budding success, it was only a few years later that the storied life of one of Macon's most renowned citizens plummeted to an untimely closing. On September 8, 1906, Blees died from heart disease in a hotel room while on a trip to St. Louis. His body was returned to Macon and buried in Oakwood Cemetery.

"The death of Col. Blees will not interfere in any way with the operations of the institutions in which he has been connected," noted The Macon Times-Democrat on September 13, 1908. "The Blees Military Academy will open on Wednesday, September 19, and will have its usual quota of students."

The academy continued to operate under the guidance of Blees' widow for three years until eventually going bankrupt, thus necessitating its closing in 1909. The property sat vacant until 1915, when it was purchased for the Still-Hildreth Osteopathic Sanatorium, which remained in operation until 1968. The academic hall underwent renovation in the 1980s and is now a senior residential facility. For many years, the building housing the academy's gymnasium was used as an armory by the National Guard but has since become the museum and home for the Macon County Historical Society.

More than a century now separates the people of Macon from the life of a fascinating man who clung to lofty dreams and visions, but the legacy Blees left behind is neither trivial nor forgotten. Instead, it bursts forth with renewed vigor thanks to the dedication of a small group of volunteers.

"Blees is certainly a large part our county's history," said White. "Our historical society—which is run entirely by volunteers—enjoys being able to share the story of his life with others." She added, "And if you can get through to one or two young minds, to share with them the impact and influence of citizens such as Blees, then everything that we do here is certainly worth the effort."

For more information on the Macon County Historical Society and Museum, please visit http://www.maconcountyhistoricalsociety. com/. *(Photograph courtesy of Macon County Historical Society)*

Company M, 4th Missouri Volunteer Infantry

Fulton

The Fourth Missouri Infantry (Missouri National Guard) was organized on March 1, 1880, with individual companies at Brookfield, Mound City, Linneus, Bethany, Richmond, Savannah and St. Joseph, according to the *National Guard Historical Annual of the State of Missouri* printed in 1939.[16] Nearly two decades later, during the Spanish-American War, the regiment became the Fourth Missouri Volunteer Infantry was comprised of companies from Carrollton, Mound City, St. Joseph (three companies), Bethany, Maryville, Hannibal, Chillicothe, Warrensburg and Fulton. The regiment mustered into service at Jefferson Barracks on May 16, 1898 and remained stateside during their entire period of wartime service, mustering out at Greenville, South Carolina, on February 10, 1899.

Although the regiment did not see any combat service during the war, Company M of Fulton, Missouri, gained a certain level of notoriety through their mascot—a dog named "Boy." As reported by the *St. Louis Post-Dispatch* on October 9, 1898, Boy was considered "every inch a soldier in his bearing and dignity." The men of the company adorned their mascot with a gold braid collar that was fastened with a buckle with a flag and crossed sabers. The boy also carried a pack saddle "on which is mounted a toy cannon over which waves a tiny silk flag," in addition to a leather strap that ran from the

---

[16] National Historical Annual, *Fourth Missouri Infantry*, XIX.

49

collar to saddle on which was inscribed "Boy, Company M, Fourth Missouri."

The dog's greatest fame came not by his accoutrements, but when, in early October 1898, he visited the White House and was received by President McKinley. It was reported that as the dog approached, President McKinley rendered a salute and Boy then "acknowledged this recognition by solemnly extending his paw, after which he sat down before the President and listened with attentively cocked ears to all Mr. McKinley's utterances." *(Photograph courtesy of Jeremy P. Amick)*

Spanish-American War Cannon

Jefferson City

On the northeast side of the state Capitol, visitors are greeted by a colossal Spanish cannon displayed near the entrance to the Missouri Veterans Memorial. Though impressive in both size and historical significance, few realize were it not for the legal wrangling of a former Missouri governor, this war relic would have been melted down for scrap during the Second World War. As early as 1899, newspapers were reporting on the discussions taking place about gifting cannons captured during the Spanish-American War to cities in Missouri.

"Assistant Secretary of the Interior Webster Davis called at the war department yesterday and secured a promise from Secretary Alger that one of the largest and finest Spanish cannons taken in Cuba and Porto Rico would be given to Kansas City" reported the *Current Local* (Van Buren, Missouri) on June 8, 1899. The newspaper added, "The secretary further promised Mr. Davis to give one cannon each to St. Louis and Jefferson City."

Captured by the United States Navy in Cuba during the Spanish-American War, a cannon arrived at the Missouri Capitol on September 25, 1901. The state of Missouri paid the freight from the Brooklyn Navy Yard to Jefferson City, which cost $74.00 through the Missouri Pacific Railway Company.

"It is an eight-inch brass gun, twelve feet long, and cast in 1769," reported the September 26, 1901 edition of the *Springfield Missouri Republican*. The newspaper further explained that the cannon weighs 6,000 pounds and was given to the state "as a souvenir at the request of the last Missouri legislature…"

Throughout the next several years, the Spanish cannon remained on display, surviving the great fire that destroyed the second state Capitol building in Jefferson City in 1911. The third Capitol was completed in 1917 and the cannon remained a stalwart exhibit on the grounds until the need for war material nearly brought its demise a quarter-century later. In late summer 1942, newspapers throughout the state began featuring articles that discussed "several pieces of obsolete artillery ranged about the Capitol grounds, relics of former wars…" wrote the September 16, 1942 edition of the *St. Louis Post-Dispatch*. This collection included German artillery captured in WWI, a cannon used in the Mexican-American War, a Civil War cannon and the Spanish cannon.

During World War II, many communities held scrap drives to collect materials that could be used in constructing tanks and other war necessities. Here in Jefferson City, many organizations and individuals fully supported disposing of the artillery pieces at the Capitol to support the war. However, Missouri Gov. Forrest Donnell, who had a "lifelong passion for sticking to the letter of the law," wrote the *St. Post-Dispatch*, first wanted to establish who had ownership of the cannons. The contestation of ownership came on the heels of a proclamation issued by the governor in October 1942 in which he stated, "The urgency of the campaign for scrap metal is exceedingly great. Our nation must have scrap to convert into war materials. Scrap which is otherwise useless can be remade into things which are useful and necessary for the successful prosecution of war."

The governor requested the Attorney General to research the matter and determine who held the title to each of the artillery pieces. Their research found the five German guns to be state property and they were immediately ordered to the scrap pile, but the ownership of the other cannons remained in question. On November 24, 1942, the state legislature adopted a resolution granting the state title to the three remaining cannons, which would then provide the legal authority to sell them as scrap.

Days later, the resolution was vetoed by Gov. Donnell, who stated the resolution was not one of the legislative subjects specifically designated in his proclamation convening the recent special session. The governor added, "(T)he State did not have the power, through such a resolution, to declare title to the cannons…," reported *The Houston Herald* (Houston, Missouri) on December 10, 1942. The veto may have had the effect of preserving the cannons, but two St. Louis men—Ross William Riley and Sidney Stearns—decided to drive to Jefferson City on December 10, 1942 and load one of the legally embattled cannons on their half-ton truck to deliver to the scrap heap. The men, newspapers reported, found encouragement through an editorial in the St. Louis Post-Dispatch calling for the scrapping of the artillery pieces.

"But they didn't move the cannon," reported the December 13, 1942 edition of the *Democrat and Chronicle* (Rochester, New York). "They called a wrecker. He called a cop and the minion of the law stopped the midnight scrap drive before it was well started."

The two were initially charged with grand larceny even though they never moved the cannon, but the charge was later reduced by the Cole County prosecutor to conspiracy to commit petit larceny. There remains a Civil War cannon in possession of the Missouri State Museum, which is perhaps one of the three cannons surviving the scrap metal drive of World War II. The fate of the Mexican-American War cannon has been obscured by the passage of years. However, the Spanish cannon remains on display near the entrance of the "Veterans Walk" on the north side of the state capitol.

"There is nothing new in the world except the history you do not know," said former President Harry S. Truman. Perhaps, when individuals visit the Missouri Capitol to take in the many historical sites, they can gaze upon the aged Spanish cannon and realize how the actions of a governor decades past helped preserve this piece for perpetuity.

Samuel W. James Sr.

Sedalia

Many fathers serve as the inspiration for decisions made by their sons. Some perhaps choose a military career because of the uniformed service of a father or grandfather while others seek employment in a profession that parallels that of an elder. In the case of the late Samuel James Sr., his pursuits appeared to have shined brightly upon many aspects of his son's life and career.

Born on a Pettis County farm near Sedalia on February 7, 1871, Samuel James Sr., was raised an only child and attended public schools in the area. As he grew into a young adult, he made the decision to continue his education and prepare for a trade by attending the former Central Business College in Sedalia.

"After finishing school, he accepted a position as a bookkeeper with the Gazette Printing Company," stated his obituary in the June 27, 1936 edition of *The Sedalia Democrat*. "He followed newspaper work for over twenty years, during which time he was connected with the Gazette, Sentinel and Capital," the paper further reported.

While he was building his civilian career, James also became actively engaged with the Company D, Second Missouri Infantry—a Missouri National Guard company previously known as the "Sedalia Rifles." As was recorded in the December 1, 1912 edition of *The St. Louis Star and Times*, James' service with the regiment began as a private on January 13, 1892. The years passed and while James continued in his full-time newspaper career, he also trained part-time with his National Guard regiment and quickly passed through her ranks, becoming quartermaster sergeant in 1893 and duty sergeant in 1894.

In the summer of 1896, he entered the officer ranks when appointed as a second lieutenant.

James Sr. was soon given the opportunity to demonstrate his military prowess in a full-time capacity when the Missouri regiments were mobilized for service during the Spanish-American War in May 1898. Despite their training and preparations, James and the Second Missouri Infantry Regiment remained in the United States during the entire conflict, totaling nine months and twenty-one days in federal service—the longest of any Missouri unit.

According to his obituary, in "April 1898, Mr. James was united in marriage to Miss Rose E. Grosshans. To this union ten children were born...," one of which was Samuel James, Jr., on May 24, 1900.

In the years succeeding his service in the Spanish-American War, Samuel James Sr., rose to the rank of major and continued in his military career "until his resignation in 1910," noted the June 28, 1936 edition of *The Sunday News and Tribune*. His full-time endeavors found him engaged in the real estate business for many years and he later studied law, eventually becoming a renowned attorney in Pettis County. Additionally, he served as a probate judge, prosecuting attorney, a board member of Lincoln University and was for several years involved in Republican politics. He passed away from heart disease at his home on June 27, 1936, when only sixty-five years old. James was laid to rest in Crown Hill Cemetery in Sedalia.

His son, Samuel James Jr., attended military encampments with his father while just a young boy and, like his father, graduated from high school in Sedalia. Shortly after the First World War erupted, the younger James followed the voluntary spirit demonstrated by his father by enlisting in the U.S. Navy on June 16, 1918. James' service card, available through the Missouri State Archives, indicates he performed his initial training at Mare Island, California (which became the first U.S. naval base on the West Coast in 1854). He then traveled to the naval training site in San Diego, where he was stationed when the war ended on November 11, 1918.

Following his discharge on July 15, 1919, the junior James "moved to Jefferson City... and married the former Miss Georgia Fowler on February 1, 1922," explained his obituary in the November

1, 1961 edition of *The Daily Capital News.* "Mr. James attended the University of Missouri School of Law and was admitted to the bar in 1929," his obituary added.

According to the website of the Cole County Historical Society, the year following his admittance to the bar, James "opened an office for the practice of law" in Jefferson City. The WWI veteran continued his law practice until October 31, 1961, at which time he died from a heart attack suffered while arguing a case in Miller County Circuit Court. The body of the sixty-one-year-old veteran was interred in Riverview Cemetery in Jefferson City.

It is a curious circumstance to consider the comparable trajectory taken in the lives of the two James men—both serving in the military, both pursuing careers in law and both passing from heart troubles at a very similar age. One may never know the pride the elder James maintained for the pursuits of his son. However, a statement in *The Sedalia Democrat,* on May 13, 1898, which described some of the men of the Second Regiment with whom Samuel James Sr., served, encapsulates the pride the elder James likely held for the young man who, like his father, "volunteered" to serve during a time of war.

"It takes nerve for a man to leave his family and friends and go to the front, but in time of need there are always true men to meet the emergency—regardless of the ties which bound them to loved ones, and regardless of business interests, responded to the nation's call, while others, when actual service was before them, were found wanting." *(Photograph courtesy of Jeremy P. Amick)*

Leof Harding

Jefferson City

A photograph captures a specific point in time, often times providing the viewer an insight into bygone days. For one local veteran, however, it is not only a glimpse into the period of the Spanish-American War, but points to a distinct moment in an extensive and fascinating military career that spans service in the regular army, Missouri National Guard and Marine Corps. The photograph inspiring such an investigation is that of Leof Harding, drawing attention to Missouri's proud military tradition and a conflict that would help establish the United States as a major player on the world stage.

Born near the community of Virgil City in Vernon County, Missouri, in 1869, records accessed through the *Find A Grave*[17] website note that Harding's father, a farmer named Jacob "Nathan" Monroe Harding, passed away the same year as his son's birth. The loss of his father, though likely devastating to his many young siblings, did not seem to detract Harding from the pursuit of a storied military career, which began with the regular army sometime prior to 1898 as noted in the May 16, 1898 edition of the *St. Louis Post-Dispatch*. Muster rolls from the Missouri State Archives indicate Harding transitioned to service with the Missouri Militia (predecessor of the Missouri National Guard) on April 27, 1898, when Col. William K. Caffee enrolled him in the Second Missouri Volunteers in Nevada, Missouri. The May 16, 1898 edition of the St. Louis

---

[17] Find A Grave, *Leof Harding*, www.findagrave.com.

Post Dispatch reported that Gov. Stephens commissioned Harding as "first lieutenant and battalion adjutant for the regiment."

As noted in the *Report of the Adjutant General of Missouri: January 1, 1917 – December 31, 1920*, the itinerant veteran soon joined the regiment in their volunteering for the Spanish-American War when they mustered into service "at Jefferson Barracks on May 12, 1898." Days later, the report went to explain, the regiment "moved to Chickamauga (Georgia) where [they] were assigned to the Third Brigade, Third Division, First Army Corps." While training in Georgia, Lieut. Otto Fleming resigned his position with Company L of Jefferson City on August 4, 1898—a vacancy that was filled by Lieutenant Harding, as noted in *A History of Jefferson City* by James E. Ford.[18]

The Missouri regiment later spent time in camp in Lexington, Kentucky, and finally at Albany, Georgia, where they remained until mustering out of federal service on March 3, 1899, never deploying overseas in support of the war with Spain. Though many soldiers returned to their Missouri communities and packed away their military uniforms, the July 8, 1899 edition of *The Portsmouth Herald* (Portsmouth, N.H.) reported that Harding chose to continue his military career when he was appointed as a second lieutenant with the Marine Corps.

Two years later, newspapers reported the officer's participation in a number of interesting assignments, which included service as judge advocate in the trial of a military paymaster "accused of scandalous conduct" and then as the officer in charge of the opening of a Marine Corps recruiting station in Pittsburg, Pennsylvania.

His military experience demonstrated an intriguing evolution when the *Scott County Kicker* reported that the lieutenant's wife gained the "unique distinction of being the only American woman" on the island-municipality of Culebra, Puerto Rico. The *Report of the Secretary of the Navy* notes that Lt. Harding was placed in command of "[t]he few men left at Culebra." Additionally, the report said, "Harding was commanded to make a survey of the Government

---

[18] Ford, *A History of Jefferson City*, 173.

land on the island" and continued "the work on the magazine and gun emplacements"—all of which earned him a commemorative diploma from the Marine Corps' commandant in recognition of his "valuable services."

The next decade was a sustained, feverish tempo of duties, which included the command of Marines at Mare Island, California, officer-in-charge of the Recruiting District of California, commander of the Marine Barracks in both San Francisco and Sitka, Alaska, and judge advocate in the trial of a naval surgeon undergoing a court martial for allegations of drunkenness.

Retiring from active duty at the rank of captain, it was noted in the August 4, 1918 edition *The Washington Herald* that Harding was recommended (and later confirmed) for promotion to major as part of "clauses in the new naval appropriation act that provide for promotion of retired officers on active duty..."

Later documentation indicates the retired officer and his wife remained in California, living in the town of Redlands where he served as an officer on the board of the community's country club. Harding passed away on March 22, 1961 in San Diego at the advanced age of ninety one. (His wife passed away seventeen years earlier.)

It is difficult to describe the curiosity that compels a person to research the subject of a photograph such as that of Spanish-American War uniformed Leof Harding, yet in this process of investigation a life emerges from the ashes of history, casting a light upon a veteran whose life teemed with interesting experiences. And if we may borrow a phrase from American novelist Tatjana Soli in her award-winning book *The Lotus Eaters*, the author encapsulates in a single sentence the enchanting process that unfolds when we seek to personify a photograph of a person... even those long deceased.

"Pictures could not be accessories to the story—evidence—they had to contain the story within the frame. The best picture contained a whole war within one frame."[19] *(Photograph courtesy of Jeremy P. Ämick)*

---

[19] Soli, *The Lotus Eaters*, 118.

Jacob Houston

Eldon

The Spanish-American War is little more than a footnote in the annals of the nation's military history, eclipsed by its position between the Civil War and World War I. Though largely forgotten, this conflict required the investment of thousands of men and contributions from scores of Missourians, including that of local farmer Jacob Houston.

Born June 6, 1874, Houston was raised in the Rocky Mount (Missouri) area and likely grew up listening to stories about the Civil War. According to a brief history of his family available through the Miller County Historical Society, two of Houston's uncles died in service of the Union Army, while another served with the Confederacy. Houston's service may have begun more than thirty years after that of his uncles but has roots extending many years previous. As noted in the souvenir book from the forty-ninth Annual National Encampment of the United Spanish War Veterans (USWV), the U.S. began to advocate for freedom on behalf of the people of Cuba—who were living under the colonial authority of Spain—as early as 1865.

"We tried to intervene in friendly fashion, and early in the year 1898 the battleship Maine was sent to Havana harbor as a friendly mission to that end," noted the Spanish American veterans in their souvenir book. "But on February 15, 1898, a terrible explosion rent (split) the Maine amidships, with great loss of life among our sailors."[20]

---

[20] United Spanish War Veterans, *Souvenir Book*, 25.

During a memorial service held in honor of Spanish-American War veterans during the USWV's 1947 meeting, John White, the organization's national commander at the time, reminded his fellow veterans of the details behind the events that led them to war 49 years earlier.

"When it was disclosed that the initial explosion came from outside the hull, and no satisfactory explanations were made by Spanish authorities, war was inevitable and the official declaration by Congress followed on April 25 (1898)," White said.

With a standing army ill equipped to respond to a war with Spain, President McKinley quickly called on the states to provide 125,000 men. In addition to supplying soldiers for both the regular army and U.S. Volunteers, Missouri furnished six regiments of infantry and one battery of light artillery, most of which were formed from volunteers in existing National Guard units.

Enlisting in California, Missouri, with Company B, Sixth Regiment of the Missouri Volunteer Infantry, Houston began his federal service on July 24, 1898 at Jefferson Barracks, Missouri, as noted on muster roles obtained from the Missouri State Archives. Carl Houston, grandson of Jacob Houston, has gazed upon his grandfather's military photograph many times throughout the years but does not recall his elder sharing any stories from his service during the near-forgotten conflict.

"It was just something I never remember him talking about," said Carl.

But utilizing several reference sources, one can piece together details of Houston's wartime experiences, including his membership in the only Missouri regiment to serve in Cuba.

The Spanish-American War Centennial Website notes that Sixth Regiment, comprised of twenty-seven officers and 1,265 enlisted soldiers, spent several weeks in training at Camp Cuba Libre near Jacksonville, Florida, before moving to Camp Onward near Savannah, Georgia, where they boarded transports on December 21,

1898 bound for Havana, Cuba.[21] Upon their arrival in the embattled island country on Christmas Eve, the Missouri regiment was attached to the Seventh Army Corps commanded by Gen. Fitzhugh Lee (a former Confederate general and past governor of Virginia)[22] and spent the next three months performing occupational duties in areas formerly controlled by Spanish forces.

Though units such as the "Rough Riders" (who arrived in Cuba months earlier) saw heavy fighting and incurred combat casualties, the Sixth Missouri lost "one officer and twenty-three enlisted men who died of disease" while another soldier "died as the result of an accident, one was court-martialed, twenty-four deserted, and **thirty**-two were discharged on disability," the centennial website goes on to explain.

Coming home after the brief war, Houston's grandson notes that the former soldier went on to build his life in a fashion similar to that of many returning veterans—marrying, raising children and tending to a farm in the rural Miller County.

"(Houston) married a full-blooded Cherokee woman," said his grandson, Carl Houston. "One day he became very sick and all of his children came by to see him. His wife was rocking in her chair on the front porch and they came out and told her that he had passed." Calmly, he added, "She just nodded her head and didn't say anything, and they all went back inside. A little while later they came out to check on her and she was dead."

Both Houston and his wife, Laura Ann Holloway, died on May 1, 1957 and were buried in Dooley Cemetery near Eldon. As noted on Laura's death certificate, her passing was attributed to "emotional shock."

---

[21] The Spanish-American War Centennial Website, *6th Missouri Volunteer Infantry*, www.spanamwar.com.

[22] Lee served as governor of Virginia from 1885-1889 and was the author of a biography about his uncle, Robert E. Lee. He was appointed to serve as consul general in Havana, Cuba by President Grover Cleveland in 1896. Serving as the commander of Seventh Corps during the Spanish-American War, Lee remained in Florida and never saw combat. He retired from the Army March 2, 1901 and passed away four years later. Library of Congress, *Fitzhugh Lee*, www.loc.gov.

Firsthand accounts of Houston's service have forever perished, but words of memorial shared by Commander in Chief John White during the reunion of Spanish-American War veterans in 1947 serves as a petition to remember Houston and the scores of citizens from Missouri who, more than a century ago, rallied to fight on behalf of the oppressed people of Cuba.

"What a tragic thing it is that so many Americans, who have never known oppression and tyranny, calmly accepting all the golden blessings of our American way of living with never a thought to the sacrifices which others made to acquire and safeguard these blessings." White added, "And as we gather here today to remember the sacrifices they made, let us renew our determination to carry on the fight for principles they held more precious than life itself." *(Photograph courtesy of the Houston family)*

James H. Debo

Fulton

Hundreds of marble headstones painstakingly aligned in rows throughout the historic Jefferson City National Cemetery serve as a lasting testimony of the various wars in which our nation has been involved and the brave individuals who participated in these conflicts. However, nearly hidden among the scores of timeworn markers is one inscribed with the name James H. Debo, a veteran of an essentially forgotten war. The veteran's tombstone might simply earn a passing glimpse by a visitor to the cemetery, but Debo's legacy of service in a volunteer Missouri regiment begs further investigation and helps to highlight the involvement of both the state and nation in the historic event known as the Spanish-American War.

Born in Muskogee, Illinois, on August 25, 1876, Debo was living in the Texas County community of Houston, Missouri, when he and several local men made the decision to enlist in Company M, Second Missouri Volunteer Infantry located in Springfield, Missouri.

As noted in a souvenir booklet for the forty-ninth annual encampment of the United Spanish War Veterans, Inc. held in Kansas City, Missouri in 1947, the United States "tried to intervene in a friendly fashion" to advocate for the freedom of Cuba from what was deemed oppressive conditions imposed by the Spanish government. The booklet went on to state that "early in the year 1898 the battleship Maine was sent into Havana harbor as a friendly mission to that end. But on February 15, 1898, a terrible explosion rent the Maine amidships, with great loss of life among our sailors."[23]

The History of the Missouri National Guard, published in November 1934, noted, "War was declared by Congress by resolution of April 1st 1898, and on April 22nd the President (McKinley) called for 126,000 volunteers. Missouri's allotment was placed at 5,000."[24] The state would eventually furnish six regiments of infantry and one battery of light artillery for the Spanish-American War. The Second Regiment, of which James Debo became a member, was initially comprised of ten companies located in Carthage, Butler, Lamar, Sedalia, Pierce City, Clinton, Joplin, Nevada, Springfield and Jefferson City. The president's call for additional volunteers resulted in the regiment increasing from ten companies to twelve with additional companies added in Springfield and Sedalia. Rosters maintained by the Missouri State Archives indicate Debo enlisted in Second Regiment's Company M—the second of the two Springfield companies—on May 4, 1898.

Reflecting on the community support for those departing for service, the Houston Herald, in their June 26, 1930 edition, ran an editorial highlighting an important event more than three decades past. "We remember when the call came for the Houston boys to mobilize in Springfield. We remember that practically every man, woman and child in the city of Houston was out wading in the mud to see the boys off to war."

A commemorative booklet printed after the war for the soldiers of the Second Missouri Volunteer Infantry, noted, "Pursuant to permission from Governor Stephens of Missouri, the regiment mobilized and rendezvoused at Jefferson Barracks, near St. Louis, Mo., May 6, 1898, and was mustered into the service of Uncle Sam on May 12th, having been reduced to the minimum strength of 1,031 officers and men."[25]

Debo and his fellow soldiers of the Second Missouri soon departed to set up camp in the former Civil War battlefield that had

---

[23] United Spanish War Veterans, *Souvenir Book,* 25.

[24] The History of the Missouri National Guard, *The Second Missouri Infantry—Pre-War,* 82.

[25] 2nd Missouri Infantry in Camp 1898, *The Second Regiment of Missouri Infantry,* 1.

become Chickamauga Park, Georgia, arriving on May 20, 1898. The next several months involved training of the new recruits in military drills and target practice with Springfield rifles, which were later replaced with the newer Krag-Jorgesen rifles. While the Rough Riders and other military units were involved in pitched combat against Spanish forces in Cuba, the Second Missouri was fighting their own battles with several afflictions to include "typhoid fever and malarial fevers," resulting from the filthy conditions of the camp.

The call to deploy to Cuba never arrived and an armistice ending the Spanish-American War was signed on August 12, 1898. Debo and the soldiers of the Second Regiment later moved camps, spending time in Kentucky and later relocating to Albany, Georgia, where they were mustered out of the service on March 3, 1899. Returning home to Missouri, Debo was married to Maggie Saila on January 4, 1901 in Springfield. Years later, when the Spanish-American War veteran was widowed after the passing of his wife, he lived with family in Nebraska before settling in Fulton, Missouri, where he was employed as a pharmacist. He passed away on April 29, 1955 and was laid to rest in the Jefferson City National Cemetery.

Without children to pass down his legacy, Debo could easily become one of many forgotten soldiers who served in a war sandwiched between the more prominent Civil War and World War I. But, as was noted by Chaplain Hamilton during the national encampment of Spanish-American War veterans held in 1947, it is the responsibility of the individual to live a life worthy of remembrance.

"We don't want to be forgotten. So many pass each year," said Chaplain Hamilton. "As my eyes sweep over this audience, I just wonder how many of us will go. That's the nature of things...it comes, and there is no use being worried about it." Sagely, he added, "The thing to do my comrades, is to so live and labor that we will be well prepared to depart from this life and into the next, and we will not be forgotten....They will keep our graves decorated." He again stressed, "We shall not be forgotten."[26] *(Photograph courtesy of Jeremy P. Amick)*

---

[26] Proceedings of the Stated Convention of the 49th National Encampment, *Memorial Service*, 75.

Fred McFadden

Osage City

Fred McFadden, a veteran of the Spanish-American War and former resident of Osage City, Missouri, is pictured while celebrating his ninety-second birthday at the former Bond Nursing Home in Russellville on December 17, 1967. Born in Clinton, Missouri, on December 19, 1875, McFadden served stateside with Company F, 2nd Missouri Volunteer Infantry Regiment during the Spanish-American War, but later deployed with the U.S. Army in the Philippines.

McFadden was an active member of Jefferson City's Admiral Charles D. Sigsbee Camp No. 26 (established in 1923) of the United Spanish War Veterans, Inc., and was well known in the community for his participation in the annual Memorial Day and Veterans Day ceremonies in Jefferson City.

The Spanish–American War veteran passed away at the veterans' hospital at Jefferson Barracks on August 23, 1969 and was laid to rest in Maplewood Cemetery in Brownington, Missouri. *(Photograph Courtesy of VFW Post 1003)*

Joseph Epps

Jamestown

Though little is known about the early life of Joseph Epps, the veteran of the conflict known at the Philippine Insurrection gained a level of national notoriety when he received the nation's highest award for gallantry—but twenty-seven years after the heroic actions which earned him the coveted distinction. Born May 16, 1870 in Jamestown, Missouri, Epps was known by most to be a quiet man and lacking in friends, said Richard Schroeder, a California, Missouri, resident who has done a fair amount of research on the life and military service of the late veteran.

"I've researched newspaper articles about him and interviewed some of his relatives (who are now deceased)," said Schroeder. "He had one close friend while growing up—a neighbor girl who was ten years older. It wasn't a romance," he added, "just a close friendship"

As Schroeder explained, the girl died when Epps was twenty-one years old and his parents passed within the following year, which inspired the quiet man from Jamestown to pull up roots and move to Oklahoma to fulfill aspirations of becoming a cowboy. Though the specific date that Epps left his Missouri home remains uncertain, the December 1, 1928 edition of the *Nashua Reporter* noted that in 1899, the Panama, Oklahoma resident "left his horse and lariat to join the army for service in the Philippines."

An article in the July 27, 1926 edition of the *Reading Times* explained that the former cowboy first entered service with Company D, First Regiment of the Territorial Volunteer Infantry from the Oolagah Indian Territory, but it would not be until his later service with Company B, 33rd United States Volunteer Infantry that he would earn a coveted and unexpected recognition.

According to the Texas Military Forces Museum, the 33rd was organized at San Antonio and "recruited almost entirely from Texas." The regiment deployed to the Philippines in 1899 to help quell an insurrection brewing on many of the islands in the region. Documentation from the National Archives and Records Administration explains that the Philippine Insurrection unfolded when the U.S. gained territorial control of the Philippines on December 10, 1898 through the Treaty of Paris. Previously, they had been under the colonial authority of Spain and "(m)any in the islands were not eager to see one colonial power replaced by another."

Under the leadership of revolutionary Emilio Aguinaldo, the islands soon erupted into struggles of armed resistance, which resulted in the United States sending troops to help suppress the guerrilla activity.

Gregory Statler penned an article for the U.S. Army Heritage and Education Center in which he states Company B, to which Epps was attached, was stationed near the Philippine town of Vigan when chaos erupted around 4:00 a.m. on December 4, 1899.

"Shots were being fired. Men were yelling and the sounds of battle were coming from the plaza...," wrote Statler.[27]

The revolutionaries or "insurrectos" as they became known, with their forces of 850 men, had begun their attack against the town held by a mere 84 soldiers from Company B.

During the battle that ensued, Epps and another soldier received orders to protect an area near a wall adjacent to a churchyard and, to prevent the insurrectos from crossing the wall. Although Company B was able to repulse the initial attack, some snipers remained behind to harass the American forces with intermittent gunfire from behind the wall.

"I want to go and get those fellows behind the wall," Epps said, according to the January 28, 1932 edition of *The Waterloo Press*. His

---

[27] Statler, *The Insurrectos Attack*, www.army.mil.

request was granted and Epps was accompanied in his mission by Private W.O. Thrafton of Texas.

The article also stated the pair cautiously approached the churchyard, at which point Epps crawled to the top of the wall and yelled at the insurrectos in both Spanish and English, ordering them to throw down their rifles and place their hands in the air. Concurrently, Private Thrafton "let loose a typical Texas whoop," giving the impression there were additional American troops at their call.

"[Epps] believed that his friend from Jamestown [who had died years earlier] was serving as his guardian angel," said Schroeder. "Before he jumped up on the wall, he heard her voice tell him, 'They can't hit you.'"

Complying with the persuasive command, the insurrectos abandoned their weapons, resulting in Epps' single-handed capture of twenty-one armed men. Congress would go on to award Epps the Medal of Honor in 1902. However, he essentially disappeared from the public eye after his discharge from the Army, thus leaving the medal unclaimed. It was not until he ran across his former captain years later that he learned of the honor he had been bestowed.

"At first," Schroeder explained, "he didn't want a big fuss made about the award. But when he learned it included a ten dollar bonus, he decided to accept it because he thought he could use the money to start up a chicken ranch in Oklahoma."

On August 13, 1926, a reluctant Epps stood at attention and received the long overdue medal.

"Epps actually received two medals," said Schroeder. "The first was the medal that was in effect twenty-four years earlier and the second was the newly designed medal," he added.

After the award ceremony, Epps, who had previously avoided any recognition, again faded into the background to live his life in seclusion. The veteran passed away on June 20, 1952 and was laid to rest at Greenhill Cemetery in Muskogee, Oklahoma.

"It is truly a unique and interesting story," said Schroeder, while discussing Epps. "To have a man who was so quiet and essentially friendless while growing up, to then go on to perform such a heroic task during his military service—it's amazing." Schroeder concluded, "It is really a great example of humility, that even when in the receipt of the nation's highest honor (for valor), Epps did not crave the spotlight. He simply wanted to move on with his life and become a chicken farmer." *(Photograph courtesy of Moniteau County Historical Society)*

CHAPTER 2
WORLD WAR I

Albert and Anton Borgmeyer

Westphalia

During the First World War, Osage County, Missouri witnessed the registration of nearly 2,900 of its residents[28], necessitated by the passage of the Selective Service Act of 1917. What these numbers fail to represent, however, are the families who would then willingly submit their children in support of the war effort, young men who would occasionally surrender their lives or health as a result.

In Westphalia, Missouri, the military service of fraternal twins serves as an enduring testament to one family's legacy of service during the war and the consequences of camp life that followed them home. Born April 25, 1897, brothers Albert (pictured, left) and Anton Borgmeyer (pictured, right) were sons of Henry Borgmeyer, the owner of the original Westphalia Hotel. Prior to the start of American involvement in World War I, the twins moved to Washington, Missouri, to begin lives independent of their Osage County upbringings.

"The two lived there a little while before they were drafted," said Roman Borgmeyer, a nephew to the twins. "They had found work there."

The June 22, 1917 edition of the *Franklin County Tribune* notes Anton was one of six Washington men who "volunteered to serve in the newly organized hospital unit," approximately two months after the United States declared war against Germany.

---

[28] Newman, *Uncle, We Are Ready*, 180.

It is uncertain as to why the aspiring soldier was not accepted for service at the time he volunteered, but on June 5, 1918, he and his twin brother were required to register for the draft. Two months later, both Anton's and Albert's draft order numbers were drawn, and they prepared to depart for military training. Though news back home concerning the war was certainly grim and depressing based upon the many newspaper accounts printed, the *Franklin County Tribune* explained in an article on September 6, 1918, that, "The boys now leaving will only get a sight of the big show."

At the time of their arrival at Camp MacArthur, Texas, in mid-September 1918, the twins' older brother, William, was fighting in France with the 1st Division, placing three of four brothers from the Borgmeyer family in military uniform at the same time. The newspaper's prediction appeared accurate since the twins remained engaged in training at Camp MacArthur, Texas, for the next several weeks. But, as listed on the military service card of Albert (accessed through the Missouri State Archives), he was discharged on November 20, 1918—nine days after the armistice—with a twenty-five percent disability rating.

"He had tuberculosis," said Roman Borgmeyer. "I can remember my father talking about it."

In an article written by Col. George E. Bushnell and accessible through the U.S. Army Medical Department website, Camp MacArthur held the unfortunate distinction of possessing the second "worst record for tuberculosis of all the large Army camps" situated in the United States during the war.[29]

The article further details that a military member "who suffers a disability from disease contracted in line of duty shall be entitled to compensation, provided that the disease has not been caused by his own willful misconduct...," which helps explain the basis for Albert's disability award.

The month following his brother's release, Anton was discharged from the Army and returned to his pre-service home of Washington. In the years following the war, both brothers married, raised children

---

[29] Bushnell, *Tuberulosis*, http://history.amedd.army.mil.

and worked at a local shoe factory, while Albert also became active in politics and served four years on the city council.

Yet the tuberculosis Albert contracted at Camp MacArthur would never fully release its grip, leading to his death from the disease in 1937, thus cutting down the former soldier when only thirty-nine years old.

As reported in his obituary, Albert "bore his illness with resigned spirit and uncomplaining courage," but, sadly, was followed in death by his wife, Marie, only nine years later. His brother went on to enjoy a lengthy career at International Shoe Company until his passing in 1960 at the Department of Veterans Affairs hospital in St. Louis.

Though the tale of twins from a rural Osage County community is simply a single story among many originating from the war, the impact of their time spent in the Army still resonates through the freedoms we now enjoy, and continues to thrive through the enthusiasm radiating from those who volunteer to take an oath to protect the nation.

With the centennial of America's involvement in World War I quickly approaching, the struggles faced by our veterans are often only remembered by time-worn granite markers scattered throughout various cemeteries, but, to many, serves as an incentive to uncover the stories buried beneath, resurrecting the history of those whose sacrifice of youth and health comprise the very foundation of our liberties. *(Photographs courtesy of Roman Borgmeyer)*

John H. Gundelfinger

Jefferson City

According to Nancy Thompson, who in 2017 was serving as chairman of the Cemetery Resources Board of the City of Jefferson, Missouri, the Old City Cemetery and the Woodland Cemetery serve as the final resting place for scores of local veterans, in addition to the number of veterans that are interred in the adjacent Jefferson City National Cemetery. Within Woodland Cemetery, however, the cemetery board has identified the graves of two local veterans of World War I, one of whom, Thompson sadly notes, has been nearly forgotten since he left behind no children to perpetuate his memory.

John H. Gundelfinger was born in Jefferson City on August 26, 1896, as noted on his WWI draft registration card. The son of William H. Gundelfinger, who worked in a local shoe factory, John followed in his father's footsteps by working for the International Shoe Company in Jefferson City prior to his military service.

"We have very little information about him other than what is found on the *Find A Grave* website," said Thompson.

Gundelfinger's draft registration card reveals several additional details, highlighting the fact that the Jefferson Citian was not required to register under the Selective Service Act until the second registration held on June 5, 1918. The first registration, which was held on June 5, 1917, required all males between twenty-one and thirty years of age to register, but Gundelfinger was nearly two months shy of turning twenty-one at that time.

On June 27, 1918, a total of 1,200 draft order numbers were drawn, which included Gundelfinger's. Several weeks later, on August

15, 1918, he began his military service when he was inducted into the U.S. Army in Jefferson City. His only sibling, a brother named William Edward Gundelfinger, was inducted into the U.S. Army on October 18, 1918 and remained with the Student Army Training Corps at Washington University in St. Louis during the brief time he spent in the military.

The twenty-one-year-old John Gundelfinger became a member of the Veterinary Corps (VC) and was first assigned to a site in North Charleston, South Carolina, which was at the time referred to as Animal Embarkation Depot 302. With the capacity for housing 10,000 animals, it was here, the book *The Quartermaster in the Year 1917 in the World War* explains, that soldiers of the VC provided "for the care and conditioning of public animals prior to their issue to troops or shipment overseas."[30]

"There has been a total of 300,802 animals purchased in the United States since the beginning of the War. All of these had to be transported from point of purchase to a remount depot, and in most instances again shipped to ports of embarkation or to a demount depot near the Atlantic Coast so that they could be readily available for shipment overseas…" as is explained in *Report of the Quartermaster General, U.S. Army to the Secretary of War.*[31]

The website of the U.S. Army Medical Department states that the Veterinary Corps was established through the National Defense Act on June 3, 1916 and, although comprised of seventy-two veterinary officers and no enlisted personnel at the beginning of World War I, grew in size to 2,312 officers and 16,391 enlisted personnel within 18 months. Though Gundelfinger's duties kept him in the United States during the war, his service with the Veterinary Corps played a critical role in ensuring the country's success by supplying healthy horses and mules that could be used to carry supplies and pull guns and other types of heavy equipment throughout France.

Gundelfinger's service kept him in South Carolina until nearly three months after the war's end, but in February 1919, he was trans-

---

[30] Sharpe, *The Quartermaster Corps*, 259.
[31] Report of the Quartermaster General, *Remount Service*, 45.

ferred to the Veterinary Corps' Auxiliary Remount Depot No. 313 at Camp Shelby, Mississippi, where he performed duties that were primarily clerical in nature until receiving his discharge from the Army on May 21, 1919. Census records indicate that after his return from the war, he lived with his parents and became involved in the real estate industry as a "land appraiser." His name would appear frequently in the local area newspapers during the summer of 1952 over a dispute with the Capital City Water Company.

"The wrangle stems from complaints by Green Berry Rd. residents about low water pressure and the company's pledge to improve the service," reported the *Jefferson City Post-Tribune* on July 14, 1952. "The company wants easement rights across Gundelfinger's property...for the laying of an 8-inch water main." Despite the argument by Gundelfinger's attorney that the water company failed to make a reasonable offer for easement rights, the Circuit Court granted the easement through a "decree of condemnation" on July 28, 1952.

As the years passed, the WWI veteran remained active in real estate pursuits. However, the sixty-seven-year-old Gundelfinger passed away in St. Louis on April 1, 1964 from complications related to a surgery, dying a single man with no children. All that remains of the veteran's legacy is a timeworn marker quietly tucked within the confines of Woodland Cemetery, but Thompson and the members of the Cemetery Resources Board are hopeful the experiences of Gundelfinger and other local veterans can be remembered and shared with the younger generations.

"I believe we need to respect the memory of all who have gone before," said Thompson. "Veterans of the earlier wars, WWII and prior, suffered particular hardships and I don't think that we can fully appreciate their sacrifices 100 or more years later. If their stories aren't retold periodically, their accomplishments and contributions fade and are forgotten." She added, "I don't want these people to be forgotten." *(Photograph courtesy of Nancy Thompson)*

Harold Linkenmeyer

Jefferson City

The fence surrounding Woodland Cemetery-Old City Cemetery in Jefferson City, Missouri, hems in hundreds of graves, many of those occupied by veterans of the nation's wars, said Nancy Thompson, 2017 chairman of the Cemetery Resources Board of the City of Jefferson. But within the confines of this hallowed space lie the resting spots of only two known World War I veterans—one of whom served in the budding American Air Service, which years later morphed into the U.S. Air Force.

Harold Linkenmeyer was born in Jefferson City on July 18, 1893, the son William Linkenmeyer, a German immigrant who later became chief engineer for the former G.H. Dulle Milling Company in Jefferson City. In later years, when the younger Linkenmeyer came of age, he embarked upon his career by becoming a machinist for the former A. Priesmeyer Shoe Company in Jefferson City. This is where he was employed, his military service card indicates, when his draft lottery number was selected.

Inducted into the U.S. Army on September 20, 1917, the twenty-four-year-old Linkenmeyer was assigned to Company M, 356th Infantry Regiment, which was "composed chiefly of men from Cole, Boone, Henry, Andrews, St. Louis and Jackson Counties" in Missouri, as was written in the official company history from World War I. As the book goes on to explain, Linkenmeyer and his fellow recruits faced many challenges while stationed at Camp Funston, Kansas, surviving "epidemics of Meningitis and other less serious diseases" in addition to overcoming a "shortage of clothing, equip-

91

ment and facilities for training" during the early weeks of their initial training cycle.[32]

But according to Linkenmeyer's military service card, he did not become embroiled in the baptism of fire the 356th Infantry later endured in the trenches of France during the summer of 1918 since he was transferred to the 328th Aero Squadron in early January 1918—a component of the American Air Service.

Described as being "hardly out of its romper stage by April 1918," wrote James Hudson in his book *Hostile Skies: The American Air Service in World War I*, the United States lacked not only "any tangible air strength," but also "plans and programs for building an air service that could fight in Europe" at the outset of the war. The book goes on to explain that the United States scrambled to prepare the American Air Service for the war by appropriating $64 million for the country's military aviation program, "which was the largest sum ever appropriated by Congress for a single purpose up to that time." [33]

In *Order of Battle of the United States Land Forces in the World War* published by the Center of Military History for the U.S. Army, historians explained that it "was necessary to train a large body of mechanics to supply the ground force" for the aviators. Additionally, the book noted, instruction for enlisted mechanics grew to include the maintenance of machine guns, a specialty that paralleled much of Linkenmeyer's experience as a machinist before the war.[34]

Located at Kelley Field in San Antonio, Texas, the young man from Jefferson City remained with the squadron only five weeks before he was transferred to the aerial gunnery school at Ellington Field in Houston, Texas, the same location where an armorer's school had been established only weeks earlier. During the First World War, "observer/gunner positions were typically held by enlisted members..." wrote 2nd Lt. Chuck Widener in an article for the Air Force News Service. The author goes on to state, "Observers who sat in

---

[32] Company "M," 356th Infantry Regiment, *Organization and Early Training*, 6.

[33] Hudson, *Hostile Skies*, 2.

[34] Order of Battle, *Air Service*, 125.

the rear cockpit of early World War I model warplanes, such as the De Havilland DH-4, quickly learned the advantages of a mounted machine gun" and soon began to claim victories while serving overseas.[35]

Linkenmeyer continued his service at Ellington Field until May 17, 1918, at which time he was transferred to the Camp John Dick Aviation Concentration Camp in Dallas, Texas. According to the website of the Texas State Historical Association, during World War I, the camp became "a personnel holding pool for graduates of ground training schools" until they were assigned to an aviation training field.[36] The Jefferson Citian remained at Camp Dick through the signing of the armistice on November 11, 1918. Several weeks after the war ended, on January 6, 1919, Linkenmeyer, was transferred to 676th Aero Squadron, whose headquarters was located on Camp John Dick. Linkenmeyer was promoted to the rank of sergeant on January 10, 1919 and, two months later, was honorably discharged from the Army.

In the years after the war, Linkenmeyer remained in Mid-Missouri and worked many years for the former Tweedie Footwear Corporation in Jefferson City. The veteran passed away on February 1, 1982, never marrying or with any children to pass down his story of service in the burgeoning American Air Service. When reflecting on his service in his golden years, one can only imagine the words Linkenmyer would have used to describe his time with the Air Service during the war. Though it is a great unknown, perhaps his description would have closely paralleled the striking statement made by fellow World War I veteran General Douglas MacArthur[37] in 1951.

"And like the old soldier of that ballad, I now close my military career and just fade away—an old soldier," MacArthur said, "who tried to do his duty as God gave him the light to see that duty." *(U.S. Air Force photograph)*

---

[35] Widener, *The Big Guns*, www.thefreelibrary.com.

[36] Texas State Historical Society, *Camp John Dick*, https://tshaonline.org.

[37] In addition to serving in World War I, MacArthur rose to the rank of five-star general and served as commander of Allied forces in the Pacific during World War II. After criticizing President Harry Truman's handling of the Korean War, MacArthur was relieved of his command on April 11, 1951.

Edgar Cole

Tipton

Described as a red-haired, short and slender twenty-eight-year-old on his draft registration card, Tipton native Edgar Cole's adult life blossomed with a career as a locomotive engineer for the railroad followed by his marriage to a local woman. The trajectory of his future soon shifted, however, when he was drafted into the Army in WWI, eventually losing his life and becoming yet another loss among several that his mother would experience in her lifetime.

Born in Tipton on January 31, 1889, Edgar Cole's mother, the former Lula Hickman, chose to live with her parents after she was widowed at a young age, as evidenced by information retrieved through the 1900 U.S. Census. Growing up as an only child in the home of his grandparents, newspaper reports indicate that Cole was employed in the eastern division of the Missouri Pacific Railroad as early as 1909, and was described as "the best-liked fireman on the 'Old Reliable,'" in the January 26, 1910 edition of *The Sedalia Democrat*. Though he grew up in Tipton and later lived in Sedalia, the June 4, 1917 edition of the *Jefferson City Post-Tribune* wrote that Cole went on to reside many years in the state's capital city and was married in Sedalia "to the girl of his choice," Miss Grace Chamberlain of Tipton, on June 3, 1917.

Having risen through the ranks at the railroad to become a locomotive engineer, Cole's life seemed to be progressing well until the Selective Service Act of 1917 required that all men "aged 21 thru 30 register at (local) voting precincts," as explained in the book *Uncle,*

We Are Ready!: Registering America's Men 1917-1918.[38] Cole registered with his local voting precinct in Tipton on June 5, 1917—two
days following his marriage and the date set forth by the Selective
Service Act as the first of three registration dates.

Cole's fate was sealed on June 27, 1918, when his registration number was drawn during a national lottery that occurred in
Washington, D.C. Several weeks later, on August 8, 1918, Cole was
inducted as a private in the U.S. Army at nearby California, Missouri.
According to his service card, Cole arrived at Camp McArthur, Texas,
on August 16, 1918 and underwent an accelerated basic military
training with Company I, 12th Battalion, Infantry Replacement and
Training Camp. Amanda Sawyer, in an article she wrote for a section
of Baylor University's website on the history of Waco, Texas, noted
the construction of Camp MacArthur began on July 20, 1917, and
was, "(s)pread out on 10,700 acres of cotton fields and blackland
farms…(and) possessed the capacity to hold around forty-five thousand troops."[39]

Sawyer goes on to explain that the camp had been used to train
the soldiers of the 32nd Infantry Division and, following the division's deployment to France in February 1918, the camp transitioned
into an infantry replacement and training site for recruits from Texas,
Arkansas, Missouri and New Mexico. Cole's hurried training at Camp
MacArthur ended in early September 1918 when he boarded a troop
ship bound for France, arriving overseas on September 23 according
to the dates that entered on his military service card.

Little evidence exists that would denote whether Cole ever experienced any combat following his arrival in France. However, records
indicate that he passed away in a hospital on November 13, 1918 (two
days after the armistice) from what was listed as lobar pneumonia.
An article by the Centers for Disease Control and Prevention notes
that of the deaths from bacterial pneumonia during the 1918-1919
influenza epidemic (also known as the "Spanish Flu"), the "median
time from illness to onset of death was 7-10 days, and significant

---

[38] Newman, *Uncle, We are Ready*, 5.
[39] Sawyer, *Camp MacArthur*, http://wacohistory.org.

numbers of deaths occurred >2 weeks after initial symptoms."[40] As such, it is unlikely Cole saw combat during the few weeks he was in France since he would have soon fell ill after processing into his new unit.

The soldier's family soon learned of his demise and his body was shipped back to the United States, where it was interred in the Masonic Cemetery in Tipton. Cole's wife later moved to St. Louis and then to Los Angeles, and remarried in 1924. She passed away in 1940 and her remains were returned to Tipton and interred in the Masonic Cemetery. Lula Cole, the late soldier's mother, found little peace in the years following the deaths of her husband and son—she would lose her mother in 1922, her father in 1929 and a younger brother in 1931. Lula Cole lived to be seventy-five years of age and was buried in a grave next to her son in 1943.

According to the 1980 edition of the book *Moniteau County, Missouri History*, the "Edgar Cole Post 304 of the American Legion was first organized around 1921..." The book further explains that the building currently used by the post was built on a lot purchased in 1949.

A century has passed since the "Great War," but the community of Tipton continues to grieve the loss of one of their own by gathering at the grave of Cole every Memorial Day to pay their respects. Local citizens like Cole left home and were thrust into hostile foreign lands, often clinging to the hope that their sacrifices would never become a long-forgotten memory.

"They shall not grow old, as we that are left grow old: age shall not weary them, nor the years condemn," wrote poet Laurence Binyon in his *Ode of Remembrance*. "At the going down of the sun and in the morning, we shall remember them." He added, "They mingle not with their laughing comrades again. They sit no more at familiar tables of home..."[41] *(Photo courtesy of Moniteau County Historical Society)*

---

[40] Brundage & Shanks, *Deaths from Bacterial Pneumonia*, www.ncbi.nlm.nih.gov.
[41] The Western Front Association, *Brothers in Arms*, www.westernfrontassociation.com.

Frank Schulte

Bay

A 21-year-old Frank J. Schulte, who grew up in the small Gasconade County community of Bay, was in the year 1917 following the path of his father and many young men of the area—trying to eke out a living as a farm laborer and hoping to someday purchase a farm of his own. In May 1917, as the nation was drawn into World War I, the direction of his circumstances were soon altered, however, by the newly implemented Selective Service Act. On June 5, 1917, all males between twenty-one and thirty years of age were required to register at their local voting precinct. Schulte's registration card indicates that although he was working as a farm laborer in Arlington, Nebraska, he made the trip home for the registration, requesting exemption from military service since he provided support to his father.

According to the Library of Congress, local draft boards were created in "each county that were to consist of three or more members who were to determine all questions of exemption in their jurisdiction." Although exemptions were available to "persons in certain classes or industries, including workmen in armories and those in agriculture," Schulte was denied an exemption.[42]

"There were three drawings of numbers to determine the order in which men were to be examined by the local draft boards and evaluated for induction," wrote John J. Newman in his book *Uncle We Are Ready!* He added, "The first occurred 20 July 1917, when 10,500 numbers were drawn in Washington."[43]

---

[42] Library of Congress, *World War I: Conscription Laws*, https://blogs.loc.gov.
[43] Newman, *Uncle We Are Ready!*, 19.

Schulte's draft order number was drawn during the initial lottery and, according to his service card maintained by the Missouri State Archives, he was inducted into the U.S. Army on October 4, 1917, approximately one month prior to his twenty-second birthday.

"My father never had much to relate about his service," recalled Harold Schulte, one of the WWI veteran's sons. "I do know that after he was drafted, he was sent to Camp Funston, Kansas, for his training."

Located on the Ft. Riley military reservation near Junction City, Kansas, the Kansas Historical Society notes that Camp Funston was "the largest of 16 divisional catonement training camps built during World War I to house and train soldiers for military duty." Additionally, the society explained, it's "main purpose was to train soldiers drafted in Midwestern states to fight overseas."[44]

One of the greatest challenges facing Schulte and his fellow soldiers at the stateside camp was not necessarily a grueling training regimen. Instead, they endured the influenza pandemic that was coined the "Spanish Flu," which is believed to have originated at Camp Funston during the war.

Military records indicate the young draftee was assigned to an organization known as the 164th Depot Brigade, which the Topeka State Journal described in their October 13, 1917 edition as "made up of companies on about the same basis as infantry, is put thru the same setting up exercises, the same vaccination for smallpox..." The July 29, 1918 edition of the Morning Chronicle (Manhattan, Kansas) shared a more critical definition for the depot brigades, humorously noting that they were referred to as "deposed brigades" by soldiers and used "merely as a storage place for soldiers in training...(that) fails to impart the spirit, which is now springing up, of belonging to a regular organization..."

The men in these brigades received their basic training and were often trained in specific specialties prior to being transferred as replacements in other units that were understrength. Such a training structure often inhibited cohesion among the troops since they were

---

[44] Kansas Historical Society, *Camp Funston*, www.kshs.org.

thrust into situations in which they had to serve with those with whom they had not trained.

"My father remained at Camp Funston and went on to train as a military policeman," said Harold Schulte, while discussing his late father's service. "He was then sent with a group to Camp Kilmer [New Jersey] for shipment overseas," he added.

The veteran's son further explained that while at Camp Kilmer, a number of soldiers with his father were struck with measles and the entire group was quarantined for several weeks. While waiting for the virus to clear up and an official release from medical staff, World War I came to an end and the soldiers were soon discharged. In the years following his military service, the veteran settled in the community of Bay, married, raised a family and fulfilled the dream of running his own farm. A charter member of the Bay American Legion Post 541, of which several of his sons became members through their own military service, Schulte passed away in 1983 and was laid to rest in Zion Cemetery in his hometown.

Estimates indicate 2.8 million men were drafted into service during World War I and Schulte, who was among the many that trained for the eventuality of service in a deadly combat zone, never saw combat because of the country's brief period of involvement in the war.

"My father never spoke much about his service because he never made it overseas," said Harold Schulte. "But his service did seem to be full of interesting circumstances—being drafted, training for war and never making it overseas because of illness among his fellow troops."

Schulte became part of an Army that grew from 127,000 in 1916 to more than four million in 1918. He may not have engaged in scenes of trench warfare that have become the highlight of WWI historical reference but, as Gen. John J. Pershing wrote in a letter to his fellow Missourian, Maj. Gen. Enoch Crowder, in October 1917, each individual was to accomplish the tasks they were assigned.

"I have the burning desire to get right into the trenches and go over the top, but I can't do that," Pershing wrote. "And so each man to (perform) the job that has been given him." *(Photograph courtesy of Harold Schulte)*

Clarence Miller

Columbia

The life of Clarence Miller can be easily summarized with a single word—responsibility. Raised in Mexico, Missouri, he left his studies at Columbia High School (predecessor to Hickman) to help take care of his four brothers and sisters after his father passed away. Years later, the young man answered another call to duty, this time when the nation beckoned for his service during World War I.

"I don't really recall him ever talking about his military service," said the late Robert Miller, a World War II veteran and son of Clarence. "I hardly even knew that he had served during the war when I was younger and now there doesn't seem to be a lot of information that I can find about his service," he added.

Born in 1895, Miller was living in Columbia when his name appeared in the July 25, 1917 edition of *The Evening Missourian*, listing his name among those registered for military service in Boone County, Missouri. The registration was the result of President Wilson's proclamation of May 28, 1917, which initially required men between the ages of twenty-one and thirty to register with locally administered draft boards "between 7 a.m. and 7 p.m. on the fifth day of June, 1917, at the registration place in the precinct wherein they have their permanent homes."[45]

Under the Selective Service Act of 1917, as the proclamation was known, local draft boards were given the responsibility for the initial registration, selection and delivery of men to military train-

---

[45] McMaster, *McMaster's Commercial Cases for the Banker*, 116.

ing camps, and was a process implemented by General Enoch Crowder—a Missouri native and provost marshal of the United States during World War I.

Though Miller, because of his age, was required to report for the first registration (two subsequent registrations were required, the latter of which extended the age requirement to those between eighteen and forty-five years of age), his lottery number was not selected until the following year. On August 15, 1918, ten days prior to his twenty-third birthday, the young man said goodbye to his family when he was inducted into the U.S. Army and departed for his training destination of Camp Jackson, South Carolina.

According to Miller's service card accessed through the Missouri State Archives, he remained at Camp Jackson and trained with a field artillery battery, preparing to serve as a replacement soldier in case the war continued. Camp Jackson was designated as the Army's Field Artillery Replacement Depot in May 1918 and, as noted in the *History of Fort Jackson* accessed through the U.S. Army's website, was plagued by the Spanish Influenza in September of the same year, resulting in three hundred deaths during the same timeframe Miller was training at the camp.[46]

When the armistice was signed on November 11, 1918, Miller continued in his military service for several more weeks, until receiving his honorable discharge at the rank of private on December 27, 1918.

The process by which the young Mid-Missourian entered the military was not unique as statistics cited in an article by Mitchell Yockelson, which is accessible through the website of the National Archives, notes that by the time World War I came to a close, "More than 24 million men registered for the draft, and almost 2.7 million men were furnished to the U.S. Army by conscription."[47]

Returning to Columbia, Miller later wedded his fiancée, Elsie McBaine, and the couple raised four sons. In later years, he became an employee of the City of Columbia.

---

[46] Fort Jackson, *History of Fort Jackson*, http://jackson.armylive.dodlive.mil.
[47] Yockelson, *They Answered the Call*, www.archives.gov.

"He used to work the swing shift," recalled Miller's son, Robert, "and when he got off, he liked to fish. I think that we fished all of the creeks around the city."

Robert acknowledges that although he served in the Army during World War II, he and his father never had any discussions about his experiences during the First World War.

"He and my brother [Raymond] were very close," Robert said, "and they talked about the military at times because Raymond had served in the infantry during the war, which really seemed to be a connection between them."

Though Roberts's brother has since passed and little information survives regarding their father's service in the First World War, he remains grateful for the service records that exist, which help shed a little light upon a father's military experiences during a war nearly forgotten. In the book *The Spirit of the Selective Service* published in 1920, General Enoch Crowder explained that a section of the nation's history was preserved through the process that mobilized an army of men in defense of the nation during WWI—a collection of information that has survived the passage of years and is now available in various archives throughout the United States.

"The pride, the sorrow, the sacrifice and the patriotism of the nation were contained within the records of the Local Boards," wrote Crowder. "Never in the history of this or any other nation had a more valuable and comprehensive accumulation of data been assembled upon the physical, industrial, economic and racial condition of a people."[48]

To learn more about military records available through the Missouri Digital Heritage site, visit http://www.sos.mo.gov/archives/soldiers/. For more information on the history Fort Jackson, South Carolina, visit http://jackson.armylive.dodlive.mil/post/museum/history-post-wwii/. *(Photograph courtesy of Robert Miller)*

---

[48] Crowder, *Spirit of Selective Service*, 355.

Adolph H. Strobel

Centertown

Born on a farm near the community of Lohman on May 25, 1892, Adolph Strobel was a self-employed farmer when he participated in the first draft registration of World War I on June 5, 1917. According to his draft registration card, the twenty-five-year-old was single and responsible for providing support for his mother, father and brother. However, J.AN. Lindhardt,[49] a local businessman who served on the Lohman area registration board, wrote on Strobel's registration card, "We believe that his parents and brother will not need to depend on him for support."

Several weeks later, on October 4, 1917, Strobel was inducted into the U.S. Army in Jefferson City. Initially assigned to Company D, 356th Infantry Regiment, the young inductee from Lohman trained alongside scores of other Missouri men at Camp Funston, Kansas. He left his company. However, on February 26, 1918 when he was reassigned to Company L of the Fourth Infantry Regiment. Serving overseas from April 6, 1918 to January 5, 1919, the young soldier went on to participate in several major defensive and offensive operations alongside his comrades, which included Second Battle of the Marne, Third Battle of the Aisne and St. Mihiel. It on October 24, 1918, during the intense conflict known as the Meuse-Argonne

---

[49] J.A.N. Linhardt was born was born on a farm near Lohman on January 9, 1866. During the early years of adulthood, he engaged in farming but later became a merchant of agricultural equipment and grain. Linhardt passed away on December 1, 1943 and was laid to rest in the cemetery of St. Paul's Lutheran Church in Lohman.

Offensive,[50] that Strobel was severely wounded and incurred an injury that would later earn him a forty-percent disability rating.

In the years subsequent to his discharge from the Army, Strobel attended the University of Missouri and lived in St. Louis for many years, where he was employed as a milk inspector for a St. Louis dairy. In 1934, he was married to the former Flora Seibert of Russellville. The couple was living near Centertown when, on October 15, 1950, Strobel suffered a fatal heart attack while driving his car. The fifty-eight-year old World War I veteran was laid to rest in the McGirk Cemetery in rural Moniteau County. *(Photograph courtesy of Audrey Scheperle)*

---

[50] The Meuse-Argonne Offensive, which involved more than a million American soldiers, was the largest military operation for the American Expeditionary Forces of World War I and has been recognized as the deadliest campaign in U.S. history, resulting in more than 26,000 casualties.

Guy Corwine

Sedalia

Military history can be uncovered in the most unexpected locations, as demonstrated by a recent visit to a Jefferson City, Missouri, antique store where a postcard was discovered that inspired a hunt for information about a Mid-Missouri World War I veteran. The postcard, which shows two men dressed in military uniforms and posing in front of a wooden building, contained no information other than the name "Guy D. Corwine" scribbled upon the back. Through review of census records and newspaper archives, it was established that Corwine (pictured on the right) was once a resident of Sedalia, Missouri. A subsequent post on a social media site dedicated to preservation of Sedalia history, helped to uncover additional details about the mysterious veteran.

"I was so excited when I saw his picture on the (Facebook) post," said Donna Leiter of Ashland, Missouri, one of Corwine's granddaughters. "I had seen the photograph somewhere before and I thought it was strange that it turned up in Jefferson City."

Information provided by another of Corwine's granddaughters, Hallsville, Missouri, resident Kay Kitch (sister of Leiter), notes that the veteran earned his teaching certificate in 1909 and taught in rural Missouri schools for several years, until he was netted by the military draft in September 1917—less than five months after the United States declared war against Germany. Military records accessed through the Missouri State Archives indicate that Corwine—who was inducted at Nevada, Missouri—was assigned to the 89th Division (which trained at Camp Funston, Kansas, the current site of Ft. Riley) and became a cook with the 89th Military Police Company.

According to the official history of Company M, 356th Infantry Regiment, a company under the command and control of the 89th Division, "the men (of the division) were drawn from the States of Kansas, Missouri, Colorado, Nebraska, South Dakota, Arizona and New Mexico." The officers of the division trained at Ft. Riley in the summer of 1917 with Major General Leonard Wood (namesake of Missouri's Army post) assuming command in August 1917. Corwine's service card shows that he served overseas beginning June 27, 1918, initially as a cook and was later appointed as a mess sergeant.

"He once told me he became a cook by default," Leiter recalled, "because he knew how to cook and no one else in his company really could." Kitch added, "My grandfather sent several postcards back home, many of which were of buildings that he saw over there (in France). Reading some of the comments on the cards were amusing…it almost sounded like he was on vacation by the way he spoke of the weather, scenery and buildings." She added, "One time, he mentioned that he had fed 2,100 refugees."

The veteran left overseas on May 27, 1919, returning to the United States and received his discharge from the Army on June 10, 1919. Six days later, Corwine married Lola Mae Wilson in Boonville and the couple raised a son and daughter. In 1943, he moved to Sedalia and continued teaching in rural schools, accruing forty-five years in the profession by the time he retired. His wife also taught at schools for a number of years in Moniteau and Cooper counties.

"One time, when I was in middle school, I believe," Leiter explained, "I asked my grandfather why he didn't cook. He told me, 'Why would I do that? I cooked for all of those men in the war and I'm not cooking anymore.'"

Leiter also noted that in later years, Corwine suffered a "major fall outside of the back door of his house" in Sedalia, breaking his shoulder, which required several months of rehabilitation at the veterans' hospital in Leavenworth, Kansas.

During World War II, Corwine relived the stresses of combat service when his only son, Maurice, became a B-24 Liberator pilot and was shot down over Dortmund, Germany on January 28, 1945, as noted on the American Air Museum in Britain website. Surviving the incident, the younger Corwine was held as a prisoner of War in Germany for several months.

"I don't think that our grandfather or grandmother ever talked about this," said Kitch. "Our mother told us about our uncle's time as a POW, but I am sure that it was very hard for them all."

Corwine later developed Parkinson's disease and passed away in 1975, receiving burial in Memorial Park Cemetery in Sedalia. More than four decades have passed since his death, yet his granddaughters have never forgotten the brief time they were able to spend with a man they deeply adored. Though both Leiter and Kitch believe the postcard's movement from Sedalia is somehow linked to their other sister, the late Dorothy Pack of Jefferson City, they are delighted by memories that have been reinvigorated by the surprising discovery buried in a booth at an antique store.

"It was truly unexpected to see the photograph resurface," said Kitch, "and it really got me and my sister talking about all of the good memories of our grandfather. It helped us remember that, being a teacher, he would always inquire about our studies and ask us about what we had been learning." She added, "That was something he always viewed as important." *(Photograph courtesy of Jeremy P. Amick)*

Francis Jobe

Elston

The old saying, "A picture is worth a thousand words," may have become something of a cliché in recent decades, summarily dismissing the large amount of work and investigation that is often necessary to establish a background on the subject that is identified through a photograph. In a recently acquired World War I era photograph with the name Francis Jobe scribbled upon the back, many immediate identifiers come to life such as a man wearing an unadorned wool uniform and campaign hat. However, in addition to casual observation, one can acquire a little more information with the investment of some basic research.

According to archived county records, Jobe was born in Elston, Missouri, on April 7, 1888 to Mephysobeth "Bosh" (M.B.) and Nancy Jobe, both of whom are buried in the Elston Cemetery.

Nearly two decades later, after the United States declared war against Germany on April 6, 1917, the Selective Service Act of 1917 was passed, which "defined five functions to mobilize men to supplement soldiers already in the army or serving in various states' National Guards," as is noted in the book *Uncle, We Are Ready!* Jobe and scores of other young recruits from Missouri were required to register for the draft, after which many were selected, classified and then inducted into military service.

According to Jobe's WWI service card available through the Missouri State Archives, the twenty-nine-year-old draftee was inducted into the U.S. Army in Jefferson City, Missouri, on October 4, 1917, nearly four months after the first registration day, which required males between 21 and 30 years of age to register with their local draft board. Little information is available regarding Jobe's initial weeks of training but his service card denotes his assignment to Company I, 134th Infantry Regiment—a regiment of the Nebraska National Guard. "The Army Lineage Book" explains the regiment was called into federal service on July 15, 1917 and became part of the 34th Division (created from troops of Minnesota, Iowa, Nebraska and the Dakotas) three months later.

Jobe would join the division in their training location of Camp Cody near Deming, New Mexico. (Camp Cody was named in honor of famous bison hunter and showman, William "Buffalo Bill" Cody," shortly after his death in 1917.) The men of the 34th Division soon earned the moniker of "Sandstorm Division" from the dust storms that seemed to blow through their training areas on a daily basis.

The 34th Infantry Division Association noted on their website that the training for the division "went well, and the officers and men waited anxiously throughout the long fall and winter of 1917-18 for orders to ship out for France. Their anticipation turned to anger and frustration, however, when word was received that spring that the 34th had been chosen to become a replacement division."[51]

Now thirty years old, Jobe, who had trained as a cook while at Camp Cody, finally set foot on French soil in mid-October 1918. He not only discovered that the men of the division would soon be assigned as replacement soldiers in other units, but that they would never experience combat since the war ended shortly after their arrival.

An end to the war did not herald Jobe's return home. His service card indicates that he went on to serve with three other units who were part of the Army of Occupation until returning to the United States and receiving his honorable discharge on July 21, 1919, after spending less than two years in the military.

In 1929 and 1930, Jobe acquired a certain level of local notoriety by lending endorsement to a new medicine known as "Hoyt's

---

[51] 34th Infantry Division Association, *Division History*, http://www.34ida.org/history/.

Compound." Through advertisements in several Missouri newspapers, the product is praised by Jobe, who shares his past history of stomach problems, fatigue and irritability, but claimed the medicine was able to "improve his system in every way."

In the *Notices of Judgment under the Federal Food, Drug and Cosmetic Act* dated February 1943, the Hoyt Corporation was prosecuted for labeling of their Hoyt Compound in a manner that "bore false and misleading curative and therapeutic claims."

In the years after the war and following his medicinal endorsement, Jobe married Margaret Schmidli on November 10, 1934 and the two never had any children. According to his obituary, the veteran and his wife resided in Jefferson City, where he spent many years as an automobile mechanic. He passed away at the Veteran's Administration Hospital in St. Louis on April 22, 1960 and was laid to rest in Riverview Cemetery in Jefferson City.

There may not be any erudite quotes adequately summarizing a man who, nearly a century ago, entered military service at the behest of a nation wholly unprepared for war. But considering the more than 4.7 million Americans who would serve in uniform during World War I, Jobe's story is a single moment of local history that can be carved out, explored and shared with future generations.

This individual—a relatively unknown farmer's son—left the comfort of his small community of Elston, to join a collective group that would train to serve in whatever capacity was necessary in the defense of their nation.

They banded together under difficult circumstances and, in the words written by then-Lt. Col. John H. Hougen[52] in 1949, became part of a team "composed of citizen soldiers, men recruited from all walks of life—from farms, the factories, the mines, the forests, the offices and the professions. In times of emergency, citizen soldiery has always constituted the indispensable pool to be drawn upon by the Nation, and so it will always be..." *(Photograph courtesy of Jean Frank)*

---

[52] Colonel John H. Hougen was eighty-nine years old when he passed away on July 14, 1978 and was laid to rest in Arlington National Cemetery.

Homer McCrea and Luther Landrum

Elston

Many stories from World War I have not survived the passage of time since the United States was involved in the war for such a short period. By the time many local residents of military service age were inducted and trained, the armistice had already been signed. But for two stepbrothers from Elston, Missouri, such delays did not keep them from the conflict since they enlisted early to serve their country.

Born November 25, 1898, Homer McCrea (pictured, center) lost his father at a young age. His mother then married widower George Landrum in 1905, uniting two families and creating a close bond between the young McCrea and an older stepbrother, Luther Landrum (not pictured).

"Luther and Homer got this idea in their heads that they would run off and join the Army," said Jean Christian, niece of the late veterans. "I know very little about their time in the service," she added, "because it's not something that was really discussed."

As is woven into family lore, Christian explained, the stepbrothers snuck away to Jefferson Barracks, Missouri, to enlist in the Army. Shortly thereafter, their father took a train to the army post in an effort to have his sons released from service. However, he was too late.

Service cards accessed from the Missouri State Archives verify that both Landrum and McCrea enlisted at Jefferson Barracks on May 9, 1917, approximately a month after the official declaration of war was made by the United States. Though the date of their enlistment indicates the two intended to serve in the same military unit, the needs of the Army soon placed them on separate paths— Landrum was assigned to Company A, 1st Machine Gun Battalion of the1st Division while his step brother was eventually assigned to Company K, 61st Infantry of the 5th Division.

A twenty-two-year-old Landrum's adventure began in earnest on October 31, 1917 upon his arrival overseas. As written in the *History of the First Division*, the machine gunners were soon issued the "Hotchkiss"—a type of machine gun used by the French and adopted by the Americans.

They soon began a brief cycle of training on the weapon followed by drills that consisted of "selecting and occupying positions and in serving the guns against an imaginary enemy position," the book further described.

Landrum and his fellow soldiers were to soon risk life and limb during some of the most hellacious episodes of the late war, which included winning "the first American victory in World War I at the Battle of Cantigny," on May 28, 1918, noted the First Division Museum at Cantigny. In later weeks, the museum shared, "the First Division participated in the major battles of Soissons, St. Mihiel and the Meuse-Argonne," the latter of which earned the young Landrum recognition that he chose to conceal from his family for several years after the war's end.

Pvt. Homer McCrea remained stateside for nearly six months following his step brother's deployment, leaving his training at Camp Greene, North Carolina, to join the battle waging in Europe alongside the Fifth Division in mid-April 1918. The horrors of trench warfare soon became a reality for McCrea as the soldiers of the division battled not only a well-entrenched German foe and filthy living conditions, but also endured merciless shelling along with heavy bombardments of mustard and phosgene gasses.

McCrea also participated in St. Mihiel and the Meuse-Argonne Offensive, during which mere survival became a triumph of its own accord. As the Society of the 1st Infantry Division notes on their website, although the men fought valiantly and overcame insurmountable odds, "[b]y the end of the war, the Division had suffered 22,668 casualties."

In the face of these tremendous odds, both McCrea and Landrum survived their baptism of fire during a war that resulted in the loss of more than 116,000 American troops in less than two years. When the conflict ended with the armistice of November 11, 1918, the step brothers remained in Europe with their respective divisions as part of the Army of Occupation.

Sadly, having survived months of German assaults that resulted in the death of many of his comrades, Sgt. McCrea died on February 17, 1919 from what is listed on his service card as "pneumonia." However, the deadly Spanish Influenza epidemic was also sweeping through American military camps during this period. Five days after the passing of his younger step brother, Private Landrum left Germany, departing for home six months prior to the remainder of the 1st Division's return to the states.

"I don't know if Luther came home on a hardship because of Homer's death," said Christain, "but considering the timing, that was likely the case."

McCrea's body was eventually returned to his family and interred in Elston Cemetery, said Christian. In the years after the war, Luther married, raised a family and worked as farmer in Mid-Missouri. As he reached his final years, he moved to Georgia to live with his daughter, where he passed away in 1992.

"Luther Landrum, a son of George Landrum of Elston, was cited for bravery during the operations of the American Army west of the Meuse from October 4 to 12, 1918," reported the February 28, 1922 edition of *The Daily Capital News*, thus revealing a secret Landrum had maintained.

The article went on to describe the three citations he received for bravery for his action in loading and firing a machine gun from an exposed position while under the constant threat of enemy shell and machine gun fire.

"He came home safe, but his brother came home in a casket," said Christian. "Homer's death was hard on him and that's why he tried to keep his awards secret." She concluded, "Nothing was shared about Homer because his death was so devastating on the family and on Luther. I think that if you can use their pictures to connect a face with their service papers and a little bit of history, then it really humanizes the sacrifice that they made. It helps ensure that what they went through won't so easily be forgotten." *(Photograph courtesy of Jean Christian)*

Otto Strobel

Lohman

It could be said of the late John "Otto" Strobel that he was a man that gave of himself in both life and death. Not only did he serve his country honorably during WWI, but after his passing, he donated his entire estate to ensure a perpetual cemetery at St. Paul's Lutheran Church in his hometown of Lohman. Yet despite all of this benevolence, Strobel is perhaps best remembered for the trips he made to Jefferson City to participate in meetings with the local Veterans of Foreign War Post—a twenty-eight-mile round trip he made by walking.

"The history of Strobel's walking feat actually got its start on the battlefields of France in 1918," reported *The Sunday News and Tribu*ne in their April 25, 1937 edition. "Marching was nothing unusual for the soldiers in those stirring days, and Strobel performed his duties so well he returned to America after the war with five medals for valor."

Prior to the veteran gaining attention because of his lengthy strolls to Jefferson City, his life's story begins on a small farm in the Lohman area when he was born on May 9, 1889.

"He spent his entire life in Lohman—except for the time he was in the Army," said Lohman historian Gert Strobel. "He was also very dedicated to his faith and really enjoyed being part of St. Paul's (Lutheran Church)," she added.

Months after America's declaration of war against Germany in 1917, a 28-year-old Strobel made the commitment to serve his country and was inducted into the U.S. Army in Jefferson City on

September 20, 1917, leaving his Mid-Missouri home for the first time in his life. According to his service card accessed through the Missouri State Archives, the recruit spent less than two months at Camp Funston, Kan., where he trained with Company M, 356th Infantry—a company that recruited several men from the Cole County area.

Though he was among acquaintances from the Lohman area during his initial training, Strobel's tenure with the company was brief since he was transferred as a replacement to Battery B, 335th Field Artillery at Camp Pike, Arkansas, on November 6, 1917.

In March 1918, he again said farewell to whatever friends he had made while at Camp Pike when he joined Battery D, 102nd Field Artillery Regiment and traveled to Camp Merritt, New Jersey. Shortly after his arrival, he was aboard a troopship bound for service in an overseas war zone. Now part of the 26th Division, Strobel and the soldiers of the 102nd were members of "the first complete American Division to be committed in France in 1918," as noted on *The Unit History of the 26th Division*, which was accessed through the website of the 26th Infantry "Yankee" Division.[53]

The website also notes that the division took part in six major campaigns of the war and "was cited (for their performance in combat) thirteen times by France, and three times by American Army Headquarters" in addition to spending two hundred and ten days fighting—the longest of all the American infantry divisions.

Returning from the war in April 1919, Gert Strobel notes that the combat-hardened soldier lived on his family's farm along with his only sibling—a sister named Antonia. In the years after the war, Strobel gained a reputation as being a hard worker, although the community's perceptions of him often limited the type of employment he was provided.

"He was not very good at communicating with people," said Gert Strobel, "which led many people to believe that because of the way he expressed himself, he might have some type of mental impair-

---

[53] 26th Infantry Division, *Unit History of the 26th Infantry Division*, http://www. yankee-division.com/history.html.

ment." She added, "All he was ever really given was menial work around town, but he was really a very bright man—an avid reader who was truly self-educated."

Newspaper accounts note that the former artillery soldier became an active member of the VFW Post 1003 in Jefferson City in the mid-1930s and even served as the post surgeon, although the duties associated with this position were not clearly described.

The most interesting of the veteran's post-war endeavors is his journey to the VFW post's bi-monthly meetings, utilizing the railroad tracks of the Bagnell Branch of the Missouri Pacific Railroad that once lay between Lohman and Jefferson City.

"Every two weeks for the last 28 months he has awakened around 3 a.m., garbed himself in his uniform cap and trod the 14 miles from his home to the city," as was explained in the April 25, 1937 edition of *The Sunday News and Tribune*. The article further noted that Strobel—a self-described "astute student of political science"—would arrive in the city several hours prior to the meeting so that he could spend time at the library reading books in both English and German.

"He loved to talk about his military service and when he got to the VFW, he felt right at home," said Gert Strobel. "After some of the meetings, the people at the Capitol knew he was coming and would let him spend the night on one of the benches inside. The next morning, he would get up and walk back to Lohman along the railroad tracks."

Strobel passed away at the Veterans' Hospital in St. Louis on December 20, 1962 at seventy-three years of age and was laid to rest in the cemetery of St. Paul's Lutheran Church, where he had been a lifelong member. Even in his passing, this often-misunderstood veteran was able to help provide for his community.

"He and his sister never made a lot of money in their lives, but they never spent anything either—if they had ten cents they would save nine cents of it," said Gert Strobel. "When both he and his sister died, they gave their entire estate—a pretty good sum of money—to the church so that a perpetual cemetery could be established." She continued, "Nobody ever paid much attention to him but he gave a lot to both his country and this community. Since neither he never married or had any children, there has really been no one to carry on his memory, and that is a shame considering what he did for the community and his service in the war." *(Photograph courtesy of Audrey Scheperle)*

William Borgmeyer

Westphalia

According to Jefferson City, Missouri, resident Roman Borgmeyer, while growing up, his father shared with him a story about an unexpected event that inspired his service in the U.S. Army—a decision that brought him face-to-face with the horrors of trench warfare and fighting against a country from which he was only a generation removed.

"My father always told me that he was working on the (state) Capitol in 1915 when he witnessed a cave-in that killed two workers," Borgmeyer explained. "He then decided to walk off the job and went and enlisted in the Army."

Though the accuracy of such accounts are occasionally diminished when filtered through generations of family retellings, records exist that can help substantiate the histories of those who have served the state and nation during conflicts long ago.

Born on November 8, 1892 in the Osage County community of Westphalia, Missouri, William Borgmeyer was the son of Henry Borgmeyer, the owner of the original Westphalia Hotel. According to census records from 1900, Henry was also a saloonkeeper and a first-generation U.S. citizen, as his father had emigrated from Germany. Military service records accessed through the Missouri State Archives indicate that on November 30, 1915, William Borgmeyer's military service began when he enlisted at Jefferson

Barracks, Missouri, and was later assigned to Battery F, 6th Field Artillery Regiment.[54]

An article by Sgt. 1st Class Kenneth A. Foss, accessed through the U.S. Army's website, notes that the 6th Field Artillery Regiment "deployed to the Mexican Border, and in 1916 it was personally selected by Gen. John J. 'Blackjack' Pershing to pursue the famed Mexican general, Pancho Villa."[55] Records maintained by descendants of William Borgmeyer reference his service during this campaign, including a photograph of the young Army private standing next to his horse while deployed along the Mexican border. But for a young man supposedly trying to escape the peril associated with his previous work at the state Capitol, he would soon find himself part of one of the deadliest conflicts in global history—World War I.

As noted by the U.S. Army Center of Military History, the 6th Field Artillery Regiment was attached to the 1st Expeditionary Division (which was later designated as the 1st Division) on June 8, 1917, two months after the United States made a formal declaration of war against Germany.

"I still have dad's service medal and it shows that he participated in five major campaigns during the war," said his son, Roman.

According to the First Division Museum website, the men assigned to the division received a callous introduction to trench warfare, which was not only characterized by anticipated threats as infantry charges and artillery attacks, but "cold, wet, cramped and rat infested" conditions producing a number of diseases including "dysentery, typhus, cholera and fungal infections such as trench foot."

Borgmeyer's service card states that his overseas service commenced July 30, 1917 and continued nearly two years. The soldier's discharge lists participation in major operations such as the Battles of Cantigny, Soissons, St. Mihiel, and the Meuse-Argonne offensive—the latter of which resulted in a condition that would haunt Borgmeyer for many years.

---

[54] Missouri Digital Heritage, *Soldier's Records*, https://s1.sos.mo.gov.

[55] Foss, *6th Field Artillery Regiment makes Ft. Drum its home*, http://www.drum.army.mil.

The last major battle of the war, the Meuse-Argonne Offensive involved 1.2 million American troops and, by the time it ended on Armistice Day (November 11, 1918), resulted in the death of more than 26,000 men. Although the division was able to defeat "in whole or part, eight German divisions," the 1st Division Museum cited, Borgmeyer was severely wounded when gassed on October 5, 1918.

Corporal Borgmeyer remained in the military until receiving his discharge at Camp Funston, Kan., on May 28, 1919, only to return home and discover that his mother passed away two months earlier. He soon embarked upon his chosen profession as a farmer in Osage County and, in 1920, married Elizabeth Jurgensmeyer of Koeltztown.

"Dad didn't really talk about the Army much," Roman said, "but I do know that after he was gassed, he had to travel to the VA hospital in Memphis [Tennessee] for regular examinations because the hospital hadn't been built in Columbia yet."

William Borgmeyer passed away on April 26, 1985 and was laid to rest in his native community of Westphalia. Though he has been gone for more than three decades, his son clearly recalls the goodbye that occurred when he received his own draft notice, thus following in the footsteps made by his father in France more than a quarter-century earlier.

"My dad took me to Linn [Missouri] to drop me off at the courthouse when I was drafted into the Army (in November 1943)," Roman explained, "and I remember that he kind of broke-up over it." He added: "He knew what I was headed for...he knew what war was."

For more information on the 1st Infantry Division, please visit. https://www.1stid.org/history. For information on the lineage and honors of the 6th Field Artillery Regiment and other U.S. Army elements, visit www.history.army.mil. *(Photograph courtesy of Roman Borgmeyer)*

Clarence Hubbard

Lohman

Distinction is a term that, when used to describe the men and women who served in the First World War, applies to a small list of individuals and includes such leaders as General John J. Pershing, who went on to serve as commander of the American Expeditionary Forces in Europe. Under Pershing's command were millions of seemingly anonymous soldiers from throughout the United States—men who did not collect accolades for their battlefield performance, but did their duty and returned home to preserve their experiences by sharing stories of their service with their families.

Born in Kansas City, Kansas, on May 9, 1896, Clarence Hubbard became one such veteran who chose to pass down his WWI experiences. He left his Kansas home at a young age to work for a farm family in the Brazito area, but was thrust into combat shortly after the United States declared war against Germany on April 6 1917.

"He made the decision to go ahead and enlist in the Army. He wasn't drafted," said Steve Jannings, the veteran's nephew.

According to Hubbard's WWI service card, he enlisted in Company L, 2nd Missouri Infantry Regiment of the Missouri National Guard in Jefferson City on May 15, 1917. Less than three months later, the 2nd Missouri was federalized and the various companies of the regiment assembled at Camp Clark in Nevada, Missouri. Hubbard and the soldiers of the regiment soon learned their "federalization" would change their National Guard company's designation to Company C, 130th Machine Gun Battalion under the 35th Infantry Division. The battalion then traveled to Camp Doniphan,

Oklahoma, spending nearly six months in training before boarding troop ships destined for France in May 1918.

"[Hubbard] never really talked much about the battles and things that they went through overseas," said Jannings, "but he did share with me many of events he found interesting and humorous."

The book *History of the Missouri National Guard* notes that the 130th Machine Gun Battalion arrived in England on May 15, 1918 and was sent to Le Havre, France days later. They were eventually sent to a French village where, the book notes, "they received a full complement of French Hotchkiss machine guns[56]...and training with them (was) instituted."[57]

Jannings remarked, "A lot of the stuff they did back then was done with mules. He a talked about it taking two men to set up the machine guns and ammunition was then brought in by mules." He added, "One man carried a tripod and the other carried the machine gun and each one weighed eighty-five pounds, he told me."

The 130th participated in some of the most gruesome engagements of the war, the most notable of which was the Meuse-Argonne Offensive in late September 1918. This battle took the lives of more than 26,000 American soldiers within six weeks' time, including fellow Company C member, Roscoe Enloe, for whom the American Legion Post in Jefferson City is named. As a machine gunner, Hubbard often had a front row seat to many of the bloody onslaughts and spent a fair amount of time living in the squalor of trenches. However, Jannings explained, it was the humorous situations he truly found joy in sharing.

"The French made cognac and they hauled it in big containers on flat rail cars," Jannings said, recalling past conversations he had with Hubbard. "One day, they got wind a train was going to come through hauling cognac so the boys got together, sized up the situation, and

---

[56] Specifically, the book refers to an 8 mm Hotchkiss machine gun. According to the book *On the Western Front: Soldier's Stories from France and Flanders*, this infantry light machine first appeared in 1909 and was often riddled with problems when used in trench warfare. However, the French-made gun proved more effective when used against aircraft. Laffin, *On the Western Front*. 28.

[57] History of the Missouri National Guard, *The 130th Machine Gun Battalion A.E.F.*, 110.

when the train arrived, they poked a hole in a barrel and filled their canteens or anything else they could find to hold liquid." With a chuckle, Jannings added, "Then they had one heck of a big party."

When the war ended with the armistice on November 11, 1918, the 130th Machine Gun Battalion incurred the battle loss of 26 enlisted soldiers, 11 officers and 176 men wounded. The battalion remained in France for several months and returned to the United States in April 1919. Hubbard received his honorable discharge on May 7, 1919. The month following his discharge, Hubbard married Cecelia Ritter of Lohman and the couple began working the farm that for years had been in his wife's family. However, Jannings said, a few years later, Hubbard chose to increase his income through a questionable opportunity.

"During Prohibition, he purchased a 1929 Chevrolet and would pick up moonshine made by a guy in Lohman and another guy in Russellville and deliver it to a speak-easy in Jefferson City. He was never caught, but the guys making the moonshine were and spent some time in the penitentiary."

In the years after the war, Hubbard gained a level of local attention for an immense collection of arrowheads and Native American artifacts found on his farm that he would display in the front room of his house. For years, Jannings explained, people would come from all around to view his collection. Hubbard passed away on January 21, 1971 and was laid to rest in the cemetery of St. Paul's Lutheran Church in Lohman. His service in the war may have appeared trifling within an army of more than four million men, but Jannings is content knowing his uncle's story has been preserved through retellings.

"I'm not sure that we have a lot of men like that anymore—he was tough and of rough character, but he was also very kind, a hard worker and a good farmer. Many don't think people realize the atrocities that happened in the war, but he talked about the Argonne forest and said that the firepower was so intense that after they left, there wasn't even a bush left standing." He added, "None of the WWI guys are with us anymore and their stories are gone. When (Hubbard) spoke about some of the things he remembered from over there, it helped me to know the man that he was and what all he experienced." *(Photograph courtesy of Audrey Scheperle)*

George Scheperle

Russellville

When handed a package of photographs and military documents pertaining to the service of a soldier from nearly a century ago, preliminary indications might suggest that uncovering the history of this long-deceased person to be a tedious process lacking in stimulation. Yet by utilizing resources such as archived regimental histories, interviews and photographs, his story comes to life, resulting in personal insight into the life of a local farmer that was molded into a soldier during the period of the First World War.

Born June 16, 1890, George Scheperle was raised in the once thriving Millbrook community near Russellville, becoming one of many local men yanked from their rural surroundings when their draft registration number was selected. The soldier's military narrative begins to take form with his induction into the Army on September 20, 1917 in Jefferson City, where the twenty-seven-year-old soon received assignment to Company M, 356th Infantry Regiment under the 89th Infantry Division.

"The (division) was organized under provisions of the draft law of May 18, 1917," stated the official history of Company M. Composed primarily of men from the Missouri counties of Cole, Boone, Henry, Andrews, St. Louis and Jackson, the company began their service in training at Camp Funston, Kansas (now Fort Riley).[58] Prior to encountering the threats posed in the trenches of the Western Front, the men of the 89th Division first had to conquer "epidemics of Meningitis

---

[58] Company 'M,' *Organization and Training*, 6.

and other less serious diseases" that assaulted the soldiers during the winter of 1918, according to company records. The division completed their training at Camp Funston in May 1918, at which time they boarded trains for Camp Mills, New York. Once there, they soon assembled on troopships destined for combat raging in France.

"He'd talk a little bit about his time in (World War I) when you got him wound up a bit, but that's been a lot of years ago and I really don't remember much about it," said Elwyn Scheperle,[59] a WWII veteran and the second of George Scheperle's three sons.

Further clarification of the soldier's experiences exists in service records available from the Missouri State Archives, denoting his arrival overseas beginning June 4, 1918. Additional details are scribbled on the backside of his "Enlistment Record," confirming his combat service two months later during the "Occupation of the Lucey Sector" when the 89th Division relieved the 82nd Division in the area northwest of Toul, France.

"The only thing I remember him talking about was his buddy," explained Ralph Scheperle,[60] the oldest son of the WWI veteran. "There were ten men in his group and one of them was named Ralph—but I don't know his last name. My father said that he told the men that he was going to go home (after the war), get married and have a son and name him Ralph because of his friend," he said.

"And here I am," he added with a grin.

Yet events cited in Company M's history not only paint Scheperle as undaunted in the face of adversity, but also revealed information about the man who would serve as the namesake for the soldier's eldest son. On October 4, 1918, less than a month after their participation in the deadly St. Mihiel Offensive—and only days before their engagement in the Meuse-Argonne Offensive—the last platoon of Company M was being relieved by the 354th Infantry in the vicinity of Beney Woods (western France) when a mustard gas attack was launched by German forces, followed by machine gun fire.

---

[59] George "Elwyn" Scheperle passed away on February 21, 2018 and was laid to rest in the cemetery of St. John's Lutheran Church in Stringtown, Missouri.

[60] Ralph Scheperle passed away on June 15, 2017 and was laid to rest in the cemetery of St. John's Lutheran Church in Stringtown.

As described in the company's history, Lt. Ralph May "called for a volunteer to go with him back into the woods and bring out the rest of the company," at which point "Corporal Scheperle stepped out," thus identifying the friendship with the soldier for whom Scheperle's son would be named years later. But this would not serve as an isolated example of Scheperle's bravery since company records go on to cite an event on November 5, 1918, when Scheperle volunteered to accompany Lt. Ralph May and a small group of fellow Company M soldiers on a mission to locate a feasible river crossing after bridges in the area had been destroyed. While "crawling across the debris and scaling the abutments of the first two bridges," the men "finally succeeded in reaching the third bridge," records state. The group was then able to infiltrate "through shell and shrapnel and in the face of galling sniping and machine gun fire," thus obtaining "valuable information as to the condition of the river and bridges."[61]

When the war finally ended on November 11, 1918, Company M remained in France with the occupational forces until returning to the United States several months later. Scheperle received his discharge on June 11, 1919, when the company was demobilized at Camp Funston, as listed on his discharge. The year following his return from war, Scheperle married Lydia Gemeinhardt and the couple settled in his native community of Millbrook. They went on to raise three sons as Scheperle worked as a bricklayer and farmer, while also practicing a trade he had learned while in the Army.

"When he was still in France after the war was over," said Ralph Scheperle, "he and another soldier attended a school to become veterinarians. Years later, he performed some veterinarian work in the community and I remember going with him a couple of times when I was a young boy." Smiling, he added, "There was a lot of stuff he saw and did during the war but somehow he managed to make it back without a scratch...and that's why I'm here."

Corporal George Scheperle passed away December 20, 1977 and is buried in the cemetery of St. John's Lutheran Church in the community of Stringtown near Lohman, Missouri. *(Photograph courtesy of the Scheperle family)*

---

[61] Company 'M," *Reorganization of Captured Territory*, 21-22.

Gus Buchta

Russellville

In many states, farmers bore the brunt of responsibility in World War I—not just from the perspective of producing the food that would be used to feed the soldiers of the United States military, but also by leaving their farms and families when drafted into military service. The late Gustav "Gus" Buchta, a Mid-Missouri farmer, embraced this responsibility and went on to carry the wounds of war in the years following his return from France.

Born in Russellville on August 27, 1893, Buchta became the sole support for both his mother and his sister, and, as noted on his registration card, was engaged in farming when he registered for the draft on June 5, 1917. The twenty-four-year-old's life quickly changed because of the Selective Service Act of 1917. As reported in the July 20, 1917 edition of the *Jefferson City Post-Tribune*, the numbers of "Many young farmers (were) drawn" including Buchta's—an event, the article further noted, that "will about complete Cole County's quota of 189 men."

"He never talked about the war, that I ever heard," said the late Dorothy Rockelman,[62] Buchta's stepdaughter, during an interview in early 2017. "Then again, he wasn't the only World War I veteran who didn't talk about what all they went through."

The farmer's service during the war begins to come into focus through several records, such as his service card available from the

---

[62] Dorothy Rockelman passed away on August 14, 2017 and was laid to rest in Trinity Lutheran Cemetery near Russellville.

Missouri State Archives. Inducted into the Army on September 20, 1917, Buchta began his military service as part of Company M, 356th Infantry under the 89th Division. "The 356th Infantry was composed of men from the State of Missouri, 'M' Company composed chiefly of men from Cole, Boone, Henry, Andrews, St. Louis and Jackson Counties," as is noted in an official history of the company.

The men of Company M trained for several weeks at Camp Funston, Kansas, where Major General Leonard Wood was serving as commander. However, as stated in a history of the 356th Infantry, in "November (1917) and the four months following, men were selected from the company to go with other units for advanced overseas service."

Buchta was transferred to a replacement battalion with whom he deployed to France in late March 1918. Several weeks later, he was reassigned to Company A, 126th Infantry Regiment—a National Guard regiment from Michigan that had been reorganized and assigned to the 32nd Division, mustering into federal service on July 15, 1917. When Buchta joined the regiment, they had been in France for nearly two months. On May 14, 1918, the regiment left their training area and "prepared to take its place in the long battle line extending from the English Channel to the borders of Switzerland, where it was destined to stay until the end of the war, except for a brief ten days in the month of September,"[63] noted the book *History of the 126th Infantry in the war with Germany.*

The regiment received instruction on trench warfare from their French counterparts who had been fighting the war for nearly four years. The 126th Infantry entered the trenches in early June 1918 and began a cycle of service on the front lines, enduring gas and shrapnel shells launched by the German forces in the Alsace region of northeastern France. On June 25, 1918, two days after the Germans made their first raid against the lines held by the 126th Infantry, Buchta was wounded in action.

"He was hit by shrapnel, "said Buchta's daughter, Dorothy Rockelman. "I know that he received some disability from the

---

[63] Gansser, *History of the 126th Infantry*, 59.

government for it after the war and eventually walked with a cane because of the injury. In later years," she added, he had to use two canes to get around."

Though it is uncertain how long Buchta was in the hospital for treatment of his injuries, his service card indicates he remained with the 126th Infantry through several deadly engagements including the Meuse-Argonne Offensive. Following the armistice on November 11, 1918, "there began to straggle through our lines in a steady stream, repatriated prisoners from the French, Russian and Italian armies...poor forlorn-looking creatures...grateful for the smallest of favors...," as was written in the aforementioned regimental history.

The men of the 32nd Division soon became part of the American Army of Occupation, marching across Luxemburg and crossing into Germany. The division remained in Germany until mid-spring 1919. However, Buchta was sent home in mid-December 1918 and was discharged from the Army on May 8, 1919.

"He got a disability from the service because of his combat injuries," said Rockelman. "After the war, he lived with his mother and did some farming, and," she added, "in the 1950s, he worked as a janitor at the Russellville School."

As Rockelmen further explained, on April 24, 1952, her mother, Lydia Hiemeyer, was married to Buchta and the couple remained members of Trinity Lutheran Church in Russellville. The WWI veteran passed away in 1977 and was laid to rest in Trinity Lutheran Cemetery near Russellville.

Rockelman realizes that although her stepfather accepted the responsibility given him during the First World War, she knows little of his personal combat experiences. Yet several archival sources provide a glimpse into the willingness of Buchta and his fellow farmers to serve their country, and their contributions both during and after the war. On April 23, 1917, former Missouri Gov. Frederick Gardner[64] held a war conference at the state capitol, stating, "Look,

---

[64] Frederick Dozier Gardner was born in Kentucky on November 6, 1869 and later attended Harvard University. During the early part of his career, he became president and sole owner of St. Louis Coffin Company and first entered politics with his election as governor of Missouri on November 7, 1916. After

if you will, from the dome of this great building, across the millions of acres of the finest farm lands over which the eagle has ever spread his wings." [65]

Acknowledging those who would soon make robust sacrifices on behalf of Missouri, Gardner added, "Look again, and you will see the man: There is the patriot. There he stands, the farmer... the mother in the doorway, the daughter by her side...ready, if the country calls, to see the father and the son go to defend the nation's honor." *(Photograph courtesy of Dorothy Rockelman)*

---

he left office on January 10, 1921, Gardner retired from politics. He passed away on December 18, 1933 at sixty-four years of age from an infection that developed in his jaw following the extraction of a tooth. He was laid to rest in Bellefontaine Cemetery in St. Louis.

[65] Missouri State Board of Agriculture, *Wartime Farming in Missouri*, 13.

Layton Longan

California

The name Layton Longan has been all but erased from the memory of the Mid-Missouri community since the young man, who was killed in 1918 while fighting in World War I, has little more than a small grave marker in a non-descript cemetery to perpetuate his legacy. Yet a historical society located in a small French village has memorialized Longan and several American servicemembers who made the ultimate sacrifice on behalf of their freedoms. In an email to the state department of the American Legion, Hubert Martin, president of a historical society in Alsace, France, sought information on the life of Longan to honor the late soldier during memorial events held in September 1918, in addition to recognizing four dozen other American soldiers who fell in battle in the mountains of Alsace during WWI.

Born on a farm north of California near Kliever, Missouri, on October 23, 1894, Longan was the youngest of three children. In 1916, his father passed away and the following year the United States entered into the First World War. As evidenced by his registration card, the twenty-two-year-old fell into the age group required to register for the military draft on June 5, 1917. At the time of his registration, Longan had worked six months for a farmer in Jamestown, although he resided in the community of Tipton. However, on July 2, 1917, he traveled to Sedalia and "enlisted in the Missouri National Guard...and with this organization was inducted into Federal Service..." reported the *California Democrat* on June 23, 1921.

Assigned to Company D, Sixth Missouri Infantry Regiment, the book *History of the Missouri National Guard* explains that both the Third and Sixth Missouri Infantry Regiments were consolidated to form the 140th Infantry Regiment under the 35th Infantry Division during WWI, and moved to "Camp Doniphan, a horseshoe-shaped site on the hard sands of Oklahoma, within the Fort Sill Reservation...."[66] Longan and his fellow soldiers had many hardships cast upon them by Mother Nature prior to their deployment overseas, spending the first part of their service in Oklahoma battling dust, which was followed by "particles of snow, mingled with the blowing sand (that) cut the skin like a knife." The cycle of adversity continued "with an epidemic of spinal meningitis, forerunner of the nation-wide epidemic of Spanish influenza of the next year," bringing yet additional misery to the soldiers who were in the final stages of preparing for the uncertainties of trench warfare.

In April of 1918, the men of the regiment boarded trains, eventually arriving in Hoboken, New Jersey, "where we quietly marched up the gangway into the (troop) ships that were to be our home for the next two weeks," wrote Evan Alexander Edwards, regimental chaplain and historian, in his book *From Doniphan to Verdun: The Official History of the 140th Infantry Regiment*. Edwards goes on to explain that the soldiers of the Missouri regiment were soon in France and imbued with the desire to join the fray after witnessing wounded soldiers being transported on a Red Cross hospital train. "The sight sobered us, and increased our desire to get to the front," he revealed.[67]

The regiment, including Longan, received their first "look at the Germans through the sites of (their) rifles" when they moved to the trenches in the latter part of July 1918. They soon received their baptism of fire under German artillery barrages and attempted raids on their trenches, the latter of which were repelled with their American Enfield rifles. For the next several days, artillery bombardments endured, eventually taking the life of young Private Longan on

---

[66] History of the Missouri National Guard, *The 140th A.E.F.*, 54.
[67] Edwards, From Doniphan to Verdun, 28.

August 14, 1918. As the regimental chaplain explained, Longan—and several of his fellow soldiers killed in the attacks, "were buried reverently, their bodies laid to rest with loving care" in a cemetery near the small village of Linthal, France.

In a letter to Longan's mother dated August 15, 1918, Lt. Albert G. Gardner—a Chicago native and commander of Company D, 140th Infantry Regiment—wrote, "We, the young manhood of our great, free nation, are fighting for the liberty of our country and the world." He added, "Your son lost his life in the face of the enemy. His duty to his country, to his home, and to his God is nobly done."

The early days of trench warfare by the regiment became the end of watch for many, but the survivors went on to fight in several major engagements of the war, remaining in Europe through the spring of 1919. Longan, however, did not return home until two years later when, as reported by the *California Democrat* on June 23, 1921, his remains were returned to the U.S. and interred in the New Salem Cemetery north of California.

Private Layton Longan—a young farm boy from Moniteau County, who answered the nation's call to colors during the "war to end all wars"—may not be memorialized in any magnificent marble or bronze monuments, yet a small historical society in France strived to ensure that his sacrifice, and that of his contemporaries, endure in the memory of the French people.

"I'm looking for information about each soldier (who died in action near Linthal)," wrote Hubert Martin, president of the historical society in Alsace, France, noting that Longan's was to be used during WWI commemoration ceremonies in Linthal in September 1918. He added, "I send you my best greetings from France and thank you so much for helping us not to forget all these soldiers who lost their life for our liberty." *(Photograph courtesy of Moniteau County Historical Society)*

Edgar Stieferman

Jefferson City

Many families have an undercurrent of military service running through their historical narratives. In this spirit, as the nation entered World War I, local families such as the Stiefermans answered the call to service through either the draft or voluntary enlistment, thus setting a steadfast example for generations of offspring who would go on to follow in their footsteps.

Edgar "Ed" Stieferman was living in Jefferson City when the United States officially declared war against Germany on April 6, 1917, thrusting the nation into the First World War. Soon, scores of young men with whom he was acquainted—including relatives—were drafted into military service. As the National Archives and Records Administration explained, on "May 18, 1917, the Selective Service Act was passed authorizing the President to increase temporarily the military establishment of the United States." This would result in three registrations, the first of which was held on June 5, 1917, "for all men between the ages of 21 and 31."[68]

Since he was twenty-one years old at the time of this requirement, Stieferman registered for the draft. His twenty-nine-year-old brother, John, also registered while another of his brothers, James, had enlisted in the U.S. Army several weeks previous and was already in training at a camp in Texas.

In the weeks that followed, draft order numbers were drawn in Washington D.C., and Stieferman's brother, John, was drafted

---

[68] National Archives, *World War I Draft Registration Cards*, www.archives.gov.

into the U.S. Army in Jefferson City on October 4, 1917. While his two older brothers were away from home learning to become soldiers, Stieferman remained in Jefferson City and worked at the former Creedon's Restaurant on Madison Street. Whether it was an overwhelming desire to join the war effort or he sought to prevent the draft from dictating with whom he would serve, Stieferman made the decision to enlist in the Marine Corps on May 15, 1918. The fresh recruit was then sent to the training camp at Parris Island, South Carolina, where he spent the next several weeks undergoing battle-focused instruction.

"After the war in Europe had begun, the Marines, with perhaps a bit more foresight than the other branches of the military, began to develop an institution of training, an institution that came to be called 'boot camp,'" wrote Van Lee in his book *Vin Rouge, Vin Blanc, Beaucoup Vin: The American Expeditionary Force in WWI*. Lee further noted, "The program was designed to build the men into tough fighters. It was also designed to weed out men who were not up to the high standards that the Corps desired." [69]

Stieferman would not go on to fight alongside his fellow Marines in iconic clashes such as the Battle of Belleau Wood (during which the Marines earned the label "Devil Dogs"). Instead, they embraced his experience in food service and assigned him to cook for the Marine Barracks in Philadelphia, Pennsylvania, which housed the Marine Guard that provided security for the local Navy yard.

Upon completing his enlistment on March 29, 1919, Stieferman returned to Jefferson City and married two years later. He and his wife went on to raise three daughters and a son. He used the culinary skills he refined in the service by operating several restaurants in Jefferson City in the decades after the war. The veteran passed away in 1955 and is buried in the Jefferson City National Cemetery.

His son, Robert "Bob" Stieferman followed a similar path when, in 1943, the eighteen-year-old enlisted in the Marine Corps during the heart of World War II. After completing his boot camp, the younger Stieferman completed training in San Diego to become

---

[69] Lee, *Vin Rouge*, 35.

a cook and baker. The Marine's service records indicate that unlike his father in WWI, he deployed overseas from March 29, 1944 to September 10, 1945, serving in support of World War II operations in the Marianas and other major battles including the invasion of Okinawa.

"Bob Stieferman stayed in the Marines until 1947," said Betty Williamson, first cousin to the veteran. "He then enlisted in the U.S. Army Air Forces in March 1947 (which became the U.S Air Force months later) and retired from the Air Force in September 1964."

The younger Stieferman married three times throughout his life and was the father of one daughter. Following his military retirement, he lived in Leavenworth, Kansas, and served as commander of a local Disabled American Veterans chapter. He passed away in 1974 and is buried in Hawthorn Memorial Gardens in Jefferson City. Since their passing, Betty Williamson has worked diligently to collect information on the WWI service of her uncle, Ed Stieferman, and to learn more about the time Bob spent in the Marines and Air Force. It is an endeavor, she affirms, that not only allows her to reflect on good memories of these relatives but grants insight into the service of which they never spoke.

"When I was little and living in Kansas City, my parents would take us to stay with Uncle Ed in Jefferson City," said Williamson. "I can remember while we were there, he was always running a restaurant and all of us kids, including his son Bob, would work there as well." She added, "Uncle Ed never spoke about his military service and since all of children are now deceased, it might not be shared. Also, I never had the opportunity to visit with Bob in later years about his service, but now that they are both gone and I don't want what they did for the country to be forgotten." *(Photo courtesy of Betty Williamson)*

John Stieferman

Jefferson City

There is a small white binder bursting with pictures and documents that California, Missouri, resident Betty Williamson maintains is a connection to her family's past. Inside it, she has collected assorted bits and pieces of information related to the history of several of her family members who served during past wars, including a beloved uncle who was drafted during the First World War.

"I have a lot of wonderful memories about my uncle, John Stieferman," said Williamson, "but I don't ever remember him talking about the time that he spent in the service."

Born near Russellville September 2, 1887, Stieferman was raised in a family consisting of five sons and four daughters. As the years passed, his father moved the family to Jefferson City, which is where young Stieferman would go on to spend his formative years. But as the drums of war began to beat and America was drawn into World War I in April 1917, "all men between the ages of 21 and 31" were required to register with their local draft board during the first registration held on June 5, 1917," explained the website of the National Archives.[70] Stieferman complied with the mandate and registered in Jefferson City.

Although at the upper end of the age range for those required to register, Stieferman's draft order number was selected and the thirty-year-old was inducted into the U.S. Army in Jefferson City on

---

[70] National Archives and Records Administration, *World War I Draft Registration Cards*, www.archives.gov.

October 4, 1917, according to records obtained from the Missouri State Archives. His service card notes that the first stop in his transition from civilian to soldier began with a temporary assignment to the 164th Depot Brigade at Camp Funston, Kansas, which was located on present-day Fort Riley. Established on July 18, 1917, Camp Funston served as a training camp for the 89th Division.

As is explained in the book *Camp Travis and Its Part in the World War*, depot brigades had the "purpose and function...to receive recruits sent by the various draft boards, clothe them, feed and house them and give them the various physical examinations and inoculations...and assigning the fit men to training battalions."[71]

In the spirit of reassignment, Stieferman was soon on his way to Camp Cody, New Mexico, to begin training with Company D, 109th Engineer Battalion in late October 1917. The battalion was constituted only weeks prior to Stieferman's arrival as a component of the 34th Division, which earned the designation "Sandstorm Division" because of the desert environment in which they trained.

In the book *Spirits of the Border IV: The History and Mystery of New Mexico*, the authors explain that in 1917, the "U.S. War Department established a 2,000-acre training camp near the town of Deming, New Mexico..." They went on to explain that the camp was initially named Camp Deming because of its location, but later renamed Camp Cody in honor of the famed William "Buffalo Bill" Cody, who passed away on January 10, 1917.[72]

Further illumination is cast upon the experiences of Stieferman's time training at the southwestern camp through *The Story of the Famous 34th Infantry Division*, a book written by John Hougen. As the author noted, soldiers at the camp were to contend with many weather-based challenges including "sand in the eyes, sand that cut the faces and, worst of all, sand that forever lodged in the food of the men."[73]

---

[71] Johns, *Camp Travis*, 225.
[72] Hudnall, *Spirts of the Border IV,* 111.
[73] Hougen, *The Story of the 34th Infantry Division*, 20.

The 34th Division began to form at Camp Cody in late August 1917 and embarked upon twelve months of intense training to prepare them to serve as combat troops overseas. As Hougen went on to explain, on August 27, 1918, "the first troops left for Camp Dix, New Jersey, from where they departed on the *S.S. 'Cretic,'*" bound for France. Yet, as the troops with whom he had trained for months began journey overseas, where they would subsequently be assigned as replacements for other divisions, Stieferman remained at Camp Cody and was reassigned to an organization known as a "Development Battalion."

Development battalions, as noted by the Office of Medical History of the U.S. Army Medical Department, were established as convalescence centers for soldiers who experienced orthopedic complications such as foot strain and associated conditions. Stieferman would remain assigned to this battalion until receiving an honorable discharge on January 31, 1919.

Stieferman later moved to Kansas City and was employed as a trackman for the Missouri Pacific Railroad. In the years after the war, he married and raised a son. The WWI veteran died on July 2, 1973 and was laid to rest in Mt. Washington Cemetery in Independence, Missouri.

"I don't have very much information or documents about Uncle John other than some family photos that were handed down to my mother," said Williamson, the veteran's niece. "And although I don't recall him ever speaking about the time he spent in the Army while we were together, it would be nice to know a little more about his service." With mirthful reflection, she added, "The one thing that sticks out in my mind is how active he was, even when he was much older. I guess it was from pumping those railroad cars up and down the track all those years. I must say, he really was the most energetic person that I have ever met." *(Photo courtesy of Betty Williamson)*

James Stieferman

Jefferson City

As a young girl, Betty Williamson enjoyed spending time with several of her uncles and building a collection of enduring memories. This treasured time with these family members, however, did not include discussions of their service during the First World War, which has left their niece to unearth information that might provide a glimpse into the time they spent in a military uniform.

"James Franklin (Frank) Stieferman was born August 22, 1891, the fourth child of Jacob and Sureldia Stieferman," Williamson explained. "It was a rather large family that eventually grew in size to five sons and four daughters," she added.

Stieferman was working as farmhand in the Jefferson City area when, on April 6, 1917, Congress granted President Woodrow Wilson's request for a formal declaration of war against Germany. Missouri native, Major General Enoch H. Crowder, quickly began to craft the Selective Service Act, establishing the mechanism for registering, classifying, and inducting scores of men into the military—a process known as the "draft." But several weeks prior to the first draft registration, a twenty-five-year-old Stieferman made the decision to enlist and was inducted into the U.S. Army at Jefferson Barracks in south St. Louis on May 13, 1917. Within a few days, the young recruit was on his way to train with his new organization—Company G, 64th Infantry Regiment of the 7th Division.

"The Seventh Division was organized January 1, 1918, from troops of the Regular Army, and by transfers from other units," reported the War Plans Division in their report, *Brief Histories of*

Divisions, U.S. Army 1917-1918. They further explained, "For the purposes of training, they concentrated at Camp MacArthur, Texas, in June 1918..."[74] Located in Waco, Texas, Camp MacArthur was named for General Arthur MacArthur—a U.S. Army general and Medal of Honor recipient who was the father of famed WWII general Douglas MacArthur. The camp covered a sprawling 10,699 acres and was at the time used as an infantry replacement and training camp, an officers' training school, and a demobilization facility.

While Stieferman was embroiled in the daily rigors of becoming a soldier at the Texas military camp, his older brother, John, was drafted into the U.S. Army and went on to spend the remainder of World War I at Camp Cody, New Mexico. In the spring of 1918, his younger brother, Edgar, enlisted in the Marine Corps and also remained stateside during the term of his enlistment. During his training, Stieferman was assigned duties as a wagoner within his company. This would have required him to demonstrate competencies ranging from the proper loading and securing of supplies on wagons to harnessing and caring for the animals used to haul his company's equipment.

As the 7th Division prepared for deployment to France in late summer 1918, an incident occurred that earned them the name "Hourglass" division. As the story goes, the division's symbol was two inverted sevens painted on the bags of the troops. However, the paint ran and the symbol appeared as inverted triangles similar to an hourglass—thus a new symbol for the division was born.

War Plans Division records indicate the division set sail for France on August 6, 1918 with the last groups arriving September 3, 1918. Stieferman's military records indicate he arrived in France on August 26, 1918. With a little more than two months until the armistice, the division—minus its artillery elements—was assigned to the 15th Training Area headquartered at Ancy-Le-Franc, a small village located in northcentral France. At the end of September, they then moved into the Toul area to relieve the 90th Division in the area known as the Puvenelle Sector.

---

[74] War Plans Division, *Brief Histories of U.S. Divisions*, 15.

"From November 9 to November 11(the division) participated in the general attack made by the 2d Army in the Meuse-Argonne Offensive," reported the War Plans Division. At the point of the armistice on November 11, the division had spent two days in active service sectors and 31 days in quiet sectors. Additionally, they took 69 prisoners and incurred 1,693 casualties while overseas. Stieferman remained in France with the division until they sailed for the United States seven months later. Following the return of the division to New York on June 20, 1919, he was sent to Camp Zachary Taylor, Kentucky, where he received his discharge less than a week later.

"After the war, he lived with us for a while in Kansas City and worked with my father at a local steel plant," said the veteran's niece, Betty Williamson. "He eventually earned enough money to purchase his own farm near Hallsville, Missouri." Williamson went on to explain that her uncle, who remained a bachelor his entire life, became seriously ill in the spring of 1952 and demonstrated focused determination in seeking assistance.

"Uncle Frank didn't have a phone and became so weak during his illness that he crawled in mud and cold weather to the nearest neighbor's home...some distance away," Williamson said. "The neighbors then contacted our family and he was taken to the hospital in Kansas City, but eventually transferred to the veterans hospital in Wadsworth, Kansas, where he died shortly after."

The legacy of scores of veterans have lived on through the memories of their offspring, but as Williamson notes, since her Uncle Frank did not have any children to pass down his history, a recipe of her memories combined with documentation preserved by her mother ensures others might have a glimpse into his military service.

"Mom and I would go down to his farm every summer and help him with canning fruits and vegetables along with other types of chores," Williamson said. "I have many good memories of those times we spent together, but I am glad that my mother saved his papers and photos after he passed so that we could have some insight regarding his service in WWI. Otherwise, it may have been forever lost." *(Photo courtesy of Betty Williamson)*

William J. Scott

Tipton

A silver prize cup spotted with age rests on a fireplace mantle in the historic Price James Memorial Library in the community of Tipton. It may appear to be little more than a paltry and forgotten relic, yet represents a connection to the past and the dedication of a woman seeking to honor the legacy of her stepson who perished while serving in the former U.S Army Air Corps prior to World War II. Scant records exist on the brief life of William "Billy" Johnson Scott. However, according to the *Find A Grave* website, he was born in Pawhuska, Oklahoma, on February 13, 1905. Census records from 1920 note that he was raised with a sister, Violet, whom was approximately two years his junior.

The *Daily Oklahoman* newspaper published on May 21, 1914 said that his father, Eugene F. Scott, was one of "the intermarried Osages" whose "[wife] and children are upon the tribal roles." The elder Scott's Native American wife passed away sometime in the years prior to 1920. *The Illustrated History of Tipton Missouri*, published in 2008, explains that Roxie James, born in 1887, was teaching music in Oklahoma when "she fell in love with, and married, the widowed father of two of her pupils. Eugene Francis Scott was a lawyer and had considerable oil interests in Oklahoma."

Scott's father and stepmother, the aforementioned historical compilation reported, maintained homes in Oklahoma, Kansas City and Tipton. Their home in Tipton has since become the clubhouse for the Tipton Country Club. Graduating from high school in the Osage Nation community of Pawhuska, Oklahoma, Billy Scott received an Ivy League education at Dartmouth College in New Hampshire and participated in the school's Reserve Officer Training Corps program. He earned a bachelor of science degree in 1928 and soon began training to become a pilot with the Army Air Corps—the forerunner to the U.S. Air Force.

Scott traveled to Brooks Field near San Antonio, Texas, for Primary Flying School and went on to attend Advanced Flying School at nearby Kelly Field. He graduated from his aviation training at Kelly Field in 1929, four years after famed aviator Charles Lindbergh completed his own training there. On March 30, 1930, Scott arrived in Hawaii "for two years of active duty on reserve status," wrote the *Honolulu-Star Bulletin* on December 17, 1931. The paper further noted that following his arrival, he received a commission as a second lieutenant.

"Organization of a wing which will incorporate all army air activities in Hawaii, has been started at the Hawaiian department air office at Fort Shafter on orders received from the war department Thursday," reported the *Honolulu Star-Bulletin* on February 27, 1931. "The unit will be known as the 18th Composite Wing..."

The young aviator was assigned to the new wing and, following his arrival on the island of Oahu, began to distinguish himself as a pilot during flights originating from Wheeler Field, a location that became a principal target in the attack on Pearl Harbor a decade later. Adventure soon abounded for the aviator when on December 22, 1930, less than nine months after his assignment to the 18th Composite Wing, he was forced to parachute from an attack plane that became inoperable near Wheeler Field.

He also began piloting gliders, often referred to as sailplanes, and in late fall of 1931 set "a new American glider record when he stayed in the air 6 hours and 36 minutes," reported the December 9, 1931 edition of the *Miami Daily News-Record (Miami, Oklahoma)*. There was little time for celebration of his recent accomplishment because of a tragedy that occurred while Lt. Scott was competing in a glider competition on December 17, 1931, an event sponsored by the Honolulu chapter of the National Aeronautic Association.

The *Honolulu Star-Bulletin* noted in their December 17, 1931 edition, "Witnesses say that Lt. Scott's [glider] lost its rudder just as he cast off from the tow cable. This caused the remainder of the tail assembly to disintegrate and an instant later one wing came off." It was observed that the glider then gained speed in its descent, crashing to the ground with "Lt. Scott tangled in the wreckage."

Later reports revealed that the glider, which had taken Lt. Scott's life, had been a gift from his father and was the same aircraft he had used to set the American distance record three weeks earlier. The aviator's body was returned to his father and stepmother, who at the time were living in the state of California, and laid to rest in the community of his youth, Pawhuska, Oklahoma. "'Endurance Without Return to Starting Point," were the bold words inscribed upon a silver cup donated by the late aviator's fellow fliers and which accompanied Lt. Scott's body when it was returned to the states.

Shortly after his father's death in 1944, Scott's stepmother moved to Kansas City and later to Tipton, where she passed away on May 6, 1976. Inspired to honor the service of her stepson, she endowed more than $886,000 to the University of Oklahoma to establish the Lt. William J. Scott Scholarship, which continues to give preference to students of the Osage Nation. The silver cup and photographs of Lt. Scott remained in the home of his grandfather in Tipton—an ornate building that has since been refurbished to serve as the Price James Memorial Library. Cloaked by case upon case of library books, the silver cup remains a tangible link to an aviation pioneer whose future was snuffed out when only twenty-six years old.

His dedication to military success was described by the *Honolulu Star-Bulletin*, reporting on December 18, 1931 that the final words muttered by Lt. Scott before he died were "I've won," revealing the young man went to his grave competing for aviation greatness. *(Photograph courtesy of Price James Memorial Library – Tipton)*

CHAPTER 3
WORLD WAR II

Eugene Earle Amick Jr.

Boonville

As a young man coming to age in pre-World War II small-town America, mid-Missouri resident Eugene "Gene" Earle Amick, Jr. possessed a strong sense of family, duty and patriotism. Born in Boonville, Missouri, on January 26, 1919, Amick served as both a mentor and role model for his younger sister, Joanne Amick Comer, who now resides in Texas. She recalls the genuine interest her older brother often displayed regarding her well-being.

"Gene taught me how to ice skate on a lake in a nearby park, taught me that if I punched a hole in a top of a soft drink bottle and sucked my soft drink through the hole it would last longer…and taught me how to play touch football," recalled his younger sibling.

The interest in his younger sister did not diminish with the passage of years. Even when Gene left home to attend college, which included studies at the University of Missouri- Kansas City and William Jewell College (the latter from which he graduated in 1941), he continued to assist his sister in establishing her own soda pop stand and allowed her to retain any profits…as long as she did not consume too much of the product between her sales.

Gene eventually joined the Navy Reserve less than three months prior to the attack on Pearl Harbor, finished his initial training and was appointed as a midshipman in February of 1942. He was then commissioned as an ensign on May 14, 1942, after successful completion of the officers' candidate course at the U.S. Naval Reserve Midshipman's School at Northwestern University.

Following his departure for military service, Amick continued to provide guidance to his younger sister. She recalls her brother giving her a Tootsie Toy naval fleet upon his departure for training and explaining to her the proper placement of the ships within the fleet so to best protect the battleships. Comer (his sister) fondly recalls keeping a small flag fastened to a wall above the bookcase on which her diminutive fleet rested and the letters she received from her brother, while he was out to sea, encouraging her to keep the flag flying high above the fleet of which he was now a part.

Ensign Amick was married on May 17, 1942, just a week prior to reporting to his new assignment as the communications officer aboard the *USS Astoria*.

During August of 1942, only three months following his marriage, the young officer's cruiser was attacked by the Japanese while attempting to protect American beachheads off Savo Island, which is part of the Solomon Island chain off of Guadalcanal. During the shelling that ensued, Radio Station No. 1 was demolished and all hands killed—Ensign Amick was commanding radio station No. 2. In order to get his radio station up and running so that communications could be reestablished, Amick realized he would need two communication reels, located in the now demolished first station.

The ensign dashed through a barrage of shellfire and miraculously reached the first station where he was able to locate the two reels. However, when making the return trip to the second station, he was struck by shellfire and killed instantly. A fellow sailor later told Amick's father that when his son's body was found, the young ensign was still clutching both reels.

In honor of the young sailor's bravery and ultimate sacrifice, the U.S. Navy chose to name a ship in his honor—the *USS Amick* (DE-168). The ship was laid down on November 30, 1942 (meaning the first parts of the keel were placed on the dry dock where the ship was to be built) and officially launched on May 27, 1943.

The destroyer escort served the remainder of the war and on September 2, 1945, she eventually played host to the unconditional surrender of the Palau Islands by Japanese forces —the same date of the formal surrender by Japan aboard the *USS Missouri* in Tokyo Bay.

The *USS Amick* served in various naval capacities where it even operated as part of the Japanese Maritime Self-Defense Force. The aging vessel was sold to the Republic of Philippines in 1976 and, according to online naval sources, was scrapped in 1989.

A handful of former sailors who served on board the *USS Amick* attended a reunion a few years ago during which they held a small ceremony to dedicate a bronze plaque at the National Museum of the Pacific War in honor of the vessel.

From the annals of Second World War arose several accounts of heroism by young men and women who would never again witness seeing the shores of America. Many of these sacrifices have been preserved for posterity. However, few servicemembers have been bestowed such a tribute as to have a naval vessel christened in their honor.

Though the *USS Amick* may have been relegated to the scrap yard of distant memory, the sacrifices made by a young Mid-Missouri native in securing our precious freedoms resonates as loudly now as it did several decades ago thanks to the efforts of a sister seeking to honor the memory of a departed brother. *(Photo courtesy of Joanne Comer)*

David Shipley

Tipton

The late Dr. David O. Shipley was known by many to be a man of stalwart faith, choosing to dedicate his life and energy to the ministry. This calling required focus and the pursuit of an education, much of which was inspired by a lieutenant who Shipley encountered while serving in a segregated environment during World War II.

"My father talked about his [military] service in general terms," said Shipley's youngest son, Douglas, "such as where he was stationed and some of the things that he did. He was quite an influential and inspirational person," he added.

Born in Tipton, Missouri, in 1925, Shipley was raised in the world of Jim Crow laws and segregation, attending the all-black Harrison School where his father was a teacher and principal. But in September 1943, before he was able to complete his high school education, the eighteen-year-old Shipley was inducted into the U.S. Navy at California, Missouri, then traveled to Great Lakes, Illinois, to complete his basic training.

"In the early months of the war, the Navy Department designated Great Lakes as the site for training African-Americans in boot camp, as well as Navy specialties," noted an article found on the Navy's website.[75] However, the article further noted that this training was "completely segregated," as was much of the country at the time.

Following his initial training in Illinois, Shipley was sent to the Naval Air Station in Pensacola, Florida, and, according to his "Naval

---

[75] NS Great Lakes, *History*, http://www.mybaseguide.com/navy/21-584.

Training Course Certificate," trained as a coxswain. It was here, the document informs, he learned to operate sixty-three-foot-long crash boats that remained on a standby status, prepared to respond to situations involving a plane crash or when small vessels encountered trouble.

The time he spent in training in the southern community would not be free of concerns related to racial discrimination and segregation. Instead, Shipley felt compelled to stand up against the injustices he encountered on the base.

"In the mess hall, white military men sat on one side, Negroes on the other," wrote Shipley in his book *Neither Black Nor White: The Whole Church for the Broken World*. He added, "A friend and I stationed ourselves inside the door and entreated our men to mix it up."[76]

Months later, noted Shipley's son, Douglas, "My father was apparently doing something between two boats and got his feet caught between them, crushing all ten of his toes. He could not walk for a while and spent several weeks recovering in the base hospital."

During his time in medical treatment, Shipley returned to the mess hall where he and a friend had previously confronted the issue of segregation. Upon noticing the situation had not changed, Shipley noted that he "refused to accept it, sitting alone in the white section to eat my meals." He added, "I continued my one-man protest until honorably discharged from the service after the war."

Though Shipley was drafted into the service prior to graduating from high school, a lieutenant named Courtney Smith demonstrated an interest in his future and "insisted that [he] should finish [his] high school work through the United States Armed Forces Institute...." The officer also recommended that Shipley continue his studies after the war, explained the veteran in an article in the August 30, 1979 edition of the Tipton Times.

Earning his GED, the inspiration provided by this naval officer would have long-term implications, especially in the years following Shipley's discharge. When leaving the service in May 1946, he not only continued his educational pursuits, but also went on to fulfill a lifelong wish.

---

[76] Shipley, *Neither Black nor White*, 24.

"My dad always wanted to be a minister," said Douglas. "When he was a little boy, he had his younger sister sit in a chair while he would preach to her."

In 1948, Shipley graduated from Lincoln Junior College (Kansas City) with an associate's degree and received his license to preach the same year. He then enrolled in Baker University in Baldwin, Kansas, earning his bachelor's degree in 1950 and was ordained the same year. He went on to complete both a bachelor's and master's degree in divinity from Central Theological Seminary in Kansas City and later earned a doctorate of ministry in marriage and family counseling from the Eastern Baptist Theological Seminary in Pennsylvania.

Although his career history is almost too lengthy to list, Dr. Shipley served as the first black chaplain for the Kansas City Police Department and became the pastor for churches of both the Presbyterian and Baptist denominations, which included nearly a decade as pastor of Second Baptist Church in Jefferson City.

The author of several books and recipient of an Image Award from the Urban League of Greater Kansas City, Missouri, Dr. Shipley—the married father of four sons—passed away on March 11, 2002 and was buried in Mt. Moriah Cemetery in Kansas City.

The veteran's account of dedication to faith and family is firmly rooted, if not inspired, by the brief time he served in the United States Navy. It was during this period that he was exposed to the disconcerting reality of segregation, but later received the compassionate support of an officer who recognized his potential. This, Shipley's son notes, was a defining moment in his father's legacy.

"I've always taken the approach to learn from my elders because it gives me a sense of who I am, where I come from...it comforts me," said Douglas Shipley. "There were many black men and women who served their country before my father and many have served since, but I think it is important to remember the struggles he and his counterparts—such as the Tuskegee Airmen—were forced to overcome. Or else," he concluded, "we run the risk of it becoming a lost part of history to our current generations." *(Photograph courtesy of Douglas Shipley)*

James Belshe

Eldon

"Seventy-something years ago," described Eldon, Missouri, veteran James Belshe during a 2016 interview, a "wide-eyed young man still in high school tried to enlist in the Army Air Forces with dreams of someday becoming a pilot." When he was told he was colorblind and ineligible to pursue a military aviation career, he returned to his high school studies.

"That's when I got drafted by the Army," Belshe grinned. "I graduated [from Eldon High School] in May 1943 and a few days later I was at Jefferson Barracks being inducted into the Army."

After only a few days at the St. Louis area post, the new recruit traveled to Camp Roberts, California, spending the next few weeks in basic infantry training followed by instruction as a "field lineman," as is noted on his discharge papers.

"They decided that I would go into communications," Belshe recalled. "We learned Morse code, semaphore [communication using flags], radios, telephones...anything that was used to communicate somehow."

When his training ended in late summer 1943, he returned home for two weeks of leave and then traveled to California to board the *New Amsterdam,* a Dutch luxury liner converted to a troop ship. The ship sailed for New Zealand, where Belshe was assigned to the headquarters company for the 161st Infantry Regiment of the 25th Infantry Division (ID). As Belshe explained, the 25th ID had already participated in several major engagements and encountered fierce resistance from well-organized Japanese forces on Guadalcanal followed by operations in the Solomon Islands. Having encountered significant casualties, the division moved to New Zealand toward the latter part of 1943 to recuperate and take on replacements such as Belshe.

"I really enjoyed my time at New Zealand," Belshe affirmed. "That's when the division was on leave, which meant that I was too." He added, "We had a big stock tank full of beer [in the middle of the camp] and you could go to town anytime you wanted. I thought to myself, 'This isn't so bad.'"

The soldier discovered that his pleasant duty conditions were temporary when, in early 1944, the division moved to an "area in the woods" in New Caledonia—a French territory comprised of islands in the South Pacific.

"I worked on the switchboard so I knew what was going on around the place," said the former soldier. "We also strung telephone lines all over our area of operations."

The men of the division were soon advised that they would become part of the force to invade the Philippines and, in November 1944, began practicing assault landings followed by a journey aboard landing ship tanks (LSTs) to Lingayen Gulf several weeks later. Upon landing, Belshe recalls, there was not any notable resistance since the "Alamo Scouts [recon unit of the U.S. Army] and Fiji Scouts had pretty well taken care of everything," but the division's push inland on the island of Luzon introduced the young soldier to ever-present threats existent in all areas of a war zone.

"The island [Luzon] was pretty well cut in two by us and other divisions," said Belshe. "Some divisions pushed south [from the middle of the island] and we pushed north. From shortly after we arrived," he added, "it basically became a running battle across the island."

Continuing his assignment in the headquarters section, Belshe explained that his duties in communications kept him several miles behind heavy enemy action. However, on March 11, 1945, he discovered his distance from the front lines did not diminish his exposure to the threats posed by Japanese soldiers.

"Two fellows and myself decided we would walk to the [tent] to get us some chow," he said. "We were walking down this little path and KABOOM!—that's all that I remember."

What Belshe later discovered is that despite the dozens of American soldiers that had secured their area of operations, a Japanese soldier managed to conceal himself along the path, shrouded by heavy brush and bushes. When Belshe and his fellow soldiers passed by the hidden enemy soldier, a grenade was rolled toward them.

"I was in the lead and was hit with shrapnel from the waist down," he said. "The guy behind me was hit in the head and killed," he solemnly added. "I don't know what happened to the third guy."

Immediately following the explosion, the Japanese soldier, now exposed, was quickly "taken care of" by machine gunners in the area. Belshe was evacuated and eventually sent to the United States for treatment, recovering at an Army hospital at Santa Fe, New Mexico. On November 23, 1945, the Purple Heart recipient received his discharge from the Army and was sent home to Eldon, still carrying bits of shrapnel inside his body that could not be removed.

In the years following his wartime service, Belshe married, raised three children and used his G.I. Bill benefits to earn an education degree while attending college in Warrensburg. He went on to retire after teaching for twenty-one years at a school in Raytown, Missouri.

His time spent in a military uniform was filled with a combination of both memorable and stressful moments but the veteran maintains that his experience overseas has been something he has never shared with others…until recently.

"Honestly, I have never talked to anyone about any of this," Belshe said, describing his time in the Army. "For me, that was always then and this is now and it just became something that I never shared. But there aren't a lot of us [World War II veterans] left and I figure there are probably some people that would like to know what we went through." Smiling, he added, "And I'm sure there's a lot more to my story, but after seventy years or so, you tend to forget a little of it." *(Photograph courtesy of James Belshe)*

Carroll T. Boyd

Fulton

Lt. Carroll T. Boyd of Fulton trained as a flight cadet in the U.S. Army Air Forces at the Missouri Institute of Aeronautics in Sikeston and was later stationed in Baton Rouge, Louisiana, and McAllen, Texas. While serving as a P-47 fighter pilot with the 412th Fighter Squadron of the 373rd Fighter Group in France, he was killed in action on September 3, 1944, leaving behind his wife and a two-month old son whom he never had the opportunity to meet. His parents, Mr. and Mrs. Bennett Boyd, were residing in New Bloomfield at the time of their son's passing. The airman was laid to rest in Brittany American Cemetery in St. James, France. *(Photo courtesy of VFW Post 1003)*

John Hohm

Jefferson City

John August Hohm of Jefferson City, right, is pictured during his installation as commander of the former VFW Post 1003 in Jefferson City on May 7, 1964. The installing officer was VFW State Commander Kenneth Pettit of Lebanon. Hohm enlisted at Scott Field, Illinois, during World War II and became a paratrooper with the 511th Parachute Infantry Regiment. He injured his back during his twenty-seventh jump when he became entangled with another parachute and, because of this incident, spent several months recuperating in a hospital in Japan. He went on to remain in Japan as part of the occupational forces and later left active duty and joined the reserves.

The veteran was called out of the reserves in the late 1950s and served on active duty as a gunner assigned to the Second Infantry Division in Korea during the Korean War. From this service, he earned a Purple Heart medal when he was wounded by a Chinese mortar in addition to suffering from frostbite and hearing loss. In the years after the war, he was employed Roark & Runge Window Company and Hamm's Beer Distributors. Additionally, he was an active member of the VFW, served as commander of American Legion Post 5 and was a life member of the Disabled American Veterans Chapter 17 and the Jefferson City Elks Lodge. During his lifetime, Hohm donated 11,000 hours of volunteer service at the Harry S. Truman Memorial Veterans Hospital in Columbia.

Hohm passed away on December 23, 2012 at the Harry S. Truman Memorial Veterans Hospital. *(Photograph courtesy of VFW Post 1003)*

Wayne Mueller

Eldon

Losing a brother during World War II was a traumatic event for Eldon resident Faye Belshe –a tragedy whose sting the decades have not diminished. In memory of the passing of her beloved sibling, Mueller now wishes to perpetuate the memory of a good-spirited young man who loved baseball and answered the nation's call to arms as a paratrooper during a time of war.

"Wayne was born in Hooker, Oklahoma, on November 15, 1923," said Belshe, when describing the youngest of her four siblings. "All five of us were born there," she added.

The Rock Island Railroad employed their father, Belshe explained, which often required that the family move to follow his work. They would later spend several years living in Kansas but, in 1939, they moved to Eldon when their father again received a transfer from the company.

"At that time, Wayne had two years of high school remaining and I can remember the first thing he did when we got [to Eldon] was walk all over town," recalled Belshe. "When he went by the school, there were kids playing baseball and the next day he went back to the school with his ball glove." Mueller's sister mirthfully added, "He loved baseball and I tell everybody that he came to Eldon with a change of clothes and a ball glove."

For the next two years, Mueller continued to flesh out his growing interest and agility in baseball by participating on several local teams and, after graduating in 1941, finally made the decision to explore making a career of the sport he so loved.

"He went down to Springfield [Missouri] to try out for the Cardinals [minor league affiliate of the St. Louis Cardinals baseball team] but it rained all three days that he was there," Belshe said. "Back then, they didn't have the artificial turf that they do now and because it was so muddy, he didn't get a chance to try out. Then," she added, "he came back home and got his draft letter shortly after that."

Leaving home in March 1943, Mueller traveled to the West Coast and completed his basic training at Camp Roberts, California –a massive training site where "436,000 troops passed through an intensive 17-week training cycle" during World War II," notes the Camp Roberts Historical Museum on their official website.[77]

The young recruit then traveled to Fort Bragg, North Carolina, where he underwent the training to become a paratrooper. While there, he was attached to the 506th PIR (Parachute Infantry Regiment) under the 101st Airborne Division. According to a history of the 506th, the regiment left Ft. Bragg at the end of 1943 and soon arrived at Camp Shanks, New York, to prepare for their overseas deployment.

The regimental history further notes that the division took part in several exercises "in preparation for the coming invasion of occupied Europe" and, on June 5, 1944, "the men of the 506th [were] parked by the aircraft that were to carry them into their first combat mission."[78]

Early the next morning (June 6, 1944), Mueller and the men of the division made their combat jumps behind enemy lines. Although they were essentially scattered far from their designated landing zones and incurred significant casualties, they were able to help secure parts of the high ground above the beaches later stormed by the seaborne forces during the D-Day landings.

---

[77] Camp Roberts Historical Museum, The *History of Camp Roberts*, http://www. camprobertshistoricalmuseum.com.

[78] 506th Parachute Infantry Regiment, *Unit History*, https://www.ww2-airborne. us/units/506/506.html.

"When Wayne landed on D-Day, he survived that, of course," his sister noted. "He sent me home a piece of the parachute, he used that day and I have kept it all these years."

Less than three months later, the 101st made their second combat jump as part of Operation Market Garden. This operation was a bold plan by British Field Marshall Montgomery for Allied airborne forces to seize roads, bridges and important cities in Holland, essentially cutting the country in half, and providing British armor and motorized columns the opportunity to reach the German border.

During this operation, wrote Mueller's older brother Paul in an article for *The Signal –Enterprise* (Wabaunsee County, Kansas), the twenty-year-old paratrooper from Eldon went missing in action (MIA) near Osphuesden, Holland, on October 5, 1944 after his group was "overrun by a German battalion." His brother further noted, "Of a group of 44 troopers, 15 escaped."

"My parents never gave up hope that Wayne was alive and might come home someday," said Belshe. "But ten months after he went missing, we were informed that they had recovered his remains," she soberly added.

Mueller's remains were eventually returned home to the family and interred in McFarland Cemetery in Kansas. In the weeks after learning of their son's demise, Faye explained, her parents struggled to find ways to cope with the unexpected loss of their beloved son.

"It was very depressing for my parents...so much so that my dad had to retire from the railroad," Belshe said. "After that, my father became more involved with Bethany Lutheran Church [Eldon] and spent his time keeping busy with volunteer activities there," she added.

The tears Faye has shed for her youngest brother have in no way diminished over the years. However, she continues to relish the moments they spent together as children and young adults and hopes that the story of his service will be cherished by all for whom he fought during the war.

"He was never married and didn't have any children to carry on his legacy," his sister shared. "All of the young folks now weren't alive back when World War II was going on so they don't fully comprehend all of the sacrifices that were made for them." With evident solemnity, she concluded, "I think it is our responsibility to share these stories with the younger generations so they can understand what my brother and his fellow soldiers did for our country." *(Photograph courtesy of Faye Belshe)*

Forest Clark

Jefferson City

When Forest Clark began working at the former Tweedie Footwear Corporation in Jefferson City, Missouri in December 1941, the United States' recent involvement in a world war was not of primary concern for a seventeen-year-old man simply focused on trying to eke out a living in rather challenging economic times. Regardless of any external concerns, Clark's life appeared to reach the height of happiness when, on March 7, 1942 (his eighteenth birthday), he wedded his fiancée, Georgia Phillips. Yet the reality of worldly affairs soon took center stage as he began to watch his friends and family drafted into the armed forces, thus securing his decision to embark upon his own military adventure.

"I talked it over with my wife and we thought that it would be best for me to go ahead and enlist," said Clark of Jefferson City. "I joined with a group of friends and by volunteering to go early [prior to receiving a draft notice]," he added, "I was sent to Europe instead of the Pacific."

Shortly after receiving his uniform on March 7, 1943—the date of both his first wedding anniversary and nineteenth birthday—the young recruit traveled to Camp Campbell, Kentucky, to begin several weeks of basic training.[79] While in the camp, Clark informed his leadership that although he had never learned to drive a vehicle (nor

---

[79] Established as Camp Campbell in 1941, the U.S. Army base was officially designated Fort Campbell in April 1950. It was named in honor of William Bowen Campbell, a veteran of the Creek, Seminole, and Mexican Wars and the last Whig governor for Tennessee.

possessed a driver license), he was interested in learning how to do so. His request was approved and he soon began training to become a military truck driver.

With his training complete in August 1943, the soldier was assigned to the 3638th Quartermaster Truck Company and sent to Camp Patrick, Virginia, boarding a troopship bound for overseas duty. The military truck company arrived in North Africa in mid-September, where, Clark explained, they spent the largest part of their time in training at a replacement center, awaiting further instructions since "there was not any fighting going on because [General] Patton had already driven Rommel out of [Africa]." Clark added, "Then they put us on a boat and sent us to Naples [Italy] because at that time the Army was pinned down at Anzio and Cassino," heavily engaged in combat against both German and Italian forces.

As Allied forces continued their northwestern push toward Rome, Clark's company supported their movements by providing logistical support, delivering supplies to the front lines including ammunition, fuel, food—"anything they needed, we hauled it," he proudly affirmed.

Although he had never operated a vehicle prior to the war, Clark jokingly remarked that by the time he left the military, he was driving tractor-trailers. And, even though he explained that his duties did not find him engaged in direct combat, there were frequent dangers associated with their deliveries such as the occasional attacks delivered by enemy aircraft.

"One night I was hauling ammunition in blackout conditions [operating the vehicles with no lights] and when I got to an ammo dump, a German plane started strafing the road I had just come in from with machine gun fire. I watched his tracer rounds hit along the dirt. When his bullets started striking close to where my truck was sitting, he shut off his machine gun, turned his plane around and returned the way he came." Pausing, he said, "The Good Lord was looking out for me because I thought that would be my end."

After he returned home from the war, Clark learned that one of his friends was killed two weeks prior to Germany's surrender when the vehicle he was driving was machine-gunned by German aircraft.

"We were operating out of Verona when the war in Europe ended" Clark said. "We stayed there for a few weeks after Japan's surrender and then boarded a troop ship in November [1945] and came home.

The veteran returned to Jefferson City and reunited with his wife, who gave birth to their only son, Dave, a couple of years later. After his discharge, Clark went back to work at Tweedie, remaining with the company until 1962. He then went to work in the communications section for the Jefferson City Police Department (JCPD), retiring in 1983 after twenty-one years of service. Following his retirement from the JCPD, he delivered mail with a local contractor for several years, but "retired for good" in 1992.

With a respectable chronicle of participation in one of the deadliest wars in United States' history, Clark affirms that although he is proud of his military service, he views himself as simply having fulfilled a perceived obligation to the country.

"There are some people who like to brag about their military service, but I've never been one to consider myself a hero. The real heroes are people like my nephew [Dale Clark], who never made it back from Vietnam." He concluded, "I was just one of a lot of guys that had a job to do and I went over there and got it done." *(Photograph courtesy of Forrest Clark)*

Hugo Ehrlich

Polish immigrant

Under the Treaty of Versailles, several German provinces became property of Poland after World War I, leaving many families to cling to their German identity while living in a foreign land. Even when they tried to carry on with their lives, the outbreak of the Second World War brought many challenging events that would result in a number of these families seeking a better life elsewhere.

Born in 1950, inside a small barn in postwar Germany, Jefferson City, Missouri, resident Inge Ehrlich Gauck entered the world to become part of a stirring tale that included a father whose immigration to the United States was set in motion by the German invasion of Poland in 1939. Gauck's father, Hugo Ehrlich (pictured above, standing, left), was born in 1916 in a small Polish village near the German border. As he entered manhood, he was not plagued with concerns related to a deadly and protracted European war when he chose to marry his seventeen-year-old sweetheart, Hedwig Beier, in 1940.

"When my parents married, their gift from the [German-controlled] government was a copy of *Mein Kampf* by Adolph Hitler," said Gauck. "Instead of reading the book," she added, "they buried it in their yard because they thought Hitler was a radical and wouldn't be around for long. They didn't believe the war would last and that they could have children and go on with their lives."

As Gauck shared, her father possessed only a third-grade education and worked on his family's farm, never losing the dream of someday owning his own property. However, in 1942, Hugo experienced firsthand the consequences of Hitler's expansionist vision when the Polish territories seized during the war were required to provide soldiers for the German cause.

In the book *The Exile Mission: The Polish Political Diaspora and Polish Americans, 1939-1956*, the author describes a "separate category of Polish citizens who had been forcibly conscripted into German military units," most of whom originated "from the areas that had been annexed directly to the Reich and were considered 'ethnically German.'"[80]

Ehrlich was not alone in his conscripted service since, as noted on the Axis History website, as many as 500,000 Polish citizens served in the Werhmacht (the unified armed forces of Germany) during the Second World War, including Ehrlich's brother-in-law, Adam Scheffler.

"Adam [Scheffler] was married to Hedwig's sister [Ehrlich's wife]," explained Gauck. "He was killed during the war, leaving behind his wife and two young children." She continued, "My father's job in the military was to operate a search light. After the bombings of different areas, he was also one of the first people to go into the area to locate the wounded and dead."

One day, however, Ehrlich's circumstances would be forever altered when he was captured by American forces.

"He was held in a prison camp," said Gauck, "but I'm not exactly sure where it was located—if it was in Europe or elsewhere. He always said that because of the humane treatment he received as a prisoner of war at the hands of the Americans, he wanted to someday bring his family to the United States."

Ehrlich was eventually released from the prisoner of war camp and a certificate he received notes his discharge from the German military on January 30, 1946, at which time he returned to Poland and was reunited with his wife and two children—Erika (daughter) and Gerhard (son).

The next few years were quite turbulent for the growing family as they joined thousands of other refugees who had lost their prop-

---

[80] Jaroszyńska-Kirchmann, *The Exile Mission*, 20.

erty as a result of the war. The Ehrlich family was later relocated to a small German village and had to live in part of a barn with other displaced families, where Gauck was born in 1950 and thus became the family's third and final child.

However dire their circumstances appeared, the Ehrlich's found solace through Public Law 774 and 555, which granted them an opportunity to enter the United States as "displaced persons" under the sponsorship of Lutheran Service to Refugees (now known as Lutheran Immigration and Refugee Service).

The family received its introduction to the United States following their immigration in 1952 through the sponsorship of St. John's Lutheran Church in May City, Iowa. The congregation helped Ehrlich find a job and provided the family a small apartment above a local grocery store.

"We didn't know English very well, so even going to the store and trying to buy something was a challenge," Gauck said. "I remember my father really liked eggs and he had to make a sound like a chicken clucking for them to understand that he wanted eggs," she smiled.

The former soldier eventually did learn English and, on November 19, 1965, earned his citizenship. In later years, he moved his family to the state of California with hopes of purchasing farmland, but instead, became successful by working as a carpenter by day and, in the evenings, moved houses for the freeways being built in Los Angeles.

Though her father passed away in 1973, Gauck is gratified knowing the struggles he overcame to give his family a better life in a country that provided the first glimmer of hope during the tumultuous period following World War II.

"My father only had the opportunity to complete the third grade," said Gauck, "but all of his surviving grandchildren have gone on to become college graduates." Grinning, she exclaimed, "What a wonderful country we live in!" She added, "He was always very proud that we lived in the United States and of all the wonderful opportunities that are available here. He proved that you can be successful by working hard...and that is the American dream come true." (Photograph courtesy of Inge Ehrlich Gauck)

199

Elwyn Scheperle

Russellville

George "Elwyn" Scheperle possesses many heartfelt memories of growing up in the Millbrook community south of Lohman, Missouri, many of which involved listening to members of his family engaged in conversations in German. Though he picked up bits and pieces of the foreign dialect along the way, Scheperle admits he never thought it would ever be of any conceivable benefit...especially during a time of war.

With World War II in full swing, the young farmhand received his draft notice in late 1944, thus sending the twenty-year-old Scheperle on an adventure that would find him directly communicating with people from a country his ancestors once called home.

"They sent me to Camp Roberts, California, for training," recalled Scheperle.[81] "It's been so long ago, but I do remember that it was not much more than a desert with a few hills around it."

In the weeks following the completion of his basic training, the young recruit went on to become a "cannoneer," learning to operate the 105mm M2A1 howitzer, which was followed by additional instruction as an automotive mechanic.

"I had grown up around a blacksmith shop in Millbrook and had watched and learned a lot about working on things there," Scheperle explained, while discussing his automotive training. "Back

---

[81] During the period of World War II, Camp Roberts was the largest U.S. Arm basic training installation and reached a peak population of 45,000 troops in 1944. Camp Roberts Historical Museum, *History of the Base*, www.camprobertshistoricalmuseum.com.

then, they expected you to be able to work on anything that needed repairs."

In early April 1945, the newly trained soldier came home to Missouri for two weeks of leave before preparing to embark for overseas duty. Boarding a troopship in mid-April, Scheperle recalls departing New York and crossing the Atlantic in a convoy that included dozens of ships.

"Every direction that you looked, you saw a ship—to the front, back, right or left," he said.

Arriving at a port in France nearly two weeks later, the men unloaded their ships and boarded trains that began dropping groups of soldiers off at different locations throughout France and Germany.

"I'm not sure where it was because things were so hectic at that time, but I arrived at a depot and they decided to put me as a replacement in an artillery unit."

Days before the German surrender, Scheperle was assigned to Service Battery, 19th Field Artillery Battalion under the Fifth Infantry Division, and notes that replacement soldiers were a necessity since the division had experienced a significant number of combat casualties in the previous weeks from engagements including the Battle of the Bulge. Though major combat offensives soon faded with the surrender of Germany on May 8, 1945, the former soldier affirms that it certainly did not herald the end of his overseas activities since he soon became part of the occupational forces.

"The division had the hell kicked out of them, so we spent a lot of time fixing vehicles and equipment that had been damaged in battle—a lot of those old trucks were in pretty rugged shape," he said. "We also pulled a lot of guard duty and even continued to do some artillery training."

Moving between German villages, the division also gained the responsibility of checking homes and buildings that might be used to conceal German soldiers attempting to evade capture, a task that soon redirected Scheperle's efforts.

"The guy that had been serving as translator [to speak to the residents when U.S. soldiers entered a German home] ended up in the hospital," said Scheperle. "Word somehow got around that I knew how to speak some German and the officers decided that I should be the new interpreter," he grinned.

The veteran admits the early days of his interpretive experience were challenging since the German he had learned from listening to family in the Millbrook community was much different from that spoken by the German citizens they encountered during the occupation.

"I learned pretty quick," Scheperle affirmed. "When we went in to check out a home, the people were usually really scared because they had been told all kinds of bad things about the Americans. But when we explained to them that we weren't there to hurt them, they were very cooperative."

As Scheperle explained, he was chosen to be part of a group of soldiers sent to the Pacific in support of the war raging in Japan. However, because of his duties as a translator, he remained in Germany until the surrender of Japanese forces. In addition to translation duties, Scheperle said, during the final weeks he spent in Germany, he also served as the Jeep driver for his company commander.

In late August 1945, the soldier's overseas service ended when he returned to the United States and was sent to Camp Campbell, Kentucky, to finish out the remainder of his enlistment by performing vehicle maintenance. He received his discharge the following July and returned to the Millbrook community.

The veteran married Edna Ott in 1950 and the couple raised one daughter. Now retired, Scheperle spent many years self-employed as a heavy equipment operator.

With insightful reflection, Scheperle insists that although his arrival in Europe late in the war resulted in his missing some of the heaviest combat endured by the division, he cannot help but grin when contemplating the ironies he experienced while serving as a translator.

"If you really stop and think about it, it's kind of peculiar," Scheperle said. "Here I was, a young man coming from Millbrook with a German background, traveling to Germany during the war and then speaking German on behalf of the U.S. while I was there."

With a spirited grin, his wife Edna added, "If they had gone ahead and sent you to Japan, you would have really been in trouble."

Edna Scheperle passed away on December 28, 2016 and her husband, Elwyn, died on February 21, 2018. The couple were laid to rest in the cemetery of St. John's Lutheran Church in Stringtown, Missouri. *(Photograph courtesy of Susan Scheperle Schenewerk)*

Walter Evenson

Columbia

With a slight accent revealing his northern upbringing, mid-Missouri resident Walter Evenson recounted his journey from childhood to service in the Navy, with an added collection of experiences in-between—all of which helped influence his final calling as a Lutheran pastor. A young boy coming to age in Minnesota, Evenson, memorized various scriptures from the Bible, but did not fully appreciate the value of the material he was learning. This would soon change as the country became involved in the Second World War, placing the young man in situations that would provide him a better understanding of these early faith-based lessons.

Graduating from high school in 1944, Evenson said, "I knew that I was going to be drafted into the Army, so I went ahead and enlisted in the Navy…I guess because my dad had served in the Navy during World War I." He was sent to Great Lakes, Illinois, for his basic training, and a few weeks later traveled to Camp Shoemaker near Oakland, California, where he reported for duty aboard his first ship.

"They put me on the *USS Harris*," Evenson explained. According to online naval records, the Harris was a commercial passenger ship built in 1921 and later converted into a troop ship during World War II. "That ship was called 'APA-2'—the number on the front of it," he added. "It stood for 'auxiliary personnel attack' and we would use it as a troop carrier to bring soldiers to the islands where fighting was taking place [in the South Pacific]."

Evenson, an inexperienced sailor with little more than initial training to his credit, boarded the ship on May 8, 1945, the day the war in Europe ended. On his first mission aboard the vessel, Evenson and the crew sailed out of Oakland with 1,500 soldiers destined for Okinawa to join the forces already there fighting the Japanese. His primary duty, the former sailor noted, was in the crow's nest of the ship watching for enemy aircraft and periscopes in the water, which might denote the presence of submarines.

While at sea, he carried a small New Testament Bible with him and began studying the scriptures he had first begun learning many years earlier. This time, he asserts, the meaning behind the words became more profound.

"I read the stories I had reviewed as a kid, but this time they really had meaning...it really began to affect me."

Though his study of the scripture continued in his down time, Evenson and his fellow servicemembers spent the next several months traveling to locations throughout the South Pacific, picking up and transporting troops in support of battles and campaigns. In early August 1945, they were ordered to follow the fleet to Tokyo Bay to prepare for the invasion of the Japanese mainland, but on August 6, 1945, the crew learned that the atomic bomb was dropped on Hiroshima. Days later, the Japanese surrendered following the bombing of Nagasaki, yet Evenson's ship continued its journey to Tokyo Bay.

"We arrived on September 8 [1945], just after the Japanese signed the surrender on the *USS Missouri*," the veteran said. "It was amazing...just amazing, to see all the cruisers, destroyers—huge ships—together in the bay."

During the next several weeks, the *USS Harris* participated in several more troop transport missions, which included locations in China and the Philippines, in addition to riding out a typhoon. In December 1945, the ship sailed to California and Evenson was granted a brief period of leave. Shortly after he returned from leave, he was assigned to the *USS Dixie* and served aboard the destroyer tender until his discharge in July 1946.

The next several years were full of activity for the veteran as he utilized his GI Bill in pursuit of his education. In 1955, he completed his education when he graduated from Luther Seminary in St. Paul, Minnesota, with a bachelor's degree in theology. He and his wife Joyce (whom he met and married while in seminary) traveled to Tanzania the fall after his seminary graduation to spend the next three and a half years as missionaries. After returning to the states in 1959, he went on to serve as a Lutheran pastor for churches in South Dakota, Kansas and Missouri, eventually retiring to the mid-Missouri area in 1992, following nearly three decades in the ministry.

"When I was on the ship," Evenson said, while discussing the impact of his naval service, "I can still remember me and the fellas sitting around—especially after supper—talking about different things like the church and our Christian faith. I remember saying that if there is a God, I want to be right with him, and if there is a heaven, I want to go there." He added, "The Navy brought me in contact with many good people who helped reinforce my desire to continue to build my faith, and also provided me with the experiences which eventually led me to the ministry."

Walter Harvey Evenson passed away in Jefferson City on September 7, 2017 and was laid to rest in the cemetery of Pyrmont Trinity Lutheran Church in Stover, Missouri. *(Photograph courtesy of Walt Evenson)*

J.R. Goff

Jefferson City

There is certainly no shortage of credit to be shared when honoring the men and women of the "Greatest Generation," who have donated both their time and resources to help bring victory to the Allied forces in World War II. Most ironic, however, is the hesitancy of those who sacrificed the greatest in accepting any accolades for their individual efforts during the conflict.

"I really didn't do anything special [during the war]," said J.R. Goff of Jefferson City. "There were so many people—such as the women who helped build [Navy] ships—that have never received the recognition they deserve."

Raised in several small Missouri communities, Goff was attending high school when he decided to leave his studies in 1943 and enlist in the Navy, thinking he "knew everything there was to know." He added, "I wanted to go get on one of them ships and join the fight. I don't really know why...I just wanted to get out there in the middle of it and boy did I ever," he chuckled.

The seventeen-year-old recruit traveled to Farragut, Idaho, for several weeks of basic training—a site, which, according to the Idaho Military Museum, trained 293,381 recruits while in operation from 1942 to 1946. The Farragut Naval Training Station is now part of Farragut State Park.[82]

Without any specialized training other than that he received at Farragut, Goff was transferred to the naval yard at Puget Sound,

---

[82] Idaho Military Museum, *Farragut, Idaho*, www.museum.mil.idaho.gov.

Washington, in the summer of 1943 to prepare for assignment to the *USS California* (BB-44)—a battleship that was undergoing a major reconstruction after incurring damage during the Japanese attack at Pearl Harbor.

"There were about 160 women that were working on that ship doing welding and all kinds of work like that, but that's not something they really ever got credit for," the veteran explained.

In early 1944, the ship was deemed seaworthy and departed for a shakedown cruise, during which time Goff received on-the-job training in a capacity that would help defend the vessel.

"I served as the first loader on one of the quad 40 mm guns," he said. The weapon, he explained, was a single gun mount with four 40 mm barrels attached and a loader assigned to each barrel.

With the shakedown cruise behind them, the ship set sail for the Western Pacific, where they participated in shore bombardment missions near Saipan. On June 14, 1944, Goff recalled, a shell from an enemy gun battery struck the *USS California*, resulting in the death of one sailor and wounding of several others.

"When that happened," said Goff, "they turned the big sixteen-inch guns toward the shore and blew that enemy gun to pieces!"

Whether by luck or skill, the crew avoided significant damage during this incident. However, the vessel would encounter a more deadly situation in January 1945 while providing shore bombardment at Lingayen Gulf in the Philippines.

"We were on General Quarters [all hands to battle stations] because there were Japanese planes attacking the ships in our group," Goff said. "One of the planes hit us and exploded...it burned to death my fourth loader," he solemnly remarked. "I used to hate even talking about that day because I lost so many of my friends."

According to online naval records, the kamikaze attack resulted in the death of forty-four crewmembers with an estimated 155 wounded.

"We really didn't even have time to clean up from the attack," Goff continued. "If I remember correctly, we were on General Quarters for three days or so."

In mid-February 1945, the ship returned to Puget Sound to undergo repairs from the damage sustained in the kamikaze attack. The young sailor had acquired enough points to qualify for a discharge, but while awaiting his release at San Francisco, he volunteered to extend briefly his service and received assignment to an attack transport named the *USS President Hayes* (APA-20).

"The Hayes made a run to the South Pacific to pick up some soldiers—I think we were gone three or four weeks," Goff said. "On the way home, I remember that some of the soldiers got so sick they begged us to shoot them," he jokingly added.

The battle-tested sailor ultimately received his discharge in February 1946 and returned to Missouri. Goff went to work for U.S. Steel in St. Louis and retired in the early 1970s after more than thirty years with the company. He was later employed as a corrections officer at Algoa Prison in Jefferson City, where he remained for another fifteen years. Married to Geraldine (Gerry) in 1957, the father of five children now enjoys sharing the quiet life with his wife at a local retirement community, asserting that although he views his military service to have been of little significance in the grand scheme of the war, it did award him with many abiding memories.

"The Navy taught me to do what I was told," he grinned, adding, "Yes, sir! No, sir!—and all that kind of stuff that will keep you out of trouble." Smiling, he concluded, "When I enlisted, I was just another young kid that thought he knew everything there was to know, but I soon found out differently. There were certainly some tough lessons I had to go through a war to learn."

J.R. Goff passed away in Jefferson City on March 17, 2017 and was laid to rest in Hawthorn Memorial Gardens. *(Photograph courtesy of J.R. Goff)*

Gilbert Schanzmeyer

Jefferson City

While the drums of war beat forth a deafening rhythm in 1943, high school senior Gilbert Schanzmeyer thought his draft number would soon be chosen and land him in combat as a member of the infantry.

"I sure didn't want to get drafted into the infantry. That's all rough kind of stuff they had to endure," laughed the Jefferson City veteran.

With an older brother already serving in the military, the graduate of Meta High School decided if he was going to serve, he would rather do it from the cockpit of a plane. Enlisting in the U.S. Army Air Forces, Schanzmeyer believed his decision to enlist might also offer him the opportunity to become a commissioned officer.

The young enlistee began his two-year training cycle by completing basic training in Texas, then on to locations in Arizona and California to complete aviation courses taught under the authority of the Western Flying Training Command. After finishing gunner training and much of his pre-flight training, Schanzmeyer was in his Basic Pilot Training School in Merced, California, when he discovered the possible dangers that could arise even in a training environment. As the veteran explained, he and a group of several dozen fellow trainees were practicing landings in AT-6s—a small trainer aircraft—when an incident on the runway nearly resulted in the loss of his life.

"There were probably 200 to 300 planes practicing a landing sequence and we were to be no closer than 500 feet apart," Schanzmeyer said. "We were supposed to concentrate on the aircraft in front of us. You weren't supposed to have to worry about any planes outside of the [landing] pattern."

On his approach to the runway, the young aviator noticed an airplane in his peripheral vision at the same altitude and on a course to collide with his aircraft.

"I shoved the stick forward so hard that I thought I was going to break it," Schanzmeyer exclaimed. "My plane dropped so fast that some of the oil that leaked from the back of the engine flew up and hit the top of the canopy inside my plane."

Schanzmeyer's quick response avoided the collision and he later learned that the aircraft that nearly struck him was piloted by the air inspector—the officer responsible for the safety of the airfield. When he returned to the operations building to check in his plane following the training exercise, the tense airman was instructed to report to a room within the building.

"They were pretty strict about safety and accidents and I thought for sure I would be kicked out of the program."

Reporting as instructed, Schanzmeyer describes the next fifteen minutes consisting of the air inspector "chewing me up one side and down the other." The verbal barrage finally reached a pause, at which point Schanzmeyer respectfully asked, "Sir, what should I have done?"

The meeting ended with the inspector telling the inexperienced pilot that he was thankful Schanzmeyer noticed his aircraft, and that his quick response helped avert a potentially deadly collision.

Schanzmeyer finished out his training as a B-25 Bomber pilot at Douglas, Arizona, and he earned his "wings" and commission as a second lieutenant on August 4, 1945. For a short time, he trained Chinese pilots who would help fight the air war against Japan. However, Japan soon surrendered and Schanzmeyer's aviation skills were no longer required.

Discharged in September 1945, he returned to Meta and entered the car dealership business with his father and brother. He also joined the Air Force Reserve and was honorably discharged in 1972 at the rank of major. In 1974, he and his brothers purchased the DeVille Southwest Apartments and the following year sold out of the car business. Retired along with his wife, Helen, his wife, Schanzmeyer says the two years he spent preparing for combat were full of intense moments that helped erase many of his youthful perceptions.

"They really pushed us to the maximum to get us through the training because they knew that the country needed pilots to help fight the war," Schanzmeyer said. "For someone from Meta who was only twenty years old at the time I was discharged," he added, "it was truly an experience where I learned more than ever believed possible and that forced me to grow up quickly."

Gilbert Joseph Schanzmeyer passed away in Jefferson City on October 17, 2014 and was laid to rest in St. Cecelia Cemetery in the rural community of Meta, Missouri. *(Photograph courtesy of Gilbert Schanzmeyer)*

Mary Hood

Jefferson City

Shortly after her graduation from St. Peter High School in 1942, former Jefferson City, Missouri, resident Mary (Roling) Hood entered a nurse training program in Boonville, an educational endeavor she pursued for a year before deciding to fulfill her yearning for an adventure while also serving her country.

"I decided to join the Navy because they always said that you could see the world," Hood grinned, "but when it was all finished, I never left the U.S."

Enlisting in August 1944, Hood became a member of the Women Accepted for Volunteer Emergency Service (WAVES)—an organization established on July 30, 1942 to help fill positions left vacant stateside because of the scores of men deploying overseas to fight in World War II. The young recruit was soon on her way to the Bronx campus of Hunter College in New York, the location that became the training base for all WAVES by 1943, according to the U.S. Naval Institute. Since the college had no residential dorms, the Navy incurred a yearly cost of $1 million to rent the entire campus for WAVES training, converting the college into a site known as *USS Hunter*. Hood remained at the campus for the next six weeks to finish her boot camp, which included drawing her military uniforms and an introduction to military traditions, customs and discipline.

"When I finished," the veteran explained, "they sent me to San Diego for a few weeks of intensive training with patients to become a hospital attendant." She added, "I was then stationed there, taking care of the boys coming back from overseas."

Balboa Naval Hospital, which is now the Naval Medical Center San Diego, was located within the grounds of Balboa Park in San Diego and treated nearly 172,000 patients during World War II. During the period of the Vietnam War, it earned the distinction of being the largest military hospital in the world.

"A lot of the [sailors] that we were treating were coming back from the Pacific with cat fever," said Hood. In the book *Occupying Force: A Sailor's Journey Following World War II*, author D. Charles Gossman describes "cat fever" as a generic term doctors used for a variety of "maladies ranging from the common cold to serious influenza-like symptoms."[83]

Although her aspirations for world travel never emerged while she was in the Navy, the veteran recalls making trips to exciting locations such as Hollywood and Tijuana, Mexico, accompanied by fellow WAVES and sailors. Hood remained at the hospital in San Diego for the rest of her enlistment, receiving her discharge in the summer of 1946. She made the decision to continue living in California for nearly four years after leaving the service. In 1950, she returned to Mid-Missouri and met her fiancée, Clarence Hood. The couple married two years later, raising three sons and three daughters. After several moves, they settled in Jefferson City, where Hood worked for local health care facilities and home health care companies.

In 2007, her husband passed away two months prior to their fifty-fifth wedding anniversary and Hood, who now resides in an assisted living facility in Grain Valley, Missouri, enjoys reflecting upon memories from her past naval service. Though the military did not provide her the overseas adventure she sought as a young woman, she maintains that her participation in the Central Missouri Honor Flight in 2009 helped to fulfill another wish—to visit the war memorials in Washington, D.C.

"While I was in boot camp in New York, we were never allowed to leave the campus and visit any of the sites or memorials, so it was somewhat disappointing. The most memorable part of that period was when I took the train to San Diego—it was the first time I had

---

[83] Gossman, *Occupying Force*, 90.

been on a train and it was so exciting for me!" she exclaimed. In reflection, she added, "But the Honor Flight was a great trip...and all of the veterans that were with us reminded me a lot of all of the wonderful boys we took care of [at San Diego]. There were even a few other women veterans on the flight with me," she smiled. *(Photograph courtesy of Mary Hood)*

Francis "Bud" Jones

Jefferson City

Throughout the years, an untold number of children have clung to dreams of a career in aviation. In the case of local veteran Francis "Bud" Jones, circumstances born of the Second World War helped transition such a dream to reality. Shortly after his graduation from Vienna High School, Jones began attending the University of Missouri in Columbia during the fall of 1941. A couple of months later, the Japanese attacked Pearl Harbor and Jones realized his educational pursuits would likely be delayed.

"I knew I would be drafted," explained Jones, "but I didn't want to be in the infantry."

Seeking to satisfy his duty to the nation while also taking advantage of an early interest he had developed in aviation, Jones traveled to Ft. Leonard Wood for three days of aviation cadet testing. Nearly a week after the completion of the testing, he was informed of his acceptance into the U.S. Army Air Corps (which later became known as the U.S. Army Air Forces and eventually the U.S. Air Force), but he would have to wait for a training slot to become available.

In May 1942, Jones was sworn into an enlisted reserve status and soon embarked upon the extensive training regimen required to become a military aviator. Completing several phases of flight instruction during which he progressed to larger and more powerful aircraft, the fledgling pilot received his first introduction to the P-40 Warhawk—a ground attack aircraft used by the Allied powers—while stationed at Luke Field, Arizona.

"In our final phase of training [at Luke Field], we spent ten hours flying the Warhawk," Jones said.

Successfully finishing almost a year of training, Jones graduated with his "wings" and was promoted to the rank of second lieutenant in August of 1943. He then traveled to the Army airbase in St. Petersburg, Florida, where he and other aspiring aviators spent about seventy hours familiarizing themselves with the P-40 under conditions structured to emulate those they might encounter in combat. With the war raging in Europe and the country in dire need of air support for the ground forces, Jones and several new pilots were soon on their way overseas. Eventually, Jones was transported to an Army airfield near Cercola, Italy, receiving assignment to the 324th Fighter Group.

"While in training, we were told that the P-40's we trained with would soon be obsolete," Jones recalled. "But when we arrived in Cercola, all we saw were P-40's lined up on the airfield."

With bombs situated under the wings and the belly of the plane, the squadron of which Jones was a member led air strikes against integral enemy targets such as railroad systems, troop staging areas and gun emplacements. On other occasions, their aircraft were simply outfitted with machine guns to be used in attacking enemy objectives. During the latter part of the war in Europe, while the Germans were being pushed out of France, Jones remarked that the enemy began to "throw everything they had at us."

Eventually, Jones' squadron made the transition to the newer P-47 Thunderbolt—a heavily armed, single engine fighter aircraft—on which he flew his final twenty-five missions.

"I got shot up pretty bad in my last few missions," Jones stated. "On one run, I got hit by four 20mm cannons. It ended up cracking the cylinder and cutting my oil line."

As a testament to the durability of his new P-47's, Jones was able to make it 180 miles back to the airbase before the engine on the plane locked up.

"The plane had an oil tank of thirty-two gallons," Jones remarked. "By the time I got back, all of the oil was either on the outside of plane or all over me," he quipped.

In September of 1944, Jones received orders to return to the states. After 117 successful missions, his combat career came to a close, but not before being awarded two Distinguished Flying Crosses, four Air Medals and numerous other decorations. Spending several months in Arizona and Alabama training new pilots in the very same combat tactics he had himself learned and employed while fighting in Europe, Jones was separated from active duty in June 1945. Continuing his military career, Jones joined the Air Force Reserve, retiring as a lieutenant colonel on May 12, 1981. On the same date as his military retirement, he also retired as a major from an extensive post-military career with the Missouri Highway Patrol.

"I couldn't have done it without my wife, Dee [whom he married in 1951]," Jones said. "She's been my best friend and loyal supporter through it all."

Jones notes that the circumstances of the war played some factor in his opportunity to take wing, asserting the experiences drawn from service in a combat zone only helped to forge his resilience.

"Don't tell me I can't do something...I'll find a way," he stressed. "That's the spirit of determination the service gave to me."

In recognition of his service in support of the liberation of France during the war, Jones was presented a French Legion of Honor Medal by Missouri Governor Jay Nixon in a ceremony that took place at the state capitol on January 23, 2012. (*Photograph courtesy of Bud Jones*)

Marvin Kaiser

Jefferson City

According to statistics accessed through the National World War II Museum, more than 565,000 members of the U.S. Army and Air Force were wounded during World War II. Many of these service-members returned home with missing limbs and other serious injuries, only to demonstrate to those in their local communities that they would not allow their lives to be defined by their unexpected wounds. These numbers include Marvin Kaiser, who was raised on his family's farm in St. Martins and later moved to Jefferson City, where he worked for the former Tweedie Shoe Factory. However, on December 1, 1942, the twenty-year-old was drafted into the U.S. Army and thrust into a situation resulting in serious consequences.

"We have never really known too much about dad's service because he wasn't the type to ever talk about what happened," said Judy Kaiser Cadice, the second oldest of Kaiser's four children.

His discharge papers indicate he was inducted into the service at Fort Leavenworth, Kansas, receiving assignment to a medical detachment of the 20th Infantry Regiment under the Sixth Infantry Division. With the regiment, he was given training as a medical aidman, learning to treat injuries and wounds that soldiers might incur in combat conditions.

Kaiser, according to the July 6, 1943 edition of the *Jefferson City Post-Tribune*, returned to Jefferson City on a fifteen-day furlough to visit with his parents. At the time, he was stationed at Camp San Luis Obispo, California, where the Sixth Division spent several months engaged in training designed to prepare them for jungle warfare. Shortly after his return to his duty station, the division moved to Hawaii and was given the mission of defending Oahu, which included "the active patrolling of beach areas as a defense against submarine attacks and the landing of small parties trained for espionage and sabotage," as noted in the book *The Sixth Infantry Division in World War II: 1939-1945*. While in Hawaii, the division continued their amphibious and jungle warfare training until January 1944, at which time they left the island and sailed for Milne Bay, New Guinea, where they would not only contend with Japanese artillery and snipers, but deadly diseases such as yellow fever, typhus and malaria.

Kaiser was soon in combat alongside the soldiers of the division, focused on treating the wounded from The Battle of Lone Tree Hill—an engagement that began during the evening of June 22, 1944 and involved more than 8,000 Japanese troops. The discharge papers for Kaiser indicate that he received his first Purple Heart when he incurred an unidentified wound on July 15, 1944. But he soon recovered from his injury and returned to duty with his division.

The campaign against the Japanese forces continued along the northern coast of New Guinea and eventually landed the division on the Philippine Island of Luzon in early 1945 to face "General Yamashita and 250,000 combat-hardened troops who were well fed and well-armed," as explained the website of the National Association of the Sixth Infantry Division.[84] The battles that ensued resulted in the second wounding of Kaiser on March 16, 1945—this time in a more serious and permanent manner.

"Technician Fifth Grade Marvin Kaiser has had part of his leg amputated as a result of a wound received on Luzon in March," stated the May 27, 1945 edition of *The Sunday News and Tribune*. "The wound was caused by shrapnel," the article clarified.

In a handwritten letter dated May 25, 1945, a friend of Kaiser's (who identified himself simply as "Luke") wrote, "Remember when you asked me how bad it was? It didn't look bad then, but you had

---

[84] National Association of the 6th Infantry Division, *Brief History of the U.S. Army 6th Infantry*, www.6thinfantry.com.

bled terrible. Then I thought it might have hit an artery. Sure enough, that is what happened."

Ultimately, Kaiser was evacuated stateside and received treatment that included amputation of his right leg at McCloskey General Hospital in Temple, Texas. He was awarded a Silver Star Medal for gallantry when, despite being wounded, left "his foxhole during an intense enemy mortar barrage to treat a casualty." His service also earned him a Bronze Star and a second Purple Heart.

Receiving his discharge on February 25, 1946, the combat veteran married Berniece Prenger in December the same year and the couple purchased a home on St. Louis Road in Jefferson City.

"Because of his injury," said his daughter, Judy Kaiser Cadice, "he walked with the assistance of a wooden leg and needed to find a desk type of job. He decided to get into the jewelry business," she added.

In the years after the war, Kaiser attended watch-making school in Southwest Missouri and, in the evenings, learned to become an engraver. He also became a gemologist and jeweler and "consistently bettered himself," his daughter explained. The veteran was employed by local jeweler Phil Dallmeyer Sr.—a WWI veteran and proprietor of Dallmeyer Jewelry in Jefferson City—before working for Warren Duncan, owner of Duncan Jewelry. Eventually, Kaiser purchased Duncan Jewelry and operated the company under that name for several years but changed the company's name to Kaiser Jewelry in the late 1960s.

Sadly, Kaiser passed away March 28, 1976 at fifty-three years of age, survived by his wife and four children. The family continued to operate their father's business following Kaiser's death, but it closed a few years later.

Cadice explained that when it came to her father's military disability, he was always "a very private man," never sharing with his family the details of his service overseas or the traumatic injury that abruptly ended his military career.

"He was a true hero...I mean I considered him a hero in everything he did—so kind, humble and always considerate of other people. But because he died at such a young age, we never had the

opportunity to learn about what he went through in the service."
She solemnly added, "I believe it is important to thank all of our
veterans because they have endured so much that many of us know
nothing about. I never had the chance to say, 'thank you' to my father
because I never knew anything about what he went through, but I
want to make sure his grandchildren know all that he sacrificed on
our behalf." *(Photograph courtesy of Judy Kaiser Cadice)*

Jim Schaffner

Jefferson City

The stories of the brave individuals who served during World War II tend to share in a consistent theme—they were called to service through the draft. This process netted many a young man, many of whom were still in the process of finishing high school, and thrust them into the middle of a war overseas where they would serve alongside scores of other drafted Americans.

A native of the Mid-Missouri area, James Schaffner's parents moved to Webster Groves near St. Louis in the early 1940s where his father found employment at a defense contractor. It was here, Schaffner said, that he graduated from high school in 1944 and embarked upon an unexpected military adventure that would last for decades.

"You've probably heard it before, but I was drafted into the Army while I was still in high school," said the veteran. "I was inducted at Jefferson Barracks in September 1944 and they sent me to Camp Robinson [Arkansas] for my basic training."

Several weeks later, an eighteen-year-old Schaffner took a train to the West Coast where he boarded a troop ship. After making several stops at various islands in the Pacific, he and hundreds of other soldiers arrived at Okinawa. It was here, he added, that he received assignment as a replacement infantryman with the 17th Regiment of the 7th Division. At the point of his arrival, elements of the 7th Division were already veterans of harrowing engagements that included service in the Aleutian Islands, Marshall Islands and the Philippine island of Leyte. However, the late arrival of the untested draftee from Missouri would not prevent him from experiencing the harm prevalent in a combat environment.

"The attack against Okinawa was launched on Easter Sunday, April 1, 1945," wrote an unidentified author in the "History of the 7th Infantry Division. "Nobody suspected at the time that it was to be the last beachhead, indeed the last campaign, of World War II."[85]

As recorded in the division's lineage of World War II service, Schaffner and his fellow soldiers would face bitter resistance while in Okinawa. In fact, some of the GI's reportedly faced an attack by Japanese soldiers who were wielding spears.

"We were in foxholes and it was raining," recalled Schaffner. "A mortar shell landed in front of my foxhole and it blew my tent away, sending shrapnel through the air and a bunch of it was embedded in my left arm."

Treated by a medic, Schaffner quickly returned to combat duty with his unit. However, within a few days he received another injury that would earn him his second Purple Heart.

"We were in an area where we could see Japanese soldiers across a ravine and they could see us," Schaffner described. "We began shooting at each other and I hit one of their soldiers, but then I was shot on the side of my left leg."

The bullet, Schaffner said, passed completely through his leg, narrowly missing his kneecap. He was evacuated to a Marine hospital in Guam and, following nearly a month of recovery, returned to his unit in July 1945.

"By the time I got back to my unit, I was wearing a Marine Corps uniform because I didn't have any of mine with me when I was sent to the hospital." Grinning, the Army veteran added, "Boy, did the guys ever give me grief over [wearing a Marine uniform] when I got back to my unit.

Upon his return, Schaffner recalls the island as "essentially secure" and the news of the Japanese surrender reaching their camp shortly thereafter. Despite the war having ended, Schaffner and many of the soldiers of the 7th Division were then placed on a troop ship

---

[85] The Patriot Files, *7th Infantry Division*, www.patriotfiles.com.

and sent to Korea to serve as part of the occupational forces. In addition to ensuring the Japanese forces left Korea, Schaffner noted that he and other soldiers from the division rotated to different outposts along the 38th parallel and conducted training in a country that would become ground zero for another war only a few years later.

Schaffner returned to Missouri in 1947, later married, and attended both the School of Mines in Rolla and the St. Louis Business School. He received a direct commission as an officer with the Army Reserve and was recalled during the Korean War, during which he was sent to Fort Benning, Georgia to serve as a nuclear, chemical and biological warfare instructor. Following his Korean War service, he transferred to the Missouri National Guard, with whom he served thirty years and retired as a lieutenant colonel. The veteran also enjoyed a career in private business and later invested twenty years in state government, which included stints as Director of Procurement and Director of Revenue under the administration of former Govern Warren Hearnes.

"That's back when I was young and innocent," grinned Schaffner while pointing to one of the photographs taken of him during World War II. "But even at my age, I'm still doing pretty good."

When discussing his combat service in Okinawa and the resultant injuries, he concluded, "When I was hit by shrapnel, it was like I had fallen on a gravel road and was all scratched up...it didn't seem like much. I recently had an X-ray done on my arm and bunch of the shrapnel is still there, all these years later." The two-time Purple Heart recipient added, "I never really thought that my injuries were all that much but I guess the Army did." *(Photograph courtesy of Jim Schaffner)*

Ralph Kalberloh

Jefferson City

With a sense of duty and patriotism signifying the character of those coming of age during World War II, Missouri resident Ralph Kalberloh was honored to answer the call to service during a time of war. And despite circumstances which later found him detained in an enemy prison camp, the combat veteran asserts his experiences have granted him a unique perspective on the true costs of freedom.

"During the [Second World War], I probably could have gotten a farm deferment, but at that time no one wanted to avoid the war," said Kalberloh.

Growing up on a farm near the rural community of Hardin, Missouri, Kalberloh left high school after finishing his junior year to enlist in the United States Army Air Forces—much to the disappointment of his mother.

The veteran explained, "I knew I would be drafted…and I thought it would be better to fly than to walk and sleep in a foxhole."

Inducted into service in September 1943, Kalberloh began his cadet training in Amarillo, Texas. Completing several months of training, he was then assigned to a B-17 Bomber crew as a tail gunner. Recalling the uncomfortable nature of the task to which he was assigned, Kaberloh noted, "[As a tail gunner], you were in a small area in the rear of the plane for sometimes eight hours—or however long the mission lasted—on your knees sitting on something similar to a bicycle seat. Looking back, I don't know how I endured that," Kalberloh quipped.

Kalberloh's newly-formed crew was soon transferred to Lincoln, Nebraska, where they picked up a new B-17 and received orders to deploy overseas. From there, they departed in December of 1944 and flew the plane to Wales following several refueling stops. Upon their arrival, the new plane was taken and assigned to another crew, while Kalberloh's group was provided with one that had recently undergone repairs after receiving significant damage during a previous air skirmish.

"The ground crew chief told us to take care of the plane, we had been given as a replacement since it had just been fixed up," Kalberloh said. "It was shot down on our first mission…so I guess he wasn't very happy with us."

Named *Dixie's Delight* in honor of the only whiskey the crew could seem to acquire during the war, the plane began taking flak while bombing targets near Berlin on February 3, 1945. The aircraft eventually sustained enough damage from anti-aircraft guns that the pilot gave the order for the crew to evacuate. Jumping from the plane along with eight of his fellow crewmembers, Kalberloh's parachute became entwined in a tree. The cords on the chute then snapped and he injured his back when he fell, slamming into the ground. Now separated from his fellow crewmembers, Kalberloh roamed the German countryside for the next five days without food, maps or money, all the while striving to evade capture. He eventually succumbed to his hunger and—on February 8, 1945—surrendered himself to a German farmer who fed him before turning him over to the town marshal.

The young prisoner was initially interviewed by a Gestapo officer before being sent to Frankfurt for further questioning. In Frankfurt, he was interrogated by an American defector originally from Chicago, but serving as a colonel with the German Luftwaffe (Air Force). His captors sent him to a prisoner of war (POW) distribution center in Wetzler, Germany, then on to a prison camp at Nuremburg. While in prison, he survived on a daily ration consisting of a loaf of bread that was made of ten percent tree flower (sawdust) and shared amongst seven of his fellow prisoners, a can of watery soup, and an occasional Red Cross parcel.

"I was just a nineteen-year-old country boy who had never been farther from home than Kansas City," stated Kalberloh. "After hearing the stories of what [the Germans] had done to the Jews, we didn't know what to expect."

Toward the latter part of April 1945, General Patton and the 3rd Armor Division were approaching Nuremburg. In response, the German military marched thousands of prisoners—including Kalberloh—ninety-seven miles to Mooseberg. However, the German plans of avoidance failed when, on April 29, 1945, Patton's troops overran the camp and Kalberloh was finally liberated from his nightmarish experience of captivity.

"I remember seeing a tank followed by a Jeep and another tank roll into our [prison] camp," Kalberloh said. "Patton was standing in the back of the jeep saluting." Tearing up, the veteran remarked, "That was...and still is...the best day of my life."

Kalberloh returned to the states in June 1945 and was discharged from the service the following September. In later years, he went on to work in the insurance industry and the Missouri Jaycees, and in 1992 retired from the Missouri Automobile Dealers Association. A past commander of the Central Missouri Chapter of the American Ex-Prisoners of War Organization (an organization which officially dissolved on September 16, 2016) , Kalberloh shared how his military experiences have affected his perception of something many have never had to live without.

"The service taught me many things—such as discipline, but more importantly, how valuable life is and that you had better take care of it," Kalberloh remarked. "It's definitely more difficult for others to appreciate the freedoms they have when it's never been taken from them...and I'll never take that for granted." *(Photograph courtesy of Ralph Kalberloh)*

E. John Knapp

Jefferson City

E. John Knapp has acquired the reputation as being a man who has enjoyed exploring various creative outlets such as poetry and painting. A retired architect, in the last several years he embarked upon another means of self-expression by putting to paper his experiences during World War II after he was encouraged to do so by his children. Modestly, he held up his book titled *Poet Flyer: WWII Poetry & Photographs Based on Aerial Combat*, and said, "I wanted to share the message of the three stages of my experience—before, during and after the war."

The story of his journey toward military service began to unfold a few years following his graduation from high school in 1935 in his home state of Michigan, Knapp explained. Employed for a couple of years as a youth swimming instructor and later as a chauffeur for a camp director under the National Youth Administration—a former government program that once provided work and educational opportunities for those between sixteen and twenty-five years of age—Knapp left the job and chose to pursue his own education. He enrolled in Lawrence Technical University near Detroit in 1937, choosing to focus on a degree in architecture because of an interest that had blossomed many years earlier.

"I watched several homes being built while I was growing up, including my grandmother's and uncle's, and decided that's what I wanted to do when I got older. I wanted to design homes."

The young man began attending classes in the evening and gained applicable experience working during the day as a draftsman for a local company. However, he decided to leave school and enlisted in the Army Air Corps in April 1941—a choice, he said, motivated by both his interest in flying and the realization he might soon be drafted. Despite the approach of war, the aviation cadet decided to marry Maxine, to whom he had been introduced by a relative, in August 1941. His participation in the war was soon secured with the bombing of Pearl Harbor in December 1941. In February 1942, he left for the Air Corps induction center at Nashville, Tennessee, to begin his training.

"We were there for a couple of months for basic training," the veteran recalled," and then I was sent to flight school at Monroe, Louisiana. While I was there," he continued, "I decided I didn't want to be a pilot and instead became a navigator."

His military specialty may have changed, but Knapp remained in Louisiana to complete his navigational studies, eventually qualifying as a crewmember and receiving his commission as a lieutenant in 1943. He then traveled to Texas and was assigned to the crew of a B-17 bomber, spending the next several weeks there refining his aviation skills.

"This was back before GPS technology so we had to learn to navigate by the stars," he grinned.

With their preparatory training completed, the crew boarded their B-17 and flew to Canada, and then on to Northern Ireland. After brief trips by both boat and train, they finally arrived to their duty assignment with the 100th Bomb Group stationed near the small community of Thorpe Abbotts, England. Knapp and his fellow aviators soon began flying missions to bomb targets throughout Nazi-occupied Europe, during which they were constantly harassed by the threats of German fighters and anti-aircraft guns. The veteran affirms that although there were many memorable missions in which he participated, including the bombing of targets "just ahead of the infantry and tanks" on D-Day, it was his crew's sixth mission that has remained forever inscribed in his memories.

"We usually got up at about 3:00 a.m. and got ready for the flight—showered, cleaned up, ate chow, all of that stuff," Knapp said.

"When I was getting on the plane to leave for the mission, our colonel pulled me off the flight...and I never knew why."

During the mission, Knapp explained, his fellow B-17 crewmembers had to make a second run at a German target that was concealed by cloud cover, which gave the enemy an opportunity to sight in on the aircraft.

"The plane was hit and exploded shortly after that," Knapp solemnly recalled.

For several years, he believed everyone aboard the aircraft had perished.

After completing thirty-five combat missions, Knapp chose to remain at Thorpe Abbott and was transferred to an intelligence section, spending the remainder of his time overseas preparing information on daily targets and flight routes. When the war finally ended in 1945, Knapp returned to Michigan, reunited with his wife (whom he had not seen for nearly three years) and went back to school to finish up his architecture degree.

"One day, I got a call from the [top turret] gunner who had been on the plane that was shot down," said Knapp. "I found out that he and the bombardier had survived and were captured and held as POWs until the war ended, but everyone else on the plane died." He added, "What a wonderful moment that was—I still remember it like it was yesterday—to hear that he and the gunner had survived!"

As the years passed, Knapp finished the training and apprenticeship to become an architect, a career he enjoyed for several decades. He later relocated to Jefferson City and used his spare time to embrace his passions of poetry, painting, and, eventually, embraced the suggestion of writing about his military service.

With decades of experience under his belt, the centenarian acquired a unique perspective on World War II, one that grew and matured from the range of experiences of which many have only read about in books.

"I have a different idea than most about World War II," Knapp said. "We really had two major enemies—Germany and Japan—and it sure was a vicious fight. But," he continued, "both of these countries are now some of our closest friends. "For me," he concluded, "that's the true measure of how we won the war and helps give meaning to the lives that were lost."

Eliud John Knapp passed away in Jefferson City on December 31, 2017. The veteran was 101 years old at the time of his death and was laid to rest in Forest Hill Cemetery in Madison, Wisconsin. (*Photo courtesy of Marsha Krech)*

Herbert Kuebler

Gasconade

Take a dash of country charm and mix with sixteen months of combat duty, then cover it with decades of life experience and you have the necessary ingredients for a captivating story of service and sacrifice during a tumultuous time in our nation's history.

In 1924, just outside of the community of Gasconade, Herbert Kuebler was born and raised on a small family farm. Like so many of his generation, Kuebler left school after the eighth grade to help his parents work the farm. Wishing to embark upon his own path, he went to work a few years later for International Shoe Company in Hermann.

"Everyone kind of worked at the shoe company then," stated Kuebler. "I was really just kind of biding my time there because I knew that I was probably going to be drafted for the war."

True to his prediction, Kuebler received his draft notice in early 1943—when he was only eighteen years old. In April of the same year, he reported to Jefferson Barracks for his in-processing into the United States Army.

"My first day there [Jefferson Barracks] they had me washing dishes," Kuebler chuckled. "Later that day, me and another guy went for a walk around the post to check things out. We ended up getting three or four more days of KP [Kitchen Police] for doing that," he mirthfully added.

Kuebler then traveled to Camp Maskell, North Carolina, for several weeks of basic combat training before traveling to Camp Forrest, Tennessee, for additional training and to participate in military maneuvers. While in training, the young soldier was qualified as a medic and learned the basics of providing first aid to injured soldiers in addition to operating an ambulance.

"I'm not sure how I became a medic," Kuebler remarked, "but it didn't really make much of a difference to me...I knew I would be treating the wounded in combat."

Kuebler was assigned to the 224th Medical Company, 17th Airborne Division, and was soon on his way to support the war effort with his newly-acquired medical skills. On August 17, 1944, Kuebler's unit boarded the *Queen Mary* in New York and arrived in Liverpool, England, several days later. Kuebler's unit remained in England for three and a half months to train and prepare for their pending combat service.

"We did maneuvers in the hills of England and learned how to give shots of morphine," stated the veteran. " We also practiced extracting the wounded and evacuating them to an aid station."

Regardless of the many memories he acquired from his service, one of the most profound was a ruined Thanksgiving dinner experience that occurred while stationed at Liverpool.

"They blamed it on the cook because he supposedly forgot to take the turkey out of the freezer," Kuebler said. "We were all looking forward to a good meal that day, but he ended up burning it and when we got to the mess hall, it smelled so bad you couldn't stand it," he chuckled. "Luckily, we were able to get some turkey from another outfit."

In December 1944, Kuebler's unit made the trip across the English Channel in landing crafts to join the battle that had been raging since D-Day. As a combat medic, Kuebler never carried a weapon and the Germans weren't supposed to fire upon them, but he recalls several incidents in which he and other medics were shot at by the enemy.

"I'm just glad they missed," he jokingly affirmed.

Initially entering combat in France, Kuebler recounted a situation in the Ruhr Valley in Germany, where intense combat ensued as American and German forces fought against one another from opposite sides of the Ruhr River.

"You couldn't get down to the river during the day because all of the shelling," Kuebler said. "We'd have to go down at night to pick up the wounded."

Kuebler was also given the opportunity to exercise his medical knowledge at the now famous Battle of the Bulge, during which he had to address a variety of wounds and injuries suffered by American troops.

"We had a lot of casualties…like gunshots," he recalled. "Almost everyone had frostbite on their feet as well. It was very cold, but I was fortunate never to get frostbitten."

While in Germany, Kuebler participated in an operation in which he and a fellow soldier were inserted into a combat zone in order to set up an aid station.

"We came in on a glider. It had two pilots, me and another guy onboard," shared Kuebler. "There was also a jeep with a rope hooked to the nose of the glider so that we could pull out of the glider once it landed."

After setting up their aid station outside of Wessel, Germany, Kuebler sordidly recounted treating serious combat injuries and a pile of American and German casualties stacked higher than a tent. The veteran would go on to provide medical support for combat operations throughout France and much of Central Europe, earning a Glider Badge and three Bronze Stars during his service. Returning to the United States on January 3, 1946, one of Kuebler's first experiences was participation in a victory parade in New York City.

"Although the parade was nice, I really didn't think that it was necessary. I just wanted to get home," he recalled.

On January 18, 1946, he was discharged from the Army at Jefferson Barracks after having served more than sixteen months in a combat environment. In 1947, he married Geneva Hackman, whom he had dated prior to his military service, and the couple purchased a home in Hermann. Kuebler went back to work for the shoe factory, where he would remain for twenty-seven years. He then went to work for Zero Manufacturing in Washington, Missouri, where, for several years, he helped build refrigerated tanks for dairy farmers until retiring in 1987.

Now decades removed from the distresses associated with treating casualties in a combat environment, Kuebler remains quite humbled by his service to the nation.

"I believe we did a pretty good job over there," Kuebler said. "There were some bad days. You were away from home and couldn't do what you wanted to." And with a trace of modesty, the veteran added, "But I really felt like I was a better person when I came home, like we really accomplished something."

Kuebler passed away on August 9, 2015 and was laid to rest in the cemetery of St. George Catholic Church in Hermann. *(Photograph courtesy of Connie Hinton)*

Cletus Kueffer

California

During the Second World War, there emerged many interesting stories from the annals of naval history, which demonstrate the remarkable performance of the sailors who served throughout the vast, hostile waters of the Pacific, enduring unfathomable risks such as the hellish explosions delivered by enemy aircraft. While serving aboard the aircraft carrier *U.S.S. Lexington*, local resident and former sailor Cletus Kueffer recalls living through such dangerous circumstances, and the lives that were lost in an effort to help bring peace to a world embroiled in conflict.

The oldest of nine children, Kueffer was raised on a farm in rural Moniteau County (Missouri) and working for the state highway department when he received his notice to report for a physical in 1942.

"My draft notice hadn't arrived yet," said Kueffer. "But I had a friend tell me, 'I'm not going to dig foxholes [in the Army],' and he convinced me to join the Navy...even though I couldn't swim," he grinned.

The aspiring sailor enlisted in Jefferson City on September 13, 1942 and was able to qualify as Third Class Painter because of his previous experience in working on bridges with the highway department—a benefit that would provide him with monthly pay of $78 instead of the $50 received by recruits without qualifying experience. Spending only thirty days in boot camp at Great Lakes, Illinois, "because the Navy was pushing us through pretty heavy back then," said Kueffer, he soon became part of a small group of carpenters and painters transferred to Quonset Point Naval Air Station in Rhode Island, where he remained until receiving orders in February 1943.

"I was assigned to the *U.S.S. Lexington* (CV-16)," Kueffer explained, a recently commissioned aircraft carrier that would earn the nickname "Blue Ghost" because Tokyo Rose—a Japanese radio broadcaster specializing in propaganda—mistakenly reported on the ship's sinking several times during the war.

According to the book *Blue Ghost Memoirs*, the vessel remained in Boston Harbor for a few "months of outfitting, tuning equipment, loading supplies and ammunition, and assembling the crew" before leaving for their sea trials known as a "shakedown cruise." [86] The ship sailed to the Gulf of Paria, off the coast of South America and returned to Boston, where, Kueffer recalled, the crew "stayed for a few days for minor repairs and little things that had to be taken care of."

In June 1943, the Lexington sailed to San Francisco to pick up a battalion of Marines and then to Pearl Harbor, loading the carrier with the initial complement of planes they would use in combat missions. As part of a task force consisting of "battle wagons" (battleships such as the *USS Iowa* and *Missouri*), heavy cruisers and destroyers, the *Lexington* began navigating the waters of the South Pacific while Kueffer worked as a painter placing identification numbers on the newer aircraft and repairing those damaged during combat flights.

"[The *Lexington*] was hit twice during the twenty-seven months I was aboard," Kueffer said. "The first time was when we were torpedoed in December of 1943 near [the island of] Kwajalein," he added.

Records maintained by the veteran note that the ship was also damaged in early November 1944, when it was bombed by Japanese aircraft. Following both incidents, the extent of the damage to the ship required it to port in Bremerton, Washington, to undergo repairs. The ship never rested for long periods and was soon back to sea and conducting operations. The ship continued its missions that would carry it through locations such as Guam and the Philippines

---

[86] Romanelli, *Blue Ghost Memoirs*, 19.

while enduring sporadic attacks by Japanese aircraft that would occasionally result in casualties.

"While we were out to sea, they had no place to store the bodies of the sailors killed in action," Kueffer said. "When it was time for a burial, everyone not on duty would go topside and the bodies would be lying on metal stretchers in canvas bags." Solemnly, he added, "Then the chaplain would say a few words and over the side [of the ship] the bodies would go."

In June 1945, Kueffer was sent back to the United States and spent several weeks assigned to the paint shop at Ottumwa (Iowa) Naval Air Station, later transferring to Clinton, Oklahoma, where he received his discharge in December 1945. In the years following the war, he lived on the farm he purchased from his great-aunt while he was still in the Navy, married his fiancée, Geneva, and raised two daughters. He worked twenty-four years for the highway department, helped form a structural painting company and farmed for several years.

A member of the Masonic Lodge, VFW, Disabled American Veterans and the United Church of Christ in California, Kueffer explained that some of his most treasured memories are from the time he spent on the high seas more than seventy years ago. It was a period he noted, full of sensational events that earned him twelve battle stars and a Presidential Unit Citation for the *USS Lexington*.

"At my age, a lot of the guys I served with are now deceased, but I consider myself pretty lucky...that I came back from all of that, that I survived all that I went through during the war," he said. "But it was all part of my duty," he added. "There was nothing wrong with me—I was healthy and I wouldn't have felt right if I hadn't gone and done my part."

Cletus Edward Kueffer passed away on April 2, 2018 in California, Missouri. The ninety-six-year-old veteran was laid to rest with full military honors in California Evangelical Cemetery. *(Photograph courtesy of Cletus Kueffer)*

Charles "Don" Lee

Holts Summit

On the morning of August 28, 1929, the *Graf Zeppelin*—a German-built passenger airship engaged in worldwide demonstration flights—passed over a small farm in northern Missouri. From the earth below, a five-year-old Charles "Don" Lee gazed up in amazement at the colossal airship.

"It was making its flight from El Paso, Texas to Chicago," said, Lee, Holts Summit, Missouri. "I can still remember seeing it pass over...it really left a vivid impression."

In 1942, the Ludlow, Missouri, native was attending William Jewell College in Liberty, Missouri, when he enlisted in a naval aviation program, a decision that would soon link him to his earlier childhood encounter. Called to active duty in March 1943, for the next several months Lee and twenty other cadets completed their military indoctrination and light plane training at locations in Kansas. The group then transferred to St. Mary's College near San Francisco for three months of "intensive physical and military conditioning," before moving on to their individual training assignments, which landed the nineteen-year-old Lee at blimp training in Moffett Field, California.

"It was called primary lighter than air [LTA] training," he said, where he learned to pilot a small class of blimp. Lee added that the Navy referred to blimps as "LTA's" while fix-winged aircraft were identified as heavier than air or "HTAs."

Lee soon graduated to advanced training at Lakehurst, New Jersey, and was introduced to the K-class of blimps during the winter of 1943. Manufactured by the Goodyear Aircraft Company for the Navy and powered by twin Pratt & Whitney engines, the former naval aviator notes that the aircraft had a complement of ten crewmembers and was capable of traveling at a speed of seventy-five knots. He received his commission as an ensign in March 1944 and was then sent to his first duty assignment as a junior pilot with a blimp crew in Key West, Florida. For the next several months, he and his crewmates operated out of an airport in Barranquilla, Colombia, flying their helium-filled aircraft above maritime convoys traveling to and from the Panama Canal.

"We had one blimp and three crews," Lee said. "Working on alternating shifts and performing fifteen- to twenty-hour patrols. We would fly at an altitude of five hundred feet searching for signs of Germans submarines that might attack the convoys."

Lee explained that although the blimp was equipped with two five-hundred-pound depth charges and a .50 caliber machine gun, their operating procedures were to contact destroyer escorts sailing with the convoys if a submarine was spotted.

"I guess we were fortunate that we only encountered friendly submarines during our missions," Lee said.

The crew was later reassigned to Chorrera, Panama, spending the next few months on patrol while also photographing submarine training activities such as torpedo firing exercises. In December 1944, Lee and his crewmates volunteered to fly a damaged blimp to a repair base in Florida. After the delivery, the crew was disbanded and Lee was sent to California, where he served with several blimp crews, eventually earning the designation of senior pilot. But with the U.S. in the process of planning the invasion of Japan, airplane pilots were needed, compelling Lee to volunteer for primary aviation training in Texas in July 1945. By the time he graduated from training five months later, the war with Japan had ended.

"At that point, I had enough points to leave the service," Lee said. The naval veteran then returned to Missouri and enrolled at the University of Missouri on the GI Bill in early 1946.

Graduating with a bachelor's degree in journalism, the former aviator continued his naval service with the reserves until 1958, and went on to enjoy a career in state government from which he retired in 1988. Lee lost his wife of fifty-seven years, Dorothy, in 2009, and the couple's son Richard lives in Springfield with their three grandsons. Despite his claims that he is just an "old widower without much of a story," the veteran's recitation of his involvement in a fascinating segment of aviation history demonstrates otherwise.

"We (the blimp crews) had the mission of protecting the shores of North and South America from submarines and we ranged far, operating up and down both coasts," he said. "It's a story that you don't hear much about and there weren't a lot of us assigned to the blimp crews, which, I guess, kind of makes us somewhat a unique part of history." *(Photograph courtesy of Don Lee)*

Robert Mansur

Jefferson City

Shortly after graduating from Jefferson City (Missouri) High School in 1939, Robert Mansur spent a year and a half studying at the former Jefferson City Junior College. It was his enrollment at the University of Missouri in 194. However, that landed him in a program that not only allowed him to complete his degree, but also sent him across the wide Pacific as a sailor in the U.S. Navy.

"While I was studying at Columbia, I enlisted in the Navy's V-7 program," said Mansur. "The program allowed me to complete my college and then attend Navy midshipmen's school upon graduation." When asked why he volunteered to enlist in the Navy and not another branch of service, Mansur jokingly responded, "I figured it would have the cleanest living and I didn't feel like digging foxholes."

Earning his bachelor's degree in business administration in May 1943, he traveled to the U.S. Naval Reserve Midshipmen's School at Columbia University in New York. It was here, Mansur said, that he underwent several weeks of specialized training to prepare for service as an officer aboard a ship.

"I then received assignment to the *USS Boyd*—DD 544—in January 1944," said Mansur. "It was a Fletcher-class destroyer that was stationed at Mare Island [California] and was at the tail end of being repaired after it was shelled [by a Japanese shore battery] during a rescue mission near an island in the Pacific."

When reporting to the ship, the young sailor recalls meeting the ship's skipper—Capt. Ulysses S. Grant Sharp—who would later become a four-star admiral and commander in chief of the United

States Pacific Command during the Vietnam War. In describing his former captain, Mansur affirmed, "He was a very competent and hands-on leader."

Soon after his arrival, Mansur was assigned as the torpedo officer and signal officer. He was then sent to San Diego for two weeks of training at the torpedo school where he learned how to track targets and fire the underwater missiles designed to strike submarines.

"The ship had two bays of torpedoes and they were located behind each of the stacks on the ship," he said.

As the veteran explained, repairs were soon completed and a week after returning from his training, Mansur was aboard the *Boyd* when it sailed for Pearl Harbor to join a task force comprised of several ships bound for operations in the Pacific. With unvarnished honesty, Mansur admits that the next two and a half years he spent on board the Boyd were relatively lackluster despite the challenges of the occasional kamikaze attack.

"At that time, there really wasn't much of a threat from submarines, so as the torpedo officer there really wasn't a lot for me to do," he said.

The ship sailed thousands of miles of ocean and participated in operations such as the beach landings during the Battle of Saipan, Battle of the Philippine Sea, invasion of Guam and the bombardment of Iwo Jima.

"Toward the end of the war, we were assigned radar picket duty with two or three other destroyers in the waters between the fleet and Tokyo," said Mansur. (Radar picket lines were a formation of several ships stationed between an enemy location and a fleet of vessels to increase radar detection range and, occasionally, to intercept enemy aircraft.) "We were there to intercept kamikaze pilots trying to find the fleet," he said. "On one occasion, they came *en masse* and while we were battling, there was a total eclipse of the moon and everything went dark—we couldn't see them and they couldn't see us." He added, "The skipper said to keep shooting whether or not we could see them."

The veteran notes that although several ships were damaged when struck by kamikaze planes, the *USS Boyd* was fortunate to avoid any further damage than that sustained earlier in the war.

After the war, the ship was "deactivated" but went on to see service in the Korean War. Mansur remained in the Navy until March 1946 and returned to his hometown of Jefferson City, working several years for Oberman Manufacturing, Farm Bureau Mutual Insurance Company, the Missouri Public Service Commission and as a doorkeeper for the Missouri House of Representatives. He has also been active with the Jefferson City Symphony Orchestra and, in 1948, joined several local musicians in reorganizing the group following its disbandment after many of its members had been drafted during World War II. For forty-six years, Mansur said, he played as first chair flute with the orchestra and also served as president, membership chairman and concert manager for the Community Concert Association.

Mansur maintains that although his military service may have been largely lacking in stimulation, his time with the Navy was punctuated with several moments he found to be both interesting and memorable.

"Much of the time, as I've said, I wasn't too busy because there just wasn't a lot of call to shoot down planes with torpedoes—in fact, the only time I fired a torpedo was during a training exercise," he said. "But there are many good memories such as the times we would drop anchor and have shore parties at different atolls whenever we weren't involved in an engagement...or the times when they would show a movie on deck." He lightheartedly added, "The food was excellent, too, but despite everything that happened—whether good or not—it really made me appreciate civilian life and I was ready to get back home." *(Photograph courtesy of Robert Mansur)*

James Marcantonio

Jefferson City

As a young man coming of age in a quaint Massachusetts community during the early stages of World War II, James "George" Marcantonio left high school in 1942 to help support his family by going to work alongside his mother at a local manufacturer building equipment used by the United States Navy.

"I was making sixty cents an hour, which was a pretty good wage back then," he grinned.

Prior to this, Marcantonio explained, he became involved with a group known as the Sea Scouts—a department of the Boy Scouts of America that provided seamanship training for interested youth of the nation.

"That's where I first acquired my interest in the Navy," said Marcantonio. "To join the Navy, I would have to be seventeen and have my parents' signature," he continued, "so I told them I intended to join when I was finally of age."

Abiding by his earlier promise and with the support of his parents, the aspiring seaman left his job and enlisted in the Navy on October 29, 1943—the day he turned seventeen years old. Several days later, he reported to Newport, Rhode Island, and remained six weeks at the location, which at the time served as one of the training sites for naval recruits during the war. When he completed his initial training, the young sailor was assigned to the Navy's Fargo Building located in South Boston, spending several weeks on a work crew performing such duties as security for the facility. However, in March 1943, Marcantonio's adventure began in earnest when he was sent to school for PT boats (Patrol Torpedo) at the training station in Melville, Rhode Island.

"That was the melting pot for guys that would serve on the PT boats," said Marcantonio. "They trained men for torpedoes, radar, machinists, gunner's mates quartermaster... just about every specialty," he added.

As he recalled, the PT boats were rather fragile in construction since the hulls were built from a type of "plywood" nearly eighty feet in length, carried limited armament such as torpedoes, small cannons and machine guns and often had a crew complement of a dozen or more sailors. The boats, Marcantonio clarified, used their speed to engage and sink various types of enemy watercraft. While training at Melville, he and the crews of the PT boats would conduct nightly maneuvers in the Atlantic Ocean in preparation for later overseas engagements.

The young sailor and a group of other recently trained PT boat crewmembers boarded a troopship bound for England on May 20, 1944. Then, on June 7, 1944 (the day after the D-Day Invasion), he and the crew of *PT-520* were stationed 3-1/2 miles off the coast of France, dwarfed in size by several of the larger battleships.

"We were basically floating next to the *USS Texas*," Marcantonio said. "At that point, one of our missions was the retrieval of personnel from the water—sometimes Americans or French pilots...other times Germans," he recalled.

The following day (June 8, 1944), an event unfolded that remains seared in the former sailor's memory—the date the *USS Rich*—a Buckley-class destroyer escort—sank after detonating mines off the Normandy Coast.

"The Rich had a crew of 215, 27 of them were killed. 52 were missing (almost all of whom were drowned or incinerated), and 73 were wounded," noted John C. McManus in the book *The Americans at Normandy*.[87]

"We were nearby and rescued some of the survivors and retrieved some of the dead," Marcantonio somberly recalled. "It's just one of

---

[87] McManus, *The Americans at Normandy*, 51.

those memories that I can't erase and I wish those that lost their lives would have been able to live to celebrate the end of the war."

In the days and months following the invasion, the men of *PT-520* completed many missions, some of which included transporting high-ranking officers and journalists. They also conducted operations with groups of American and English PT boats along the Seine River in France, using their speed and armament to intercept and sink German boats.

"The Germans fired back at us, but we were quicker," he affirmed. "If they had hit us where we stored the torpedoes...that would have been it for us. Luckily, that never happened." He added, "On one occasion, they hit the antenna on our boat and the shrapnel damaged our [U.S.] flag."

Toward the latter part of December 1944, Marcantonio returned to the United States and, after a brief period of leave, was transferred to operations as part of the Seventh Fleet in the Philippines aboard the smaller boat, *PT-250*.

"To be honest with you, we kind of just fell into a regular routine for some time, traveling from base to base around the different islands," he said. "Our presence was more for goodwill purposes because there weren't any battles we were involved in. We were essentially waiting for the invasion of Japan."

In early summer 1945, the sailor was transferred to *PC-1241* (Patrol Craft), where he served as a boatswain's mate while snipers aboard the ship targeted, shot and detonated floating mines that posed deadly hazards to the U.S. fleet. The war ended with the Japanese surrender aboard the *USS Missouri* on September 2, 1945, and the following spring, Marcantonio received his discharge and returned home to Massachusetts. He eventually moved to Missouri to attend Central Methodist College (now University) in Fayette, Missouri, and then met Fern Wood, whom he married in 1952.

In later years, the WWII veteran and his wife raised three children and settled in Jefferson City. He went on to retire from the former Jefferson City Correctional Center. As Marcantonio has come to realize, the most intense memories of his life center on his days in the military and the time spent alongside a group of men whose contributions have often gone unnoticed.

"The PT boats were an important part of the war," Marcantonio affirmed, "and it was a type of duty that a person had to volunteer for because you didn't have that much protection in combat, and you were almost always in a dangerous environment." He added, "And when you were on those boats and realized that they were made out of wood and what could happen if you were hit," he paused, chuckling, "you just had to be a little crazy to want of be a part of it. We were a different breed." *(Photograph courtesy of James Marcantonio)*

Walter McHugh

Jefferson City

While growing up, many have been influenced by someone they held in high regard—perhaps an individual that seemed to be larger than life and who has traveled to exotic locations or participated in remarkable events of which others have only dreamed. In the late 1930s in a suburb of St. Louis, a youthful Walter McHugh recalls listening to the tales shared by a next-door neighbor, thus inspiring the young boy to embrace a "fib" with hopes of someday fulfilling a dream.

"The man living next door was a retired Marine—a big, strapping guy that really impressed me as a young boy," said McHugh. "No one in my family had served in the Marines and I really enjoyed visiting with him. I admired him so much I decided to join," he added.

Aided by his neighbor, McHugh was able to disguise the fact that he was only fourteen and enlisted in the Marine Corps Reserve.

"To be honest with you, the recruiter didn't give a damn about my age…they were just happy to have someone that was interested," the veteran laughed. "But my dad found out about it six months later and blew his top. Then he went down to the Marine Corps recruiter and got me out of it."

As the years passed and McHugh finally came of legal age, he took a "500-question exam" administered by the Navy for the Marine Corps. After missing only two questions on the entire exam, McHugh said, he enlisted in the Navy in 1944 since he was promised assignment to a Marine Corps Air Squadron.

"They sent about 180 recruits down to Jacksonville, Florida, and hammered us pretty good for about six weeks. They made us physically fit there," he grinned.

From there, the young sailors were sent to schools in different locations throughout the country while McHugh received assignment to the Naval Air Technical Training Center in Norman, Oklahoma. It was here that he underwent training in aviation ordnance. However, he soon discovered the course of instruction would be used to conceal an assignment of a covert nature.

"Although I learned some about ordnance, they taught us to carry coded messages—that's what the guys who scored high on the (Navy entrance) test were selected to do," he affirmed.

The messages, McHugh recalled, were transmitted verbally and often sounded like oddly structured sentences, but the intended recipient understood the meaning of the communication.

"For the next couple of years, I carried messages to ships around the South Pacific," he said. "Once I got aboard, they knew I was coming and took me right to the person I was supposed to deliver it to. When I was convinced it was the right person, I gave him the message and then went to work as an ordnance man on the ship." Pausing, he added, "I never spent more than two weeks in one location and then I was off delivering another message."

After the war ended and the need for coded messages was no longer critical, McHugh returned to the states and finished out the last six months of his enlistment on military police duty in San Francisco, until receiving his discharge in 1946. While still the Navy, McHugh married his childhood sweetheart, Frances Gretchen Schirr, with whom he was reunited upon his return from the war. He soon went to work for the Pittsburgh Plate Glass Company (PPG) as a salesperson for the paintbrush division until a relative's "suggestion" fulfilled his desire to serve with the Marines, although with unexpected consequences.

"My sister had married a Marine captain and he had something to do with the Marine squadron at Lambert Field in St. Louis. He talked me into enlisting in the Marines [in August 1950] and six weeks later I was in Korea, which was one hell of a big mistake!" he grinned.

In September 1950, his squadron boarded a troopship in California that carried them to Japan, where they were then loaded on landing ship tanks (LSTs) operated by Japanese civilians. McHugh and his fellow Marines were then sent to the Korean mainland and became part of the Battle of Inchon—an amphibious invasion involving an estimated 75,000 United Nations troops. McHugh fought inland with the 1st Marine Division and helped establish an airfield a few miles northeast of Inchon, from where they launched aerial attacks against enemy forces. However, weeks later, he and scores of other Marines were sent to the Chosin Reservoir to help rescue an estimated 30,000 American troops surrounded by 120,000 Chinese soldiers.

"We were using whatever type of equipment we could to get the wounded out of there," he said. "There were cart paths we used for roads and you could only fit one piece of equipment down it at a time. Also," he continued, "the paths were surrounded by steep mountains on either side and the Chinese would shoot at us and our equipment as we passed."

Though he hesitated in providing much detail regarding certain combat activities, the eleven months McHugh spent in Korea earned him seven Purple Heart medals from shrapnel and bullet wounds.

"None of them [the wounds] were very serious," he humbly submitted. "I was lucky...others weren't."

Returning to St. Louis in August 1951, he and his wife in later years raised four children. The veteran returned to his employment at PPG and eventually relocated to Jefferson City, where he became the owner of Brady's Glass and Paint, which he operated until his retirement.

His life, McHugh admits, has been full of many unexpected twists and turns, but he often enjoyed reflecting on the years he spent in uniform and the man, who so many years ago, first inspired his decision to become a Marine.

"After the war, I never saw my neighbor again and I have no idea whatever happened to him," McHugh said. "But I really enjoyed those days when I could listen to him tell his stories about serving in the Marine Corps...everything he said just awed me," he added. "And after I went on to serve with the Navy in the Pacific and the Marines in Korea, it really helped give me an appreciation for everything that he had talked about. I understood what he had been through."

Walter Leo McHugh passed away October 27, 2017 at his home in Jefferson City. The ninety-one-year-old veteran was entombed with military honors in Riverview Mausoleum. *(Photograph courtesy of Walt McHugh.)*

Gilbert Hofstetter

Fortuna

In his days of youth growing up on a small farm between the rural communities of Latham and Fortuna, Kay Hofstetter remembers his older brother Gilbert leaving home to help his grandparents on their farm. During WWII, his brother would again leave, this time to serve his nation. This departure, Kay said, resulted in his brother laying down his life in service to his country, leaving behind grieving parents and eleven siblings to carry on his memory.

"He was the second oldest of twelve kids," said Kay Hofstetter, describing his family. "Everybody liked Gilbert. He had coon hounds and he and his buddies enjoyed going coon hunting when they had the opportunity," he added.

While working on his grandparent's farm, the twenty-one-year-old Gilbert Hofstetter was inducted into the U.S. Army at Jefferson Barracks, Missouri on October 14, 1941. From there, he traveled to Ft. Riley, Kansas, and completed boot camp and then went through cavalry training. Weeks later, the young farm worker from Mid-Missouri was sent to Ft. Bliss, Texas, where he and his fellow soldiers were assigned to the 7th Cavalry Regiment and continued to train as horse cavalry. This would become, however, the last time many of these soldiers were to serve on horseback during the war. A website dedicated to the history of the 1st Cavalry Division and its subordinate units explains that in February 1943, "the entire 1st Cavalry

Division was alerted for an overseas assignment as a dismounted unit [foot soldiers]."[88]

Several months later, in June 1943, Hofstetter and the soldiers of the division traveled to California and boarded troop ships. A few weeks later, they arrived in Australia and completed months of amphibious and jungle warfare training. In January 1944, they left for New Guinea and, weeks later, sailed for islands to the north, where they would soon acquire their first taste of combat against Japanese forces.

"The next important step in General MacArthur's plans was a proposed landing in the Admiralty Islands, lying west of New Britain," wrote Trevor Dupuy in his book *Asiatic Land Battles: Japanese Ambitions in the Pacific.* He added, "The Admiralties were important because of their airfields and harbors..."[89]

The 7th Cavalry Regiment exemplified the stalwart courage of the American soldier during the Admiralty Campaign, performing assault maneuvers and later conducting "mop up operations...all over the northern half of Los Negros Island," the previously mentioned 1st Cavalry website explained. This was followed by the invasion of Manus Island, all of which resulted in forty-three dead and seventeen wounded for the regiment by the time the campaign ended on May 18, 1944. Hofstetter had received his baptism of fire and for the next five months, conducted extensive combat training in preparation for yet another major combat operation of the war—the Battle of Leyte in the Philippines.

Operating under the 6th U.S. Army, Hofstetter and the men of the 7th Cavalry Regiment were part of a force totaling nearly 100,000 combat troops that on October 20, 1944, following naval bombardment of the eastern coast of the Philippine island, began to "sweep toward the beaches of a front eighteen miles long," wrote Dupuy.

---

[88] 1st Cavalry Division, *WWII, Pacific Theater*, www.firts-team.us.
[89] Dupuy, *Asiatic Land Battles*, 62-69.

"Gilbert was killed on October 21 (1944)," said Kay Hofstetter, when describing his older brother's overseas service. "According to one of the soldiers that served with him, he was shot by a sniper."

Shortly thereafter, back home in Missouri, Hofstetter's family would discover the callous manner by which families were at one time informed of the death of a loved one serving in the military.

"When he was killed, I can remember seeing my mother walk down to get the mail and then going to sit down on the steps," said Kay Hofstetter. "I could tell that something was wrong and I went and got my dad." With a somber pause, he lowered his head and added, "It was the telegram from the Army saying that Gilbert had been killed. I don't know how my mom stood it."

The recipient of a Bronze Star and Purple Heart, Corporal Hofstetter was initially laid to rest in the Philippines inside the Leyte Military Cemetery. However, in February 1949, his remains were returned to the United States and buried with full military honors in the Jefferson City National Cemetery following a service held in California, Missouri.

While recounting details of the funeral ceremony held decades ago, Kay Hofstetter noted, "I just remember seeing both the flags— the U.S. and the Army flag—on each side of his casket. He also had two Army guards standing by his casket and it was a very impressive site for a young boy."

In the years following Gilbert Hofstetter's burial in Jefferson City, Kay Hofstetter explained, his mother never missed an opportunity to visit her son's grave every Memorial Day until her passing in 1993—a tradition that the late soldier's younger brother has strived to carry on.

"He gave his life in service to his country and for me. On Memorial Day, it's not a sacrifice to go to Jefferson City to honor his memory," said Hofstetter. "I have always gone and will continue to do so as long as I can." *(Photograph Courtesy of Kay Hofstetter)*

Henry Nilges

Loose Creek

It takes one only a few minutes of mild conversation with Henry Nilges to realize the full breadth of historical experience and knowledge possessed by the former soldier. Having come of age during a tumultuous and profound moment in our nation's history, the retired local farmer was decades ago pulled from his rural surroundings and thrust into the center of a war waging in Europe, coming face-to-face with a world not easily understood.

Born near Loose Creek in 1925, Nilges was the proverbial country youth who recalls, "walking about four miles to school."

After graduating from eighth grade in 1939, he left school to remain home and begin his career working on the family farm.

"Back then, there really weren't any jobs in town...unlike there are now" Nilges remarked.

However, his developing agricultural endeavors were soon interrupted when he received a draft notice in December 1943. He reported to Jefferson Barracks (a historic U.S. Army post founded in 1826 and located in south St. Louis) for his physical examination and in processing, and was officially inducted into the U.S. Army in January 1944.

"I was selected to serve in the infantry," Nilges recalled. "I don't know how they decided where a person would serve. I guess they just went by their physical, education and where they were needed."

The young farmer then traveled to Camp Blanding, Florida to complete his basic combat training.

"We were supposed to complete twenty weeks of training," Nilges explained, "but they cut it down to seventeen weeks because replacements were needed to serve overseas."

The next leg of the farmer's journey carried him to Camp Shelby, Mississippi, and assignment with the 65th Division, where he and his fellow trainees began receiving instruction in infantry tactics and troop movements.

"It was terribly hot at Shelby," explained the veteran, "and they made us eat salt tablets regularly."

The division prepared for their deployment in December 1944 by packing all of their equipment on rail cars destined for New York. Nilges and his fellow soldiers then boarded a troop train to meet up with their equipment. Once in New York, the division boarded the troop ship *USS Monticello* and spent fourteen days in transit to the port in Le Havre, France. Upon arrival their January 1945, they were loaded on military trucks and driven to Camp Lucky Strike near Le Havre, France, which served as one of the many staging points for the thousands of soldiers preparing to enter combat in Europe.

"It was colder than heck there," noted Nilges, "and they took us to this field where there was about a foot of snow."

All members of the unit were then issued a cot, picked up three "K-Rations" and set up their tents in certain areas of the snow-covered field. Due to logistical complications associated with the overall war effort, the unit was unable to link up with their supplies and their food stores quickly diminished.

"We quickly ran out of food to eat," said Nilges. "It got to the point where he only had a spoonful of carrots and a cup of coffee daily...whatever they could find."

But it would be a fortuitous visitor from back in Missouri who would soon locate Nilges and help to ensure the young soldier's stomach found some relief from the extended lack of nourishment.

"My brother Gus heard that I was at Camp Lucky Strike and tracked me down while I was there," Nilges smiled.

With a more reliable source of supplies, Gus' unit was fortunate to have regular meals. He quickly invited his brother over to share dinner with his unit.

Leaving the camp at the end of February 1945, Nilges and the division received their introduction to combat when they were assigned to relieve the battle-worn 26th Division.

"The Germans had dug in on the Saar River along the Siegfried Line," Nilges explained. "They [26th Division] had driven the Germans back to the river but it had become something of a stalemate and nothing seemed to be moving."

According to Nilges, the Germans were so well entrenched that mortar attacks had little—if any—effect on their defensive positions. The division was waiting until the weather broke in spring to move in on the Germans' location. Eventually, the U.S. Army was able to break through in the north and drove the Germans back. The 65th Division fought across Germany, where Nilges continued to serve as a gunner in the third platoon. In May of 1945, their wartime journey took them into Austria and eventually into Czechoslovakia, during which time the war in Europe officially ended.

Throughout his journey, Nilges recalled hitting what he describes as "action spots," where Hitler's trained SS troops resolved not to surrender, but instead to fight. After the Germans' surrender, Nilges returned to Austria and worked for a brief time processing residents from other nations who had been conscripted to serve in the German military.

"We would take displaced soldiers turned loose by the Germans after the war and gather them in one location," recalled Nilges. "Once we got a truckload of people together from one country, we would haul them back to their homeland," he added.

From Austria, the war veteran was sent to Germany and spent some time guarding an ammunition dump. Shortly thereafter, the 65th Division was dissolved and Nilges was assigned to the 9th Division. His squad was then moved into the Bavarian Mountains to guard the border. Remaining in Europe for several months after the close of the war, Nilges received notice that he would be going home and, in May 1946, received his discharge from the Army. The combat veteran returned home to help his family work the farm in Loose Creek. In 1959, he took over the farm and continued to work it until his retirement in 1989.

With a timbre of mild humility, Nilges recalled of his military service, "I was in the Army until the end of the war and saw enough to know what a lot of veterans went through. I was just a greenhorn when I was drafted and had never been any farther than Jefferson City." He quickly added, "A lot of folks don't understand what happened during the war and I don't think that it is taught right in school, but I am sure proud to have been part of the experience." *(Photograph courtesy of Henry Nilges.)*

Norbert Struemph

Jefferson City

In the annals of military history, submarine service has gained a certain level of mystique, inspiring the vision of a sleek, fast underwater craft possessing the ability to move about in relative secrecy in the world's oceans. Though such visions might possess a quantity of truth, local submarine veteran Norbert Struemph recalls his own underwater service being far from romantic, fraught with peril and necessitating a lengthy separation from family.

While growing up in the rural community of Vienna, Missouri, Struemph was raised one of twelve children. After completing the eleventh grade, he made the decision to go to work and left for St. Louis, becoming a riveter for the Curtiss-Wright Corporation.

"That's where I was when Pearl Harbor happened," recalled Struemph. "I remember walking downtown and people were standing in line for four or five blocks waiting to sign up [for the military]."

On June 5, 1942, six months after the attack on Pearl Harbor, Struemph joined scores of other patriotic Americans and enlisted in the United States Navy. Days later, he was transferred to the Naval Air Station once located on the site of Lambert-St. Louis International Airport, to undergo his initial training. In training, he and other sailors attended dances and special events hosted by a local USO, where he soon met a young woman named Phyllis Fites. The couple married weeks later in November 1942.

"Sometime during our boot camp, these guys came down to talk to us and said they were looking for volunteers for the submarine service," Struemph said. "I didn't know much about it, but I decided to volunteer because it meant that I would receive extra pay," he added.

After passing the requisite tests, the recruit was sent to Groton, Connecticut, and was indoctrinated into his new duty assignment by learning to work on and operate the diesel engines and associated electrical systems used aboard submarines. The next step of his journey took him to California, where he boarded a boat for Pearl Harbor. Shortly after his arrival, he received the news of the birth of his first child, which, he added, was a joyous event tempered by his exposure to the continuing efforts to recover bodies of those who perished during the attack on Pearl Harbor.

"Every morning, ambulances would line up on the piers to pick up the bodies of sailors that had been killed in the attack," Struemph said. "They had guys in the water with torches cutting the metal and removing the bodies from the compartments inside the ships that had been hit."

Following a brief stay in Hawaii, the sailor was sent by ship to Fremantle, Australia to work aboard the *USS Orion*—a submarine tender that stored supplies used to perform certain repairs on damaged submarines. It was here, Struemph said, that he worked for several weeks before receiving assignment to his submarine, the *USS Narwhal (SS-167)*. The Narwhal, naval records indicate, returned to port in Fremantle, Australia, in late 1943 after completing several war patrols. With Struemph aboard the Narwhal as a machinist's mate, they soon deployed for the Philippines transporting special cargo in support of the localized guerilla movement.

"We began missions of hauling Filipinos that were loaded down with grenades, radios and all kinds of equipment. They were trained to fight by the United States," said the veteran. "We would sneak up some shallow tributary at night to avoid detection by Japanese warships. Then," he continued, boats would come from shore to pick up the Filipinos and carry them off to fight the Japanese."

In addition to delivering troops, Struemph recalls missions where their sub also transported soldiers and Filipinos who had escaped from Japanese imprisonment. Once everyone was aboard, the *Narwhal* would "back out" of the tributary and quietly slip into waters with more depth and concealment.

"One time, our captain brought the *Narwhal* up a little bit and raised the periscope," Struemph said. "He saw nothing but wings, tires and parts from airplanes floating everywhere from a battle that had taken place. He quickly retracted the periscope and we went back down and got out of there before we were detected."

On a separate occasion, Struemph recalled, the submarine slipped through shallow waters between the islands at night and used their six-inch guns to detonate tanks used by the Japanese to store fuel. Although the submarine experienced many narrow escapes in areas crawling with Japanese warships, the crew survived the war and returned to the East Coast. The *Narwhal* was decommissioned on April 23, 1945 and her two six-inch guns were removed for display at the Naval Submarine Base at New London, Connecticut.

The war in Europe ended shortly after their return stateside. However, Struemph and many of the crew of the *Narwhal* remained at New London for preparations to serve aboard a new submarine to be used in the planned invasion of Japan. Fortunately, he explained, the war ended when Japan signed the surrender documents on September 2, 1945, resulting in his discharge the following month.

In the years following his wartime service, the veteran and his wife raised seven children and later moved from Vienna to Jefferson City, where he retired from the maintenance section of Jefferson City Parks and Recreation.

Reflecting on his service, the veteran maintains even though he and his fellow submariners frequently lived and operated under very stressful conditions, Struemph's time in the service included many good memories, one of which made him think about the family back home awaiting his return.

"One time, while we were in Australia, some guys I was on leave with got in trouble at a bar and ended up getting locked up in the local jail," said the veteran. "I was not involved in the scuffle, but had no way to get back to the ship and there was no place for me to stay that night." He paused, "But an Australian guy took me home to stay with his family. The next morning they took me fishing and I really had a good time," he smiled, recalling the event. "With all of the things that went on during the war, it was nice to meet good people such as them during my Navy time and to be treated as if I was just another member of his family even when mine was so far away."

Norbert Xavier Struemph passed away in Jefferson City on November 3, 2017. The ninety-five-year-old veteran was laid to rest in Visitation Cemetery in Vienna. *(Photograph courtesy of Norbert Struemph.)*

Paul Mueller

Eldon

Faye Belshe realizes all too well the sacrifices of the "Greatest Generation." The Eldon, Missouri, resident still clearly recalls "all the boys" leaving home for overseas service during World War II, which included three of her brothers. Unfortunately, her family would be forced to endure an inordinate amount of "sacrifice" before the war ended—a reality punctuated by decades of suffering by an older brother.

"My brother Paul was seriously injured in an accident while serving in Belgium on October 5, 1944," said Belshe. "He suffered from his injuries for the rest of his life."

Born in Hooker, Oklahoma, in 1917, Paul Mueller's family later moved to Kansas, where he spent many of his formative years and graduated from high school in 1934. But it was in 1938, Belshe said, that her brother received his introduction to the military by attending Citizens' Military Training Camp at Fort Riley, Kansas—a four-week program that provided young men with a basic military instruction without an obligation for future service.

"Our parents moved to Eldon in 1939 and Paul came to live with us for a year or two," explained Belshe. "He then moved back to McFarland, Kansas, in 1941, was married and became father to his first child, Janice."

However, his new domestic responsibilities would be placed on hold when Mueller was drafted into the U.S. Army in 1942 (three days prior to his daughter's first birthday) and returned to Fort Riley, Kansas, but this time for several weeks of basic training as an enlisted soldier. It was sometime during his training, he was assigned to the 9th Armored Engineer Battalion of the 9th Armored Division. Trained as a combat engineer, the soldier's battalion was re-designated the 993rd Engineer Treadway Bridge Company after the armored divisions underwent a major reorganization and were stripped of their organic bridge companies.

Family records indicate that Mueller's next stop in his military pilgrimage was the Desert Training Center near Needles, California, for desert maneuvers in early 1943. Several weeks later, he traveled to Ft. Polk, Louisiana, for swamp maneuvers, all the while learning to operate a twenty-ton truck that carried the pontoons used to construct bridges for river crossings.

"Paul and his company went to Boston in May of 1944 and boarded a troop ship for England," recalled the veteran's sister.

An article about a reunion of 993rd Engineers appearing the August 4, 1971 edition of the *New Castle News* (New Castle, Pennsylvania) notes that the Mueller and his fellow engineers "arrived overseas with little time to spare, because the Normandy Invasion came June 6, 1944 and the 993rd followed the assault troops into Fortress Europe late that same month." The newspaper further explained that the 993rd became part of the "famed 'rat race' across south central France toward Germany" shortly after their arrival and spent most of their time overseas attached to the Third Army under the command of Gen. George S. Patton.

Although Mueller and his comrades learned to survive on as little as three or four hours of sleep each night before preparing for the next day's movement, it was an event that unfolded in Belgium on the evening of October 5, 1944 that would provide him an extended— yet undesired—period of rest.

"What happened," said Belshe, "is they were behind the front lines in Belgium and couldn't have any lights on because it might give away their position [to the enemy]. He and another soldier were sleeping in their pup tent that evening when Paul heard a truck approaching their tent." Solemnly, she added, "Paul sat up and that's when this truck ran through their tent and over his mid-section, mashing his insides. The truck also ran over the head of the other soldier and killed him instantly."

On the same day of his injury, Mueller later discovered, his younger brother, Wayne Mueller, was killed in action in Holland while serving as a paratrooper with the 101st Airborne Division.

For the next three years, Mueller was moved from one military hospital to the next, undergoing several surgeries to address his serious injuries. He received his discharge from the Army at the hospital at Ft. Bliss, Texas, in 1947 and returned to Kansas to try to rebuild his life with his wife and young daughter.

"After the war," Belshe explained, "my brother ended up getting a job with the post office and stayed with them for fifteen years. He and his wife also ended up having two more children, both boys," she added.

As Mueller explained in an article in the October 10, 1996 edition of *The Signal-Enterprise* newspaper (Wabaunsee County, Kansas), his years of suffering from his military injuries combined with the loss of a brother and a friend inspired him to find ways in which to honor their legacy.

"I try to fly our flag here at home almost every day," wrote Mueller, "but on October 5th I fly the large flag from my brother's casket in memory of him and my buddy."

Corporal Paul August Mueller passed away at eighty-six years of age on November 30, 2003 and was laid to rest in McFarland Cemetery in Kansas. Though he and his brothers are no longer here to share recollections of their experiences, his sister has remained dedicated to the preservation of her family's military legacy.

"Paul wore a brace on his leg his entire life after he was hurt," Belshe said. "When he left for the service he weighed 180 pounds and he must have lost close to 100 pounds after the incident—he was nothing but skin and bones. Tearfully, she added, "He was one of so many that were hurt over there [in World War II] and I think his sacrifice should never be forgotten. Everyone should know what all of the boys have done for them. " *(Photograph courtesy of Faye Belshe.)*

Ralph Popp

Brazito

The Allied nations prevailed during World War II by working in concert to defeat the tyranny entangling several European and Pacific locations. However, what few people realize, one local veteran affirmed, is that not only did the men and women of the military help the Allies succeed, but there were also contributions made by those known as "man's best friend."

Born and raised in the Brazito community, Ralph Popp was in his senior year of high school at Eugene when he received his draft notice in January 1945.

"I was eighteen years old at the time and didn't even get to finish high school before they sent me to Camp Hood, Texas, for basic training," said Popp.

When his boot camp was finished, Popp explained, most of the recruits were immediately sent to fight in overseas locations, but he was instead assigned to a rather unique section of the U.S. Army.

"They put me in the K-9 Corps to train dogs for scouting purposes," he said. "The only reason I can think that I was even selected for such a thing was when I had been asked about my hobbies, I told them that I was interested in coon hunting with hunting dogs," he added.

Popp then traveled to Ft. Robinson in the northwestern corner of Nebraska, becoming part of the Army's War Dog program. The program was born out of an initiative first "intended to train dogs to perform sentry duty for the army along the coast of the United States," as noted in an article by Dr. Arthur Bergeron, Jr., accessed through the U.S. Army Military History Institute website.[90] As part of the Quartermaster Corps, the program later became the "K-9 Corps" and was expanded to train scouting and patrol dogs, messenger dogs and canines that could detect trip wires, booby traps and mines.

During the months he spent at Ft. Robinson, Popp explained, he was placed in a platoon with more than two dozen soldiers and assigned two dogs that he would train for scouting purposes.

"The primary dogs we trained on the post were Doberman Pinschers and German Shepherds," Popp said. "The dogs I trained were German Shepherds and they were so smart that you could teach them to count the number of fingers you held up by barking," he grinned.

The soldier also remarked that the dogs, in anticipation of the invasion of the mainland of Japan, were trained to become "fierce fighting dogs," and the only ones that could handle them were the individual soldiers to which they were assigned.

"We taught the dogs how to detect people hiding in caves or up in trees," Popp added. "The time we spent in Nebraska was kind of like a basic training for the dogs."

In April 1945, his platoon placed their dogs in cages and boarded rail cars bound for Camp Butner, North Carolina, where they joined the Fourth Division, which had recently returned from combat service in Europe.

"We had to take care of our own dogs the entire time because no one else could handle them," Popp said, "or else they'd attack."

While stationed in North Carolina, they continued training in preparation for the invasion until Japan surrendered weeks later, which meant the end of the war and thus heralded the conclusion of the K-9 Corps.

"Everything was dissolved in the K-9 Corps and the dogs were taken somewhere to be 'deactivated,' they called it," said Popp. "I'm not sure what happened to my two dogs, but they tried to get all of

---

[90] Bergeron, *War Dogs*, www.army.mil.

them back to the original owners because they had only been loaned to the Army by their owners."

Many of the dogs, the veteran said, were unable to be separated from the ferocity that had been ingrained during their training, resulting in their having to be euthanized to avoid any potential dangers they might pose to civilians.

"I had to take part in bringing some of the dogs to a veterinarian—the ones they couldn't deactivate," Popp solemnly noted. "That was a very difficult thing for me to have to do."

With nearly a year remaining in his term of service, the soldier was transferred to Ft. Sill, Oklahoma, where he became a supply sergeant with an artillery battery until receiving his discharge in 1946. He returned to Mid-Missouri, finished earning his high school diploma and, in 1947, married Irma Sommerer, the woman who had patiently awaited his return from the service. Raising one daughter, Lora, the couple was married for sixty-one years when Irma passed away in 2007. In 1959, the veteran founded Popp's Lawn and Garden Center in Jefferson City, operating the company for four decades. Following his retirement, he enjoyed spending his free time gardening, working around his farm and supporting Immanuel Lutheran Church at Honey Creek.

His military service, he noted, may not have possessed the flare and excitement of many of the combat veterans of the Second World War, but he affirms that it was a story that represented a unique type of sacrifice made by our canine friends.

"Really, it was a sacrifice for so many citizens to give up their dogs for military service during World War II," he said. "I know I was very close to my dogs and I miss them as much as anything." He added, "For many people, I'm sure saying goodbye to their dogs was like saying goodbye to a son heading off to war...not knowing if they would ever return home."

Ralph Popp passed away December 4, 2016 and was laid to rest in the Immanuel Lutheran Church Cemetery at Honey Creek, Missouri. *(Photograph courtesy of Ralph Popp.)*

Virgil Shikles

Enon

For an account of a veteran's military service to survive the passage of decades, it often needs a conduit through which to be shared. Loretta Raithel of Russellville had suspicions that once her brother-in-law, Virgil O. Shikles, passed away when only fifty-five years old, followed by the death of his son in 2004 and his wife several years later, there was really no one left to preserve his legacy of service in World War II.

"When my sister passed in 2012, [Shikles'] military records and photographs could have easily been discarded, but I have hung on to them to help preserve the memory of what he had done in the war," Raithel said, sifting through papers related to the military service of her brother-in-law.

Virgil Shikles was born October 27, 1913 and raised near the rural community of Enon, the second oldest in a family of six children. Records indicate the twenty-six-year-old registered for the military draft in Washington, Missouri, on October 16, 1940, more than a year prior to the attack on Pearl Harbor. According to the National Archives and Records Administration, "President Franklin D. Roosevelt signed the Selective Training and Service Act, creating the country's first peacetime draft and officially establishing the Selective Service System." The act required all males between the ages of 21-36 to register during the first draft registration held on October 16, 1940, the date listed on Shikles' registration document.

At the time of registration, he was employed by the former Missouri Pacific Railroad headquartered in St. Louis. In his position as a "trackwalker," he was responsible for walking sections of the railroad's track system to examine the condition of joints, rails and ties, ensuring there was no damage that could lead to a train accident.

Statistics from the National World War II Museum state, "By the end of the war in 1945, 50 million men between eighteen and forty-five had registered for the draft and 10 million had been inducted in the military. Of those drafted, Shikles received his own call in early 1942, approximately six weeks after the U.S. declared war.

The "Enlisted Record and Report of Separation" for Shikles shows he was inducted into the U.S. Army at Jefferson Barracks in St. Louis on January 21, 1942, beginning a period of military service that would extend nearly four years. As the weeks passed, Shikles was assigned to the 401st Coast Artillery (CA) and began training at Camp Haan, California—a military reservation established in 1940 to serve as a Coast Artillery Antiaircraft Replacement Training Center. In April 1942, the 401st CA was re-designated the 401st Antiaircraft Artillery (AAA) Gun Battalion.

Equipped primarily with the M1 90mm antiaircraft guns, which were towed behind vehicles, Shikles trained as a radar crewman for the battalion, learning to assemble and disassemble the battalion's mobile radar equipment in addition to operating the radar to detect and locate possible aerial threats. The battalion would also participate in desert maneuvers at Camp Young, California.

Shikles and the 401st AAA Battalion went on to train at Camp Pickett, Virginia, before "boarding an LST in April, 1943, for an unknown destination overseas," reported the July 21, 1944 edition of the *Folsom Telegraph* (Folsom, California). The paper further noted the battalion landed at Arzew—a port city in Algeria—where they were attached to the Fifth Army.

Following a short period of training, the battalion boarded LST's (Landing Ship Tanks) in early August 1943 bound for Tunisia, met up with a convoy of American troops and then sailed for Sicily. Weeks later, they were sent to the Italian front, where they began defending supply depots, roads, bridges, airfields and critical military installations. The battalion continued to move up with the front lines and, on May 1944, "the whole Italian front exploded into action and the big drive for Rome was on," noted the November-December 1946 edition of the *Coast Artillery Journal.*[91]

The journal further listed the challenges encountered by U.S. forces during this campaign, "Enemy aircraft flew in low from several directions toward the points of attack making 90mm fire extremely difficult. Radar control was often unsatisfactory due to terrain interference and large quantities of [chaff] dropped by the Germans."

By the time the war in Europe ended on May 8, 1945, Shikles earned five Bronze Stars for his participation in five major campaigns in Italy. The 401st AAA Battalion remained overseas until boarding ships bound for the United States in October 1945. Within days following his return, Shikles took a train to Jefferson Barracks, where he processed out of the U.S. Army and received his discharge on November 6, 1945, having served more than three years and nine months in military uniform.

"After he returned home, he married my sister, Evelyn Scott, in February 1946," said Loretta Raithel. "They later moved to Kansas City, Kansas, and raised a son, Gary." She added, "He then went to work for General Motors until he became so ill with Parkinson's disease that he was no longer able to maintain his employment."

The World War II veteran passed away on August 12, 1969 at the age of fifty-five. His son, Gary, who later served with the U.S. Navy during the Vietnam War, also died from complications related to Parkinson's in 2004, he was fifty-six years old and had no children. Like his father, he was laid to rest in Enloe Cemetery near Russellville.

"All of my brother-in-law's records went to my sister and when she passed away in 2012, I made sure to hang on to them because they would have disappeared since his family is all gone," said Raithel. She continued, "Those guys in WWII never really talked about their service...at least the ones that I knew. It's important to save their stories, and those of other WWII veterans, so others can appreciate what they went through during the war." *(Photograph courtesy of Loretta Raithel)*

---

[91] United States Army Artillery, *Coast Artillery Journal,* 6.

Robert Miller

Jefferson City

During more than nine decades of life experience, Jefferson City resident Robert Miller accrued many good memories throughout the years and met a number of interesting individuals, many of whom he calls "friends." Despite all of the encounters he has to call upon in cheerful reflection, the time that he served in the Army during World War II remains the most poignant of his memories.

As a young man growing up in Columbia, Miller began making eyeglasses for a local optical company after graduating from Hickman High School in 1940.

"The company transferred me to their office in St. Joseph, and that's where I was working when I received my draft notice in 1942," said the veteran. "I remember driving to Columbia in my 1932 Ford to report to the draft board and I got pulled over by the highway patrol for speeding along US Highway 40," he said. "When I told the officer where I was going, he said 'drive on.'"

Following his induction, the recruit completed his basic training at Camp Kearns, Utah, and then reported for training as a medical technician at Fort Oglethorpe in Atlanta, Georgia. While in Georgia, he learned a variety of laboratory techniques such as how to perform blood tests and, in May 1943, reported to the ophthalmology clinic at McClellan Air Force Base in California. The soldier built upon his previous eyeglass experience by learning to refract patients' eyes so that "the captain, an ophthalmologist, could go play golf at the base course," Miller said.

Because of the test scores he had received on his military entrance examinations, Miller was soon accepted into the Army Specialized Training Program (ASTP)—a college program "designed to keep troops busy until their services were needed." Spending a short time at Stanford University, the soldier transferred to Indiana University and spent several months in college courses related to engineering and chemistry. In March 1, 1944, Miller departed Indiana University for Camp Campbell, Kentucky "to help form the 20th Armored Division." He added, "Students from many of the ASTP colleges were included in the personnel arriving at the camp to help make up the division."

Assigned to Company C, 220th Medical Battalion, Miller worked in the company's medical supply section and, for the next several months, learned the duties of his new position in addition to participating in various training exercises. By Christmas, the division was prepared for overseas deployment and set sail for Europe weeks later, arriving in Le Havre, France on February 17, 1945. Miller affirms that his movement with the division is well chronicled in the book *20th Armored Division in World War II*, but summarizes his time served overseas as "moving south through France, Belgium, and Holland into Germany."

Miller added, "We were close to the front lines and there were casualties, so the medical team I belonged to was very busy. I also remember it being cold with snow...and all that we had to keep warm with during the daytime was our uniform with an overcoat."

The veteran further explained that occasionally there were field hospitals set up and they could enter for a short time "to try and warm up," but then "it was back to working in the cold to get the much needed medical supplies."

After crossing the Rhine and Danube Rivers, Miller clearly recalls encountering one of the most distressing situations of his entire military career—the liberation of Dachau concentration camp on April 29, 1945.

"I did not go in [the camp] but I stood by the entrance for some time," he solemnly remembered. "It was a horrible site—the people...

they were just skin and bones. All any of them wanted to do was to get home as quickly as possible."

While in Salzburg, Austria, the division learned of Germany's surrender and remained in Europe for the next several weeks. They returned home later that summer to begin preparations for the invasion of Japan, but after the Japanese surrendered weeks later, the soldiers of the division soon began receiving their discharges.

Leaving the service in February 1946, Miller returned to Mid-Missouri and married his fiancée, Grace, later that year. The couple raised a son and a daughter, and Miller used his GI Bill to earn a bachelor's degree in engineering and later returned to school to earn his master's in public health. In 1983, he retired from the Missouri Department of Natural Resources.

Relaxing in his charismatic home office surrounded by mementos from his past, Miller stresses that of all his interesting and intriguing encounters, the ones that seem most ingrained in his memory are those related to the time he spent alongside the soldiers of the 20th Armored Division.

"I have been so fortunate in my life and in my time in the Army," Miller affirmed. "And when you witness things, like the horrors of Dachau, it is truly something that you never forget and hope that the younger generation remembers." He added, "It was certainly my privilege to have been able to serve my country during the war and I don't believe anyone owes me anything for having served."

Robert Miller passed away on March 16, 2016 and was laid to rest with military honors in Riverview Cemetery in Jefferson City. *(Photograph courtesy of Robert Miller)*

Raymond Miller

Columbia

A travesty in the preservation of military history is failing to capture the stories of our nation's combat veterans before they are silenced by the grave. Fortunately, the voice of one local veteran has endured, thanks to the foresight of placing on paper his personal military experiences during combat—a legacy that concluded with a brother's visit to the war memorials in the nation's capital.

Born September 1, 1923 in Columbia, Missouri, Raymond Miller graduated high school in 1941. According to his biography titled *Action in Europe*, he worked in several low profile jobs, eventually entering a machinist program sponsored by the U.S. government.

"Raymond was one year younger than me and was a starting tackle for the Columbia Hickman (high school) football team," recalled his brother, the late Robert Miller of Jefferson City.

Completing the course, Miller, "took a job in defense at Curtiss-Wright Aircraft Company in St. Louis," he wrote in his book. In September 1943, he wedded his fiancée, Helen Lewis, and was drafted into the U.S. Army the following year, after having received a deferment "for defense employment."

Raymond's writings explain that as a young draftee, he entered service in July 1944, traveling to Camp Hood, Texas, to undergo his conversion to a United States soldier by completing several weeks of basic infantry training. Weeks later, he reported to Fort Meade, Maryland, to receive his issue of clothing and equipment. From there, he boarded the *USS Wakefield* anchored at Boston Harbor—a luxury liner turned troop carrier bound for the war in Europe carrying thousands of soldiers.

"Aboard the ship, everywhere you looked, there was a poker game or dice game in progress," Miller recalled, describing his time aboard the vessel.

When the inexperienced soldier arrived in Liverpool, England less than two weeks later, he moved by train to Southampton Port, loading on a British troop ship for movement across the English Channel. On December 21, 1944, five days after the Germans launched the major offensive known as the Battle of the Bulge, Miller arrived at an infantry replacement center, where he received his rifle and assignment to Company C, 334th Infantry Regiment of the 84th Division.

As the company prepared to enter combat, Miller wrote that a lieutenant who, after asking Miller his name, stated, "You are the squad leader of the new men in 3rd squad" — an unexpected appointment that found the soldier serving in a leadership capacity without any previous combat experience. His baptism of fire came on January 7, 1945, when he participated in his first combat in the town of Marcouray, Belgium, fighting from foxholes while enduring both enemy artillery barrages and the frigid weather.

"I was very cold, tired and hungry," said Miller. "It was impossible to dig a foxhole in the frozen ground," and he and a fellow soldier found a bomb crater full of snow, crawling inside to benefit from some semblance of protection. He remained with his company for the remainder of "the Bulge" and, the following month, became part of a river crossing that characterized the violence and dangers of the remainder of his time in Germany.

On February 23, 1945, Miller was part a group of Company C soldiers scheduled to cross the Roer River in boats as part of an assault on a nearby German village. Departing in the early morning, the boats became targets for shelling and rifle fire as soon as they touched the frigid water. By the time the nightmarish incident ended, Miller's boat was separated from the group and several soldiers had been killed or wounded. Miller and his group eventually reunited with the company and went on fighting across Germany.

During the early days of May, the "84th Division met the Russians at the Elbe River," heralding the end of the war "for all practical purposes," Miller transcribed.

Throughout his remaining weeks in Germany, Miller kept busy playing on the regimental softball team and served with a quartermaster company as part of the occupational forces. In June 1945, he accrued enough points to return home.

"After he came home from the war," said Miller's older brother, Robert, "we both played softball on a team in Columbia. Raymond played third," he continued, "and I played left field. He knew all the players on the opposing teams and how they played, and would tell me where to play [to intercept their hits]."

In later years, the younger Miller would go on to work for the postal service. His first wife, Helen, passed away in 1972, and he retired from his postal job the following year. The veteran then moved to Florida, where he met and married his second wife, Audrey, who passed in 1999. Though he had no children, Miller remained in Florida until his death on July 26, 2007.

"Before he passed," said Robert [who himself served with the Army's 20th Armored Division in WWII], "we would talk on the phone every night...about the war and things." He added, "He had said that he didn't know where he wanted to be buried, so I brought him here [Jefferson City] to be buried with full military honors."

Although the Battle of the Bulge survivor never received the opportunity to visit, in person, the World War II memorial in Washington, D.C., his older brother devised a way for them to make the trip together.

"I knew Raymond would have wanted to have been on the [Central Missouri] Honor Flight," Robert remarked, "so I brought his military photograph with me and had our pictures taken in front of the memorials. That," he concluded, "made me feel as though he was with me...that he we had the honor of making the trip together." *(Photograph courtesy of Robert Miller)*

Marvin Strolberg

Jefferson City

The education Marvin Strolberg received during a military experience that spanned two wars and two branches of service was invaluable, the veteran noted, however, the details of his time in uniform have not been something he has dwelled upon in recent years. More accurately, he affirmed, they are more of a distant memory that required "dusting off" during a recent interview.

"I can tell you it's been many, many years ago and I've probably forgotten a lot of the particulars of what happened," humbly admitted the veteran when discussing his military service from decades earlier.

Growing up in Minneapolis, Minnesota, Strolberg completed his junior year at Miller Vocational High School when he decided to postpone his education and join the Merchant Marines after learning they were in dire need of men to serve. World War II was a frenetic period for U.S. shipyards as cargo vessels were being built faster than men could be recruited and trained to serve on the crews. A critical component of the nation's defense, the ships operated by the Merchant Marines were needed to deliver equipment and other supplies necessary to support the war in Europe and the Pacific.

"In 1944, they sent me to Sheepshead Bay, New York," said the former mariner, discussing his arrival at U.S. Maritime Service Training Station. "That's where we did all of our training," he added.

Throughout the next several months, the aspiring seaman underwent military-type training that included physical fitness activities, instruction on drill and ceremony, which was then followed by an introduction to the details of seamanship in such areas as mast-rigging, ground tackle and mooring lines. In May 1945, he and approximately four dozen fellow mariners graduated from their training and were assigned to details aboard the various ships transporting supplies overseas.

"I spent the next three years or so going back and forth across the North Atlantic aboard several different cargo vessels," Strolberg said. "We delivered supplies all over Europe and I can remember we would haul everything from grain and coal to tanks and Jeeps."

Statistics vary regarding the number of mariners who lost their lives during World War II. However, in *Merchant Marine Survivors of World War II*, the author references a 1946 War Shipping Administration report citing the loss of 733 merchant vessels, which included "more than 6,300 American merchant seaman (who) were either killed outright or went missing."[92]

"We all knew that ships were being sunk by German submarines and about half of my graduating class [from Sheepshead Bay] lost their lives during the war. But," he added, "it was just one of those things that you tried not to dwell on because we had a job to get done."

The young mariner's service came to a close in 1948 and he returned to Minneapolis, where he was able to receive his high school diploma because of credit earned for the time he served in the Merchant Marines. He then enrolled in classes at the University of Minnesota, but the Korean War erupted in June 1950 and soon caused another delay in Stolberg's educational pursuits.

"Back then, the draft for the Korean War was going on and they weren't giving any kind of credit for my service in the Merchant Marines during World War II," he said. "So I decided to join an Air National Guard unit [in St. Paul, Minnesota]."

Months following his enlistment, Strolberg's unit was activated and sent to Kimpo (also referred to as "Gimpo") Air Base in Seoul, South Korea, where he was attached to the Fourth Fighter Interceptor Wing and served as senior clerk for an Air Force legal officer.

---

[92] Gillen, *Merchant Marine Survivors of World War II*, 177.

"I got to Korea on Christmas Day in 1951," he said. "I clearly recall that it was the worst day of my life because I had already been through service in a war and it wasn't something I was looking forward to going through again."

Spending twenty-one months on active duty, nine of which was served overseas, Strolberg returned to the United States and was discharged from the Air Force in October 1952. He returned to school to finish up his degree and in 1953, married his fiancée, Betty. He and his wife went on to raise three children, and Strolberg traveled across the United States while engaged in a number of business endeavors. For twenty-six years, the couple lived in Camdenton, Missouri but have since relocated to Jefferson City to be closer to their daughter and grandchildren.

"He has always enjoyed visiting with others who have spent time in the service," said Strolberg's wife, Betty, adding, "but he has never been one to brag about his own service."

While looking at a photo of the nearly four dozen mariners with whom he graduated from training at Sheepshead Bay, Strolberg remarked, "We had a very critical function to perform [in World War II] and we did our jobs, but we lost a lot of men doing it." "As I said," he solemnly concluded, "about half of the guys I went through training with lost their lives out there in the ocean...and that's something that you never forget even after all these years." *(Photograph courtesy of Marvin Strolberg)*

The Sad Sack

During his 1,200-mile trek across Europe as a gunner on an M-18 Hellcat Tank Destroyer, World War II veteran Norbert Gerling experienced his share of stress under combat conditions. He was not alone in his journey, the Henley, Missouri, veteran recalled, since a beloved military cartoon character kept him and his fellow soldiers company, providing laughs and a little relief from the hardships surrounding them.

"[*The*] *Sad Sack* was a typical GI—just like Beetle Bailey," Gerling beamed. "There always seemed to be one or two guys just like him in every unit in the Army," he added.

The Sad Sack comic strip made its debut in *Yank*, The Army Weekly—a magazine published by the United States military during World War II—in the May 1942 issue.[93] The cartoon was the creation of Sgt. George Baker, a native of Massachusetts who grew up in Illinois and was later hired by Walt Disney Studios in 1937, assisting with the production of animated films such as *Pinocchio*, *Dumbo* and *Bambi*.

Drafted by the U.S. Army in June 1941, five months prior to the attacks on Pearl Harbor, Baker was assigned to the Signal Corps to produce animation for military training films. He grew appalled by the cheerful and tailored manner in which the average soldier was portrayed to the public, and embarked upon a campaign to depict

---

[93] The Best of Harveyville Fun Times!, *Meet... Sad Sack*, 47.

soldiers in a more authentic manner, resulting in the birth of *The Sad Sack*.

The fictional comic featured the antics of a clumsy and often-times inept soldier of the U.S. Army, who was usually involved in absurd and outrageous situations, inadvertently distressing sergeants and officers within his unit. As Gerling noted, although he enjoyed the photographs and articles in *Yank* magazine, *The Sad Sack* strip served as the magazine's focal point.

"Whenever mail call would come, the magazine often came with it," Gerling explained, recalling his enjoyment of the publication while in Europe more than seven decades ago. "Sometimes GI's would pass them along to each other, and whenever you found one, you read it and then gave it to someone else to enjoy."

Gerling added, "[*The Sad Sack*] was a typical, run-down soldier who seemed to stumble his way into trouble. The humor was great and everybody got a kick out of it...it was something that took our minds off the combat and gave us a little relief."

Jefferson City, Missouri, veteran Raymond Herigon, who landed on the beaches of Normandy, France, on June 9, 1944 and fought his way across Europe with the 4th Infantry Division, also recalled the iconic comic strip, and serving with those who reminded him of the amusing character.

"We all read [*The*] *Sad Sack*. We'd get copies of [*Yank*] every so often," Herigon said. "There was a guy in our unit who reminded us of him—he was always playing tricks on the officers. The guy could whistle like a German shell coming in and he would hide behind tents and scare the heck out of the officers," he grinned.

But as the combat veteran explained, comics—and the antics they inspired—were integral in helping everyone forget the horrors of combat, if only for a little while.

"We were always playing tricks on each other...we had to," Herigon said. "Otherwise we would go nuts."

In the years following the war, Sgt. Baker's creation continued through a short-lived daily comic strip in newspapers, became a comic book series published by Harvey Publications and inspired a motion picture starring Jerry Lewis in 1957.

The memory of The Sad Sack may have become a near-forgotten phenomenon, yet the soldiers who fought their way across the frontiers of Western Europe remain grateful for the chuckles provided through the blundering frolics of a cartoon character with whom they often felt personally connected.

"[*The*] *Sad Sack* was put out for a reason," Gerling paused, "it was meant to give us a lift...and sometimes we'd only have one magazine for two or three tank crews, but we'd share them among us. But he truly was a very funny character that provided us with a little entertainment and a few smiles in very difficult times."

Ruth Stephenson

Moberly

Lying in her bed while in hospice care, Ruby "Ruth" Stephenson's body may have become weakened by illness, but one can easily discern the increase in vigor that occurs when she describes the fourteen months she served in the U.S. Navy during World War II—a brief moment of her past that not only allowed her to serve her country, but introduced her to a fellow sailor with whom she would share most of her life. Surrounded by her three children, Stephenson shared stories of the journey that led her to uniformed service, memories that were supplemented by recollections of her family.

"Mom had a brother that died in infancy and she was raised as an only child," said Elaine Cook, Stephenson's daughter. "She was raised in Fayette [Missouri] and graduated from high school there."

For two years, Stephenson attended school at Central Methodist University until deciding it was time to "strike it on her own," the veteran softly whispered.

"The first time she applied (for the Navy), she was told that her eyesight was too poor," said Romie Stephenson, the youngest of her two sons. "But they later relaxed the standards and she was able to join in 1943." With a grin, Romie added, "She decided on the Navy because she thought they had the best looking uniform."

The young recruit was soon on her way to become a member of the Women Accepted for Volunteer Emergency Service (WAVES)—an organization established on July 30, 1942 to help fill positions left vacant stateside because of the scores of men deploying overseas to fight in World War II. Her first stop was at the Bronx campus of

Hunter College in New York, the location that became the training base for all WAVES by 1943, and where she remained for the next several weeks to finish her boot camp and undergo medical training that would qualify her as a "Pharmacist's Mate."

As Stephenson recalled, her first (and only) duty assignment was at a small medical facility at Camp Elliott in San Diego, California—a former Marine Corps and naval site where the first Navajo Code Talkers were trained. (A portion of the site is now situated on the Marine Corps Air Station Miramar.)

"She spent about a month working on one of the wards," said Fred Stephenson, the oldest of her two sons. "Then," he added, "she spent the rest of her time in the admissions and discharge office."

While at Camp Elliott, her family shared, the young WAVES member met Frederick Stephenson, Sr.—the man with whom she would fall in love and then marry on April 21, 1944.

"Dad had been in the Navy since the late 1930s and was at Pearl Harbor when the Japanese attacked," said his daughter, Elaine. "After he and mother were married, she became pregnant and had to leave the Navy because at that time women couldn't be in the service and pregnant."

Receiving her discharge in October 1944, Stephenson returned to Mid-Missouri, giving birth to her first child, Elaine. A few months later she moved back to California to wait for her husband to finish out his enlistment.

"In California, mom lived in an apartment across the hall from Phyllis Diller—this was back before she became a famous comedian," said her son, Fred. "They became good friends and Phyllis would babysit Elaine when mom had to go run errands and mom would watch Phyllis' brood whenever she needed to go do something."

When Stephenson's husband was discharged from the Navy on February 10, 1947, the family returned to Fayette, where their second child, Fred Jr., was born months later.

"Dad worked for a while at a grocery store in Fayette but wanted to become a professional photographer," said Elaine. "We moved to Houston [Texas] in early 1949 so that he could enroll in the University of Houston's photography program."

The couple and their growing family spent the next few years living in housing in Memorial Park dedicated to WWII veterans attending college. While there, the couple welcomed their third and final child, Romie, in 1953.

"Our dad graduated with his photography degree and worked a few years for Susan's of Hollywood [in Texas]," said Fred. "He then worked for Southwest Industrial Electronics and stayed with them until his retirement in the early 1970s, after he became partially disabled from a stroke." Fred added, "Mother was a homemaker for several years and later worked for Sears. She retired from there in 1984."

After the passing of their father in 2001, Stephenson relocated to Moberly, where she has resided until her transfer to the hospice care unit at a local hospital. Reflecting on the stories they have heard their mother share throughout the years, the veteran's children are proud of their mother's service and continue to find pleasure in helping to share her experiences.

"I personally feel that they aren't accurately teaching the history of World War II anymore," said Romie, "and people need to understand the sacrifices that others—such as my mother and father—have endured for them."

His older brother, Fred, added, "And it's not just about those who fought in the war, but they should also learn about how the entire country was united and everyone on the home front gave something, too...through sacrifices such as rationing." Pausing, he concluded, "These are stories that need to be preserved and shared so that these lessons are never lost."

Ruth Stephenson passed away on December 22, 2015 and was laid to rest alongside her husband in the Houston (Texas) National Cemetery. *(Photograph courtesy of the Stephenson family)*

Bruce "Duane" Sublett

Eldon

In our nation's history, there are examples of events concealed from public awareness—many of which have since emerged from various archival sources. One notable surfacing includes the atomic testing that took place during World War II. Even more elusive than information on some of these events are the individuals who witnessed them and are willing to discuss their experiences. Bruce "Duane" Sublett is one such person, who as a young man traveled to Fulton to receive instruction as a welder shortly after finishing the eighth grade.

"I graduated the [welding] school in December of 1942," recalled Sublett, formerly of Eldon, Missouri. "Then I was sent to Richmond, California, as a sixteen-year-old welder in Kaiser Shipyard."

His new career was curtailed when "breathing too much smoke working in the bilges of a ship" necessitated a visit to the doctor and his return to Mid-Missouri in 1943. For the next few months, Sublett worked several welding jobs, eventually moving to Chicago in early 1944 to work for a company that built excavation equipment. But in May of the same year, he was approaching his eighteenth birthday and chose to enlist in the Navy before being caught by the draft. He soon finished his basic training at Great Lakes (Chicago), Illinois, during which, he recalled, "They wanted us out there in a hurry because of the war...and they knew we were going to be part of a special operation."

The young sailor then traveled to California for amphibious training in San Diego and, in October 1944, received orders for the

USS Bracken—a newly commissioned attack transport with a complement of two hundred sixty-one enlisted men and twenty-two officers. The ship's crew spent the next several weeks training the crews of subsequently commissioned transport vessels before finally embarking on their first seafaring mission in May 1945. Sailing for Pearl Harbor, the following months were spent delivering troops and supplies to South Pacific locations including Midway, Leyte and Samar. Later missions involved the transport of occupation troops to Japan in addition to bringing Allied prisoners of war to Manila, Philippines.

"We were on the move, I tell you," grinned Sublett. "We covered that Pacific...and even went through a typhoon, losing landing craft off the side of our ship. It was so bad that you couldn't even go topside," he added.

The ship also transported a group of nurses Pearl Harbor. After undergoing repairs, the crew the set sail for Bikini Atoll in the Marshall Islands in early 1946. It was here the *Bracken* became one of many target ships used in the atomic bomb experiments known as "Operation Crossroads."

"There were a bunch of experiments brought on the ship to test for radiation from the atomic bomb fallout," Sublett explained. "Part of this," he continued, "was a stall on the starboard side of the top deck that had four live sheep in it."

The veteran notes that the crew of the *Bracken* was evacuated to another ship a safe distance from the blast site, while their former ship was anchored approximately a mile from the detonation point.

"We all waited on deck and watched the plane drop the bomb," he said. "It exploded and it was the *dangdest* blast you've ever seen. I can tell you that it just leveled everything."

Later returning to the *Bracken*, he remembers the Geiger counter clicking from high radiation measurements. The sheep, he explained, did not survive the blast with the exception of one that he describes as being "almost dead." The Bracken remained near Bikini for a second test three weeks later, this time to check for the radiation emitted from an underwater atomic blast.

"When we returned to the ship after the second bomb, we were only allowed to stay on it for an hour," Sublett said. "The Geiger counter was really hot then."

For the next two weeks, the *Bracken* was sprayed both day and night with a water and with chemical mixture that turned the hull white, Sublett said, all in an attempt to remove the radiation from the ship. Sublett came back to the United States via a different ship, but later discovered the *Bracken* had been towed to the open seas near Kwajalein, where she was then scuttled (sunk).

The sailor remained in the Navy for several months and finished out his enlistment in June 1947, having served more than three years in uniform. He returned to Mid-Missouri and worked many years as a welder until becoming the co-owner of a Gulf Station in Columbia. He later branched into the towing business, an occupation he maintained until his retirement in 1995.

Despite being witness to a thrilling and unique moment in American history, Sublett asserts that his participation in the atomic testing has remained somewhat of an enigma.

"None of my military records even show that I was there [Bikini Atoll]," Sublett said. "It was something that I personally witnessed and is likely something that no one will ever see again." He concluded: "And then for us not to have our service recognized for our participation in a very important part of the war...it just makes it clear that our story should be shared whenever possible." *(Photograph courtesy of Amy Sublett)*

John Sullivan

Jefferson City

With a recollection of events as lucid as though they occurred yesterday, Jefferson City resident John Sullivan beams with pride when sharing the story of his service in the skies above Europe during a war several decades passed. Raised in the mid-Missouri area, Sullivan graduated from Jefferson City High School in 1941, just months prior to an event which drew the country into World War II.

"I had begun working for my uncle who was an electrical contractor," Sullivan said. "But after the Japanese attacked Pearl Harbor, I knew I could join [the military] or be drafted."

With an interest in flying, the eighteen-year-old traveled to Ft. Leonard Wood to enlist in the U.S. Army Air Force Aviation Cadet Program in May 1942. As he recalls, the program was seeking pilots, navigators and bombardiers. He completed six weeks of basic training in San Antonio and was sent to Ellington Field in Houston for pre-flight training. While in Houston, he took classes on communication skills such as Morse code in addition to basic courses on weather and physics. The next step in his aviation preparation took place in Laredo, Texas, where he was introduced to several aspects of aerial gunnery.

"We learned how to operate .50 caliber machine guns and all types of military weapons," Sullivan recalled. "There was also a point in the training where we fired in flight at moving targets with a .30 caliber machine gun while in the back seat of an AT-6 fighter trainer."

Later practicing firing techniques from on board an actual bomber, Sullivan graduated in 1943 with his gunner's "wings." From

Laredo he traveled to Childress, Texas, for the final part of his training—bombardier and navigation school.

"At that time bombardiers were getting navigational training as well," he said.

Graduating in February 1944, Sullivan was commissioned as a second lieutenant and transferred to Westover Field, Massachusetts, and assigned to the crew of a B-24 Liberator—an American heavy bomber. Throughout the next several weeks, he and the crew of the plane flew practice missions to become accustomed to the aircraft, reinforcing their navigation training and conducting mock bombing runs. However, in May 1944, the time for practice was over as they boarded a troop ship in New Jersey bound for the war in Europe.

Arriving in Scotland in early June, he and the crew were assigned to the 93rd Bomb Group, 330th Squadron, at an airbase in Hardwick, England. From this location, the crew would embark for bombing missions throughout Europe. Sullivan's crew flew their first mission in July 1944 and over the period of the next six months would participate in thirty-five missions, during which not a single crewmember was lost. However, Sullivan noted, there were many occasions during which the dangers were real and numerous, and much too often aviators were lost in combat.

"There was a mission we flew across the (English) Channel to drop supplies to the 82nd Airborne fighting in Holland to secure bridges in the area," Sullivan recalled. "We encountered a lot of small arms fire on the way in, but couldn't return fire because the Germans would set up their offensive in the middle of areas populated by civilians."

The commander of their squadron, Sullivan explained, received damage to an engine of his B-24 when it was hit by 20mm fire. He was able to drop his supplies but later crashed in the English Channel, killing everyone on board the plane.

In November 1944, Sullivan returned to the United States and married "Bee," his fiancée who had awaited his return from the war. Sullivan went on to complete the final year of his enlistment as a property officer at an Army post in Big Springs, Texas. In December 1945, he returned to Jefferson City, enlisted in what became the Air

Force Reserve and went to work full-time in the electrical industry.[94] Sullivan retired from the Reserves in 1965 at the rank of major, and has been enjoying retirement from his electrical career for the last several years.

The recipient of a Distinguished Flying Cross, a World War II Victory Medal and several Air Medals, Sullivan described his service in a war zone as experiences often laced with a little luck.

"There were missions where we would fly into a black cloud made up of 88mm shellfire from the Germans," Sullivan said, "and we would sometimes come through without a scratch. Moments like that are why I feel fortunate that I was able to survive the war without any of my crewmembers being seriously injured or killed... because there were many who didn't make it home."

John L. Sullivan passed away in Jefferson City on May 10, 2016. The WWII combat veteran was laid to rest in Riverview Cemetery. *(Photograph courtesy of John L. Sullivan)*

---

[94] The U.S. Army Air Forces became the United States Air Force on September 18, 1947. The following year, the Air Force Reserve was established.

Emma Verslues

Jefferson City

While World War II continued to unfold during the early 1940s, a young woman from the state of California believed there might be some means through which she could support the war effort, giving something back to a nation desperately in need of volunteers. In the spring of 1945, Emma Verslues walked into her local Navy recruiting station with hopes of enlisting, but instead received the shocking admonishment, "You're too young and heavy."

The aspiring recruit was not discouraged and took the advice of the Navy recruiter, visiting the Army recruiting office where she found the opportunity for which she was searching—enlistment in the Women's Army Corps (WAC). The predecessor to the WAC—the Women's Army Auxiliary Corps (WAAC)—possessed no military status and was intended "for the purpose of making available to the national defense the knowledge, skill, and special training of the women of the nation," read Executive Order 9163, signed by President Franklin Roosevelt in May 1942. But on July 3, 1943, the president signed into law the WAC bill, which then granted military status to the women in the organization.

"A few days after I enlisted, they put a group of us on a bus and sent us to Fort Des Moines, Iowa," said Verslues. (Ft. Des Moines was selected as the first training site for the newly established corps.)

The book *United States Army in World War II: Special Studies: The Women's Army Corps* explains that the WAC basic training lasted approximately four weeks and "followed quite closely the first four weeks of the men's basic course," after which, the new enlistees would be transferred to an assignment in the field or attend advanced training.[95]

Finishing her basic training in early summer 1945, during which, Verslues joked, the physical activity "took the weight off of me," she remained at Fort Des Moines to attend two advanced trainings—first, clerk training that introduced her to the fundamentals of typing and file keeping, and then moving on to basic medical training.

"The medical classes taught us how to do things like take a temperature and gives shots," Verslues said. "We would practice giving shots using a lemon and I remember saying to myself, 'I hope I never have to do this on a real person,'"

By the end of summer, Verslues recalls that she and her fellow WACs eagerly awaited the receipt of orders for their first duty assignments.

"I made a lot of good friends while I was there, but we were all separated when our orders came," she said. "I was sent to Walter Reed [Army Medical Center] in Washington D.C."

The young WAC spent a short time at Walter Reed, and later transferred to Ft. Meyer, Virginia, working as an assistant to the hospital's nurses and helped bathe, feed, and occasionally write letters for servicemembers receiving treatment, many of whom were blinded or missing limbs because of their service in overseas combat zones.

"I really enjoyed taking care of people even though it could be a real tear-jerker at times," she said. "But helping those boys that were hurt get better...there was just nothing better than that."

While living in Virginia, Verslues was married and gave birth to her first son, which inspired her to leave the WACs in January 1947 so she could focus on her growing family. Her husband, who was serving in the Army, was discharged in the late 1940s and the couple moved to Columbia, Missouri. Years later, after giving birth to her second son, Verslues attended nursing school at Boone County Hospital, earning her "cap, pin and uniform" in the early 1950s. However, she later moved to Jefferson City, Missouri, after she and

---

[95] Treadwell, *United States Army in World War II*, 635.

her husband separated, and began working for Von Hoffman Press, from where she retired in the mid-1980s.

For the last several years of her life, the Army veteran embraced her hard-earned retirement and affirmed, while pointing to the American flag proudly displayed on her front porch, that her country and the military are two inspirations for which her devotion has never wavered.

"I love this country because it has done so much for me. I can go to sleep at night without worrying about where my next piece of bread is coming from." With a tear, she added, "And if I were able to turn back the hands of time, I would go back in the service because not only did I make some great friends, those were some of the most memorable times of my life."

Verslues passed away on January 9, 2017 while in hospice care at the Harry S. Truman Memorial Veterans Hospital in Columbia, Missouri. *(Photograph courtesy of Jeremy P. Ämick)*

Jim Donley

California

In 1942, California resident, Jim Donley embarked upon a journey that would take him from his Clarksburg home and thrust him into the center of a war raging in Europe, leaving him with memories that would carry forth into his daily reflections more than seven decades later. A 1939 graduate of Clarksburg High School in rural Moniteau County, Donley went to work assisting his father on the family farm, never suspecting an approaching adventure.

"You could hardly buy a job back then," said Donley. "So in 1941, me and two friends left and went to work for Beechcraft [building training airplanes] in Wichita, Kansas."

As the next year unfolded, the United States declared war on both Germany and Japan, and the young man soon realized it was a matter of time before he would be captured by the ever-present draft.

"I figured they would get to me eventually, so I went ahead and joined," he smiled. With a little aircraft experience to his credit, he believed the U.S. Army Air Forces would best align with his interests and abilities.

He traveled to the state of California in 1942 to attend an aircraft mechanic school and then received assignment to gunner school at Tyndall Field, Florida.

"We fired everything from BB guns to machine guns," he recalled. "A lot of the training was shooting from the back of a moving truck so that we could learn how to lead a target," he added.

From there, he went to Boise, Idaho, where ten-person crews were assembled for the first phase of a three-phase flight training program aboard the B-24 Liberators—an American heavy bomber.

"There in Idaho, I took mostly engineering training," Donley said, which consisted of his monitoring of many of the mechanical operations of the plane during flight.

The crew then traveled to Utah for their second phase of training, which, Donley explained, was primarily bombing run practice for the pilots. Finally, the crew moved on to Sioux City, Iowa, for the last phase of their aviation instruction.

"That was mostly bombardier training for the crew—we would fly over targets and drop our practice bombs," the veteran said.

After a brief stop in Kansas, the crew received orders for Miami, Florida. In early November 1942, they were on their way overseas with orders to report to Seething Field, England, as part of the 712th Bombardment Squadron under the Eighth Air Force. Upon arrival, Donley was advised that when he completed twenty-five missions, he would be allowed to return home from the war, and so he began a cycle of bombing runs as the gunner inside the belly turret of the B-24.

"One mission that stands out in my mind was the first time Berlin was hit in daylight...I believe it was our thirteenth mission," Donley said. "That number had the boys pretty superstitious, but we came through it alright."

The crew's fifteenth mission was also memorable for the young airman, but mostly for reasons that characterized the dangerous nature of the activities in which they were involved.

"Our co-pilot got wounded pretty bad when a piece of flak came through the windshield of the plane. It ended his flying career."

When Donley approached the point of completing half of his required missions, he discovered that the requirements were changed and he would now have to complete thirty missions before he would be allowed to return home.

"I flew in the waist gunner's position for the remainder of the missions," Donley said. "We quit using the belly turret in the later flights because we were getting pretty good fighter [plane] escorts by that time."

Completing his final mission on June 3, 1944—three days before D-Day—Donley returned home from war having completed thirty combat missions aboard the bomber striking targets throughout Central Europe. He arrived back in the states in September 1944 and after a brief period of leave, reported to Keesler Field, Mississippi, where he spent the next year instructing trainees on aircraft instruments and later working in an equipment repair section. Following his discharge in the fall of 1945, he returned to Clarksburg and married his fiancée, Margaret Birdsong, the next year. Donley was later employed by local electric cooperatives and the utilities division for the City of California, Missouri, but went on to retire from Co-Mo Electric Cooperative in 1987.

Though his experiences during the war are now several decades in hindsight, the World War II veteran maintains his encounters in the hostile skies play a frequent role in his daily reflections.

"All you thought about back then was to get out of the war alive and to get back home," he said, adding, "and it was something you're never gonna forget...something you think about almost every day." *(Photography courtesy of Jim Donley)*

Bill Wheeler

Jefferson City

Bill Wheeler reflects on his lengthy military career with a sense of pride, recalling the many changes he witnessed between his service in World War II and into the Cold War. But, as the former Air Force pilot noted, he would not have received the opportunity to don a military uniform were it not for an older brother who laid down his life more than nine decades ago. While living in a house on East Miller Street in Jefferson City, Missouri, a nineteen-month old Bill Wheeler started to drown while playing in nearby Wears Creek in November 1919. It was then that his nearly four-year-old brother, Jack, played the part of the hero by rescuing his struggling sibling from the creek.

"About a month later, Jack died of scarlet fever and diphtheria," said Bill Wheeler, who know resides in Savannah, Georgia, recalling the bravery of his older brother. "All because of Jack...because of what he did," he sagely remarked, "I was able to live, to go on to have a good career in the Air Force."

In the years following the family tragedy, his parents moved the family to St. Louis in 1931 and Wheeler went on to graduate from Normandy High School in 1935. Then, Wheeler explained, he worked for local companies and began drilling with an Organized Reserve unit prior to the outbreak of World War II.

"The draft came and I think being in that reserve unit gave us a low draft lottery number," Wheeler laughed, when discussing his induction into the U.S. Army at Jefferson Barracks in April 1941.

Initially assigned to the infantry, the recruit trained at Ft. Leonard Wood, Missouri, and later traveled to Louisiana for what he described as "war games." A short time later, Wheeler recalled, he was informed that the Army Air Corps was seeking applicants.

"I applied, passed the tests and was accepted," said Wheeler. "First, I was sent to Brooks Field in Texas and spent a lot of time in the library studying math—algebra, calculus and the like. Everybody wanted to be a pilot and I had heard that you had better know your math if you wanted to become a pilot."

His regimen of self-study paid off when he advanced to primary flight training at Ballinger, Texas, and was introduced to the PT-19 Fairchild—a two seat, single engine aircraft. Several weeks later, he attended his basic flight training using a more advanced aircraft at Goodfellow Field in San Angelo, Texas.

"Then," Wheeler continued, "I was sent over to Mission, Texas [Moore Field], to train on the AT-6, which was a much heavier, more complex airplane than those we had used up to that point. We learned to shoot targets and perform aerial acrobatics," he added.

In December 1942, one year following the attack on Pearl Harbor, the young airman was commissioned a second lieutenant and received his pilot's wings. Given the choice of either becoming a fighter pilot or flying "heavier airplanes," the young aviator chose the latter.

"I was transferred to Hondo [Army Air Field], Texas," Wheeler said. "That's where I began to fly the AT-7, which was the first multi-engine plane that I flew and held about six passengers. We would use the plane to train navigators because that was back before we had all of the fancy electronics they have now for aerial navigation."

Remaining at the base throughout World War II, the pilot recalls not only amassing more than 10,000 hours of flight time while train-ing navigators, but also worked with a "secretive atomic unit" and in an administrative capacity to help track operations on the large base.

"It was while I was stationed at Hondo that I was introduced to Mary," recalled Wheeler, an unforgettable event he described as "love at first sight." (Five weeks after first meeting, the couple married.)

As Wheeler explained, he left the service in September 1945 and returned to St. Louis, finding employment at a local shoe factory and flying with a reserve unit at Scott Field (now Scott Air Force Base), Illinois, on weekends. A year later, he reenlisted when offered a regular commission in the Air Force. (The U.S. Army Air Forces was established as the U.S. Air Force in 1947).

He went on to fly C-119s in McCord AFB in Seattle and later became a B-47 Stratojet pilot with the Strategic Air Command (SAC), stationed in several locations throughout the United States including five years at an air base in England.

"While I was with SAC," he said, "the B-47 I piloted was equipped with a hydrogen bomb—it had the capability of destroying an entire city. We had orders that if something happened [during the Cold War], we were trained and prepared to drop the bomb on a specific target in the Soviet Union."

The married father of three children noted that he retired from the Air Force at the rank of colonel on March 1, 1970, with nearly thirty-two years of military service to his credit. For several decades, he has lived in Savannah, Georgia, but insists his success in life remains attached to one Mid-Missouri community.

After listening to her father share his story of military service, Wheeler's daughter, Dana Bradley, stated with evident solemnity, "For me, my dad's story represents a full circle moment. Uncle Jack gave him life and then he went on to give life to three children and two grandchildren."

Tearfully, Wheeler himself added, "If Jack hadn't pulled me from that creek years ago, I wouldn't have been here to live the wonderful life that I have." He concluded, "I feel as though I should thank the citizens of Jefferson City as well for giving me the privilege of calling this my hometown—it always has been and always will be." *(Photograph courtesy of Bill Wheeler)*

Van Williamson

California

Much of Van Williamson's life has been that of travel, as past employment has moved him to and from several locations throughout the United States. But as the California, Missouri, resident related, the pace of such movement is something to which he grew accustomed while storming across Europe with the 20th Armored Division in World War II. Born and raised in the Kansas City (Missouri) area, Williamson began repairing motor boats at a local marina while still in high school. However, after graduating in 1942, he received a piece of paper notorious for its potential consequences.

"I turned eighteen and got my draft notice two weeks later," said the veteran. "That's how they did me...they didn't even give me a chance to enlist," he chuckled, when describing the beginnings of a three-year military journey.

In March 1943, Williamson donned an Army uniform and traveled to Camp Campbell (now Fort Campbell), Kentucky, to complete his basic training. He went on to attend a gunnery school at Ft. Knox, Kentucky, learning the mechanics and operation of lighter weapons such as pistols and rifles, in addition to the heavier artillery and anti-tank guns. Later in his training cycle, Williamson explained, the Army recognized the potential value of his previous marina experience and sent him to a military boat repair and maintenance course in Milwaukee, Wisconsin.

"The Army obviously recognized what I had done in working with boats in Kansas City and knew that I was the person to do that for the Army, too," he said.

According to Williamson, he received notice that his division would travel to Europe to relieve the men who had been fighting it the Battle of the Bulge since the middle of December 1944. Boarding a troopship in early February 1945, Williamson arrived in Le Havre, France days later, missing the "Bulge" by only a couple of weeks. Despite the timing of his arrival, the young soldier did not realize he was only weeks away from participating in another lethal engagement.

"When we got to Laon, France, they began to break us up into whatever we'd be doing—whether you were going to be a tank driver, a mechanic, halftrack operator...," he said.

Attached to the 220th Armored Engineer Battalion under the 20th Armored Division, Williamson began the move across France and into Belgium as U.S. forces fought toward Germany. Though he recalls several skirmishes along the way, Williamson affirmed that one of the most ingrained of his wartime experiences was the crossing of the Rhine River in April 1945.

"I was on a boat helping push the bridge pieces together so that tanks and other equipment could cross into Germany," he said. "We got the bridge up...mostly...before the fighting started—but when it did, that was a fight!"

Although his service in a combat environment was punctuated with stressful moments, Williamson noted that there were instances of unanticipated respite from the action, specifically when they liberated the German army of some precious provisions.

"Sometime after the Rhine, we captured a German train that was carrying beer," the former soldier grinned. "We took all that we wanted of the beer and drank it while traveling to the next place," adding, "but I didn't care much for that stuff...it was a lot different than what I was used to."

As the division pressed on, they crossed the Danube River on April 28, 1945, and, the following day, became one of three U.S. Army divisions to liberate Dachau concentration camp. According to an article on the United States Holocaust Memorial Museum website, as American forces approached the camp, they discovered thirty railroad cars filled with corpses of former captives.

"There were a lot of guys that looked half-dead," Williamson somberly recalled, "and of course, there were many more that never made it."

With their liberation duties behind them, the division continued to Salzburg, Germany, and remained in Europe until late July 1945, returning via troopship to Camp Kilmer, New Jersey.

Following a brief period of leave, Williamson continued in his service with the Army, believing he would soon deploy to the Pacific, but when Japan surrendered in September 1945, he married his fiancée, Betty, since he knew his time in uniform was close to an end. He received his discharge on February 12, 1946 and in later years went to work for the Caterpillar Corporation, which carried him to several locations throughout the United Sates. In 1979, he moved to Mid-Missouri, and now lives in the small community of California.

When asked why memories from his participation in a war now seven decades past appear undiminished by the passage of time, Williamson responded with the insight of a man who has witnessed more than his share of unpleasant situations.

"A lot of people have tried not to remember their service because they want to forget about it," he paused, "people died...and they don't want to remember that, but many of us World War II veterans are still here and we have a story to share." He added, "We did what we were sent to do, to put it simply, and it was an important moment in my life." *(Photograph courtesy of Betty Williamson)*

Lucky, Lucky Me!

George Allison Whiteman

Longwood

The memory of many notable events and people from Missouri's military history is preserved through marble shafts, statues and various types of monuments. One local community, however, came together after the Second World War to ensure the sacrifice of one of their native sons killed during the Japanese attack on Pearl Harbor would live on for ages through the naming of Whiteman Air Force Base (AFB) near Knob Noster, Missouri.

The story of Whiteman AFB begins with the birth of George Allison Whiteman on October 12, 1919 in the small town of Longwood, located several miles north of Sedalia. He went on to attend local grade schools and graduated from Smith-Cotton High School in Sedalia. According to the December 7, 1971 edition of *The Sedalia Democrat*, Whiteman made the decision to attend the Rolla School of Mines "because the Armed Forces told him if he attended college, he could enter the Army Air Force as an officer, and might possibly become a pilot."

Spending two years matriculating at Rolla, the article goes on to explain that the aspiring pilot was informed by military recruiters he was "too light" to serve in the Army Air Corps. Not discouraged, Whiteman enlisted in the Coastal Artillery but was eventually able to join the Air Corps and was sent to pilot training at Kelly Field in Texas. On November 15, 1940, he earned his pilot wings and commission as a second lieutenant. Adventure appeared to be on the horizon for the new officer when he was assigned to a unit at Hamilton Field, California, that was scheduled for service on

Martinique—a French island located in the Caribbean. But when the unit's commander requested six pilots to volunteer for service in Hawaii, Whiteman's fate was soon established.

Arriving in Hawaii in the early part of 1941, Whiteman and his fellow volunteers traveled to their assigned duty stations at Wheeler Army Airfield located on the island of Oahu adjacent to Pearl Harbor. In an interview with the staff of *The Sedalia Democrat* that appeared in print on December 7, 1958, Major Charles King—who served with Whiteman in Hawaii—shared the details of the aviator's death.

"The [Japanese] plane swooped low and strafed some of the men who were swimming and then zoomed away," noted King, adding, "that while the men were running back to the unit to report the incident, word came through to load ammunition in the Curtiss P-40s and disperse them in the area." King went on to explain that while men were rushing out to load ammunition on the planes, "12 Japanese Zero's started strafing the field" while Whiteman, the first pilot to reach his aircraft, "climbed in and started the engine."

The account given by King further notes that Lt. Whiteman headed for the runway without having the time to grab his flying suit equipment or giving the gun crews time to replace the gun cowling on his aircraft. While proceeding down the runway, King stated, two Japanese pilots spotted Whiteman's P-40B, named *Lucky Me*, and began strafing the aircraft with machine-gun fire.

Although Whiteman's plane was able to lift off, he was attacked head-on by the Japanese pilots. As King described to the newspaper, "The lieutenant veered his plane to the right and tried to make a belly landing on the beach, but a combination of Japanese bullets and the fire resulted in a flaming crashing and Lt. Whiteman's death."

The first Missourian killed in World War II, Whiteman was laid to rest in the Schofield Barracks Post Cemetery in Hawaii on December 9, 1941. The airman's remains were later returned to Missouri and reinterred in Sedalia's Memorial Park Cemetery. A year following his death, Whiteman's parents received the Silver Star and Purple Heart medals posthumously awarded to their son.

While Whiteman's parents attempted to cope with the grief from the loss of the oldest of their eight sons, they were once again victims of tragedy when Whiteman's younger brother, Marshall, was killed in action on April 9, 1953 while serving with the Marine Corps in the Korean War.

According to the Sedalia Convention & Business Bureau, the Sedalia Glider Base was established in November 1942, approximately two years after Lt. Whiteman graduated from his flight training. Undergoing several expansions and changes in the ensuing years, in 1954 the Air Force announced it was seeking nominations from civic groups for the renaming of the airfield.

"The United States Air Force plans to rename the Sedalia Air Force Base in memory of some nationally prominent deceased figure," reported *The Sedalia Democrat* on June 24, 1954. The article further noted, "Sedalians feel the qualifications for the name of Whiteman are fulfilled with his acts at Pearl Harbor when he endeavored to take his plane into the air and fight the invaders."

During a dedication and renaming ceremony on December 3, 1955, the Sedalia Air Force Base underwent the official transition to Whiteman Air Force Base, nearly fourteen years following the death of its namesake.

Newspaper reports subsequent to Whiteman's death characterized the inspiration provided by his sacrifice at Pearl Harbor as hundreds of aviation cadets wished to expedite their training to avenge the attack that took the Sedalia airman's life. In a letter of condolence to the parents of Whiteman printed in December 10, 1941 edition of The Sedalia Democrat, Missouri Secretary of State Dwight Brown expressed not only his appreciation for the sacrifice made by Whiteman, but summarized his affection for the valiant and patriotic manner in which Whiteman's mother viewed the unexpected loss of her son.

"I have read with interest the statement credited to you: 'We have got to expect to sacrifice our loved ones if we want to win this war,'" Brown wrote. He added, "These are the words of an American woman devoted to the American way of life. Your expression is an inspiration to every man and woman in the land." *(Photograph courtesy of Museum of Military History)*

Louis "Leroy" Poire

Jefferson City

The Bikini Atoll in the Marshall Islands is the visage of paradise—lovely beaches, palm trees and brilliantly colored fish swimming through stunning blue waters. Yet this hidden gem situated between Hawaii and Australia in the South Pacific was once "ground zero" for the testing of nuclear weapons by the United States, an event witnessed firsthand by Jefferson City resident Louis "Leroy" Poire. Born in 1927 in the small community of Hale, Missouri, Poire attended "a little country school" and, after completing the ninth grade, left his studies to help with the never-ending list of chores on his family's farm.

"It was during the latter part of World War II and I decided to enlist in the Navy four days before I had to register for the draft," Poire recalled. With a grin, he added, "I didn't want to end up in the Army or Marines."

The twenty-two-year-old recruit began his active service on October 31, 1945, traveling to the Naval Training Center in San Diego to complete several weeks of basic training. From there, the former sailor explained, he boarded the *USS Alabama* and sailed up the coast of California to San Francisco.

"Once we got to San Francisco, the Navy put a bunch of us on a plane and flew us to Pearl Harbor," he said. "Then, they put us all up in barracks and within a few days, everyone shipped out of there for various assignments...all except me," he added.

The day following the departure of his fellow sailors, Poire recalls sitting in the barracks when Delbert Poire—his older brother who was also serving in the Navy—walked in to greet him.

"I found out that my brother was serving aboard the *(USS) PGM-32* and he and the skipper arranged to have me held back so that I could be assigned to his ship," Poire said.

Commissioned February 9, 1945, the *USS PGM-32* was classified a "motor gunboat" and could sustain a complement of sixty-five crewmembers. Once aboard the ship in early 1946, Poire and the crew of the gunboat departed Pearl Harbor to participate in an event of major consequence and possessing a legacy that has been obscured by the passage of decades.

"We sailed for the Bikini Atoll and once we arrived, we anchored for several days," said Poire. "Then when they got ready to drop the atomic bomb, we pulled anchor and sailed in a circle about eleven miles from where the bomb exploded"

Codenamed *Operation Crossroads*, in 1946 the U.S. began to "test the effect of nuclear weapons on naval warships," noted the Atomic Heritage Foundation. The operation consisted of two tests—the first test occurred on July 1, 1946 with the detonation of a bomb "over the target fleet at an altitude of 520 feet with a yield of 23 kilotons."[96] On July 25, 1946, a second and final test was performed when an atomic bomb exploded ninety feet underwater. This test, the foundation described, created "a 900-foot 'base surge' [of falling water] which rolled over many of the target ships, painting them with radioactivity that could not be removed."

In describing the first detonation, Poire said, "They wouldn't let us look at the explosion or take any pictures. It really wasn't a loud explosion, but you could kind of feel it. I remember looking at the mushroom cloud rise into the air and thinking that it would eventually cover us up!"

Following the underwater detonation that occurred several days later, the former sailor recalls sailing back into the target area where

---

[96] Atomic Heritage Foundation, *Operation Crossroads*, www.atomicheritage.org.

the six scientists they were carrying aboard their ship began taking samples of the water to test for lingering radiation levels.

"After a day or so in the target area, they put the Geiger counter on us and we had to abandon ship because of the radiation in the bilges," he said. "They took us to a transport carrier and we stayed there about five days." He continued, "Two men would then spend three hours at a time aboard our ship to keep anyone from bothering it."

In August of 1946, Poire left the Bikini Atoll aboard a cargo ship, returning to San Diego and then traveling to Chicago, where he received his discharge from the Navy several weeks later. Spending only a year in active service, the sailor received a five-year reserve commitment, receiving his final discharge in 1951. Returning to his father's farm, he went on to marry the former Marjorie Muller in 1947 and the couple raised four children. In the decades following his naval service, Poire entered the construction trades and moved to Jefferson City in 1969, where he and his wife continue to reside.

When asked if he believes his presence at the historic testing of nuclear technologies was a unique and rare experience, Poire affirmed, "I never really thought much about being involved in the experiment—it was one of those situations where I went where I was told and did what I was told to do."

He added, "I do feel like we were kind of guinea pigs in a sense, even if we weren't directly in the target area. With the effects of radiation, I believe it was the reason my brother had kidney problems before he died and why I've had kidney issues as well." Following a brief silence, he concluded, "I don't think the government really even wants to recognize us for having been there." *(Photograph courtesy of Louis Poire)*

Lloyd Workman

Vienna

In late spring of 1944, Lloyd Workman left his home near the community of Vienna, Missouri, to travel to the sprawling city of St. Louis, where he was able to acquire employment with the Goodrich Tire Company. It was simply a period of waiting, he explained, since he realized the long tentacles of the military draft of World War II would soon reach him.

"I got my notice for a draft physical in the mail and was sent to Jefferson Barracks in August of 1944," he recalled. "It wasn't but a few days and I was inducted into the U.S. Army and sent to Camp Fannin, Texas, for training," he added.

Located near Tyler, Texas, the former Camp Fannin served as an infantry replacement training center during World War II. During his seventeen weeks there, Workman recalled, he participated in a twenty-mile "march with a full field pack," in addition to receiving an introduction to machine guns.

"We trained with the A4 and A6 [variants of a .30 caliber Browning machine gun] during our training cycle," he explained. "As the gunner, I carried the machine gun and I had an assistant gunner that carried the tripod and the ammunition."

When his initial training was completed, Workman returned home for several days of leave before reporting to Ft. Meade, Maryland, in the early days of January 1945. From there, he was sent to Camp Shanks, New York, to board a British troopship that carried him and other replacement soldiers to Liverpool, England. Eventually, the veteran explained, he was sent by train to the port city of Southampton and ferried across the English Channel to France. Following additional rides by train and military truck, the young soldier arrived in Metz, France, and was assigned to Company C, 22nd Infantry Regiment of the 4th Infantry Division.

"The Battle of the Bulge had recently ended and they gave me a machine gun right off the bat," he said. "At one point, we were in a pillbox on the Ziegfried Line and became pinned down by German machine gun fire. My assistant gunner was fifteen feet from me but couldn't get the tripod over so I could return fire."

As Workman explained, another platoon on his flank was able to "take care" of the enemy attack. Shortly after this event, the young soldier asked his platoon leader to give him a Browning A6 machine gun since it could be fired by one person and he would not be dependent on the tripod carried by an assistant gunner. Although his request was granted, it was not long after this event that he was introduced to the range of threats that emerge in a combat zone.

"We were on the move one morning at about daylight, at the time of day when there's really not enough light to make anything out," he said. "A guy to the left of me from another platoon stepped on a bouncing betty [a German mine], I believe, and when it exploded, a piece of the shrapnel hit me in my leg," he added.

As the veteran described, he heard the unknown soldier calling for a medic to come provide emergency medical care. Workman and his fellow soldiers continued forward on their mission and it was not until sometime later that his own injury, though minor, was reported to medical personnel. For the injury, Workman was later presented a Purple Heart. This was not the only medal he would receive since he was provided an opportunity to demonstrate his mettle in combat several weeks later, during an event that resulted in his receipt of the nation's third highest military combat decoration

On April 3, 1945, after his company had been surrounded by enemy forces, "Private Workman seized his [Browning A6] assault machine gun and ran forward of the company lines to repel the enemy force. Time and time again, he held the enemy at bay...until mortar fire could be adjusted upon them," wrote Major General George P. Hays in the citation for the Silver Star that Workman was awarded.

The 4th Infantry Division continued fighting toward Germany and, after reaching the Rhine River, were relieved by the 11th Army. The division moved south and when the war in Europe came to an end on May 8, 1945, Workman believes they were "somewhere near" the borders of Austria and Czechoslovakia.

"I was one of the first from our company sent home after the war because they planned on sending me on to fight in the Pacific," Workman recalled. "But there was a huge public outcry over that practice and my orders were changed for Camp Butner, North Carolina, where the division was inactivated."

The combat veteran was eventually transferred to Ft. Benning, Georgia, spending the remaining months of his military commitment helping to train officer candidates. On July 5, 1946, he received his discharge from the U.S. Army at Ft. Leavenworth, Kansas. After returning to Missouri, Workman married, raised two daughters and completed a lengthy career with the Carpenters Union. Though decades have passed, he views his experiences in WWII as an obligation that he was able to survive and remain in good health.

"I didn't have any choice since I was drafted like so many others, but I'm glad that I did it," he affirmed. "I've been told that I was lucky...and I was. I could have been hurt a lot worse." He added, "I learned to take orders, to do what I was told, and I got to come home when a lot of guys never did." *(Photograph courtesy of Lloyd Workman)*

CHAPTER 4

KOREA, VIETNAM AND THE COLD WAR

Charles Bestgen

Tipton

When describing his service to the nation during the Korean War, Charles Bestgen emits a jovial personality that belies the many hardships, losses and injuries that he has both witnessed and experienced during his time spent overseas. Born in 1930, Bestgen was raised in the Moniteau County community of California, Missouri, in a family possessing a respectable legacy of military service—his father was a veteran of World War I and his two older brothers served during the Second World War. After graduating high school in 1949, a nineteen-year old Bestgen went to work for California Manufacturing Company. He soon settled into his post-high school life, but the draft notice he received in October 1951 interrupted whatever plans he had made for his future.

"It wasn't too much of a shock to me," said Bestgen, while discussing the receipt of his draft notice. "I wasn't the only one that got one," he added with a smile.

Several days later, the young inductee arrived at Fort Ord, California, where he underwent a sixteen-week regimen of intense infantry training that transformed him into a soldier and rifleman for the U.S. Army.

"It didn't get real cold [at Fort Ord] but there were some mornings when there was ice on the ground," he said. "The ice didn't last long and then it got so hot you couldn't stand it. I guess that's California for you!" Bestgen chuckled.

After completing his training in February 1952, the soldier came home for two weeks of leave and then returned to California to board a troopship bound for service overseas. Arriving in Inchon Bay, Korea, he was soon assigned as a rifleman to Company A, 32nd Infantry Regiment of the 7th Infantry Division. As Bestgen explained, although he was given an M-1 rifle when arriving in country, he was soon assigned an air-cooled .30 caliber machine gun to use in defensive emplacements and later when participating as a member of combat patrols.

"You could really put a lot of lead out with that machine gun," the veteran affirmed. "I think I walked all over Korea packing that thing," he grinned.

Bestgen recalls beginning a cycle of "living on the front lines in bunkers" for thirty days at a time, followed by a return to their base camp for thirty days. However, he further explained, this cycle was soon interrupted when during the month of July 1952, he and his company began frequent combat patrol in the evenings.

"We went out many a night and I don't see how we did it," he said. "On one patrol, we had a guy get his arm blown off by a burp gun [a 7.62mm Soviet weapon]—those things would just tear you up." He solemnly added, "He died before we were able to get him back to camp."

Bestgen considered himself "lucky" since he was frequently fired upon by enemy soldiers yet never wounded. His providence soon expired when his company received orders to join other elements of the first battalion in attacking and securing ridges known as Jane Russell Hill and Sandy Ridge during the Battle of Triangle Hill on October 15, 1952. While fighting under conditions that required close quarters combat near trenches and slopes filled with Chinese and North Korean troops, Bestgen was proceeding toward the company's objective when an artillery shell from an enemy barrage landed behind him and exploded.

"I ended up with shrapnel wounds to my left leg," he said. "They evacuated me to an aid station and removed some pieces of the shrapnel from my leg, but I was eventually sent to the United States for several surgeries," he added.

In the end, Bestgen recalls, he was sent to the hospital at Camp Atterbury, Indiana, where he underwent an estimated four surgeries, some of which included skin grafts. On April 11, 1953, while still recovering from his treatments, the soldier married his fiancée, Margaret Ann, whom he had met before the war. After spending more than eight months in the hospital, he was discharged on July 24, 1953.

The combat veteran returned to his Mid-Missouri home where he and his wife went on to raise four children. After the war, he returned to his previous employment with California Manufacturing and retired after nearly forty years of service to the company. In 2012, Bestgen received the unexpected and memorable opportunity to travel to Washington D.C., to see the nation's war memorials—including the Korean War Memorial—as part of the Central Missouri Honor Flight

The decades have passed and the Korean War has become little more than an ancient memory to many young citizens, thus highlighting its distinction as the "Forgotten War." Despite its fading remnants, the veteran affirms that remembering his time in combat and the soldiers with whom he served are experiences that will never fade from his reflections.

"Yes, the 'Forgotten War'—that is more or less what it's become," he somberly noted. "It's truly a shame that a lot of people don't know anything about the war...all of those brave men that gave up their lives." He briskly concluded, "I know the costs. I was there and will never forget." (*Photograph courtesy of Charles Bestgen*)

Carl Houston

Tipton

In 1952, Tipton resident Carl Houston was beginning to establish himself as a young man recently out of high school. But the realities of war and vagaries of daily life would soon deliver him a draft notice and two years of military service away from friends, family and a girlfriend who would later become his wife.

Born and raised ten miles east of Eldon, Houston graduated high school in 1949 and began working at the Wesseling Jordan Company (footwear manufacturer). In 1951, he transferred to the company's new Tipton facility when the Eldon location closed. Houston's introduction to military service came in May 1952, when he received a draft notice and was inducted into the U.S. Army at Camp Crowder, located near the community of Neosho, Missouri.

"I knew that my time was coming," said Houston. "Everybody my age was going [to Korea] or had already gone."

Houston was sent to Fort Leonard Wood for nine weeks of basic combat training. "During my basic training we were told that ninety percent of us would be going over to Korea," Houston recalled.

Shortly thereafter, the newly minted soldier traveled to Fort Belvoir, Virginia in order to complete nine weeks of heavy equipment training. As was his suspicion, Houston received notice towards the end of his military school that he would soon deploy to Korea. When departing Fort Belvoir, Houston was instructed to report to Ft. Lawton, Washington (outside of Seattle), in about twenty days. This "delay in route" provided the young soldier the opportunity to return to Eldon for ten days of leave prior to his pending overseas service during which he would spend with his family and girlfriend.

During the middle October 1952, Houston reported to Ft. Lawton. "The camp was on the middle of a mountain and you couldn't see anything for the fog," said Houston. "You couldn't see the peak of the mountain above, but you could hear the bellow of the boats in the water below."

Houston and his fellow soldiers were then moved to Navy Pier 91 where they boarded a troopship on October 25, 1952—his twenty-first birthday. Although an important milestone in the life of many, Houston lamented, "I never felt like less of a man in my life. Once I got onboard the troopship," he continued, "I got seasick immediately and spent the next three days in my bunk. I was so sick that I couldn't even take my boots off!" he laughed.

One of his friends brought him a dry turkey sandwich, which he was able to keep down. After visiting the top deck of the ship and breathing some fresh air, the young soldier began to feel better, though he recalls not feeling "entirely like myself" for the remainder of the trip.

After almost three weeks at sea, the troopship ported in Yokohama, Japan. Houston then boarded a troop train that traveled through Tokyo to Camp Drake where he and his fellow troops received brand new M-1 rifles still packed in grease. At this point, everyone had to clean their rifle to the extent that they were able to get one shot off in order to ensure it functioned properly. They again boarded the troop train and returned to the port at Yokohama. After boarding the same ship that had delivered him to Japan, Houston and his comrades spent an additional three days at sea before arriving at Pusan, Korea. From there, Houston boarded another troop train for a three-day trip that would deliver him to a location near Seoul.

"All of the windows had been shot out and it must have had two or three inches of slack in every coupling," joked the veteran, during a discussion about his trip along the rickety Korean rails.

He was then assigned to the 8th Army, 79th Engineer Battalion, beginning a lengthy deployment that would see him living in tents and foxholes with a loaded rifle for a pillow. During his time in country, Houston operated a bulldozer assisting in the construction of roads, helipads and bridges so to improve upon the country's infrastructure and support troop movement. On one occasion, the young soldier would find that even bulldozer operators were considered potential targets for enemy snipers.

Houston's unit was camped in an area known as "No Man's Land," in the process of clearing the site for the construction of an enemy prisoner of war camp. The campsite was situated on a mound along a river composed of tall grass that would die off every year, fall to the ground, and grow again the next year, eventually forming into several layers of dead, dry grass.

"One day the enemy began firing at us with tracer rounds from across the river and set the grass on fire in the area we were camped," Houston said. "We had to take the dozers to the top of the hill to put out the fires or else we would be burned out."

While plowing out the fires with the dozers, enemy soldiers began firing on Houston and the other dozer operators.

"You could hear the bullets bouncing off the dozer, but with the ten-foot blades we were kind of protected," the veteran said. "Also, you kind of sat down in a 'nest' on the dozer, so you weren't that exposed."

Houston also remembers the great difficulty his unit encountered in trying to keep their equipment in running order.

"You couldn't find parts for anything," he said. "We actually had a sign in our camp that said, 'We have done so much with so little for so long that now we can do anything with nothing,'" Houston joked.

Towards the latter part of his deployment, Houston received word that he could find all the parts he needed at the 919th Airbase approximately sixty miles from his camp.

"I jumped in a Jeep and drove to the base as fast as I could without getting bounced out," he recalled. "When I got to the air base I found that it had been bombed the night before and there was nothing left."

In March of 1954, following seventeen months in country, Houston boarded a troop ship in Inchon, Korea, that would take him to San Francisco. From there he traveled to Camp Carson,

Colorado, where he received his discharge from the service. Traveling from Colorado to Eldon by bus, the veteran went back to work at the shoe factory and in April 1955, was married to his pre-service sweetheart, Ellen Enloe. In 1957, Houston purchased a garage and welding shop in Tipton, which he operated until his retirement in 2002. The former soldier is a member of the American Legion Post 304 and for many years worked at a local funeral home to keep busy during his retirement.

Although Houston recalls the two Christmas holidays he missed because of his service, what prevails most in his memories is the amount of compensation he received in the Army.

"I started out with $71 a month in pay," said Houston. "After seventeen months, a couple of stripes and combat pay, I was up to $122," he chuckled. *(Photograph courtesy of Carl Houston)*

Harold Schulte

Linn

Growing up on a small farm near the small community of Bay, Missouri, Harold Schulte recalls tossing a baseball around with his brothers when not busy helping his father with chores. As the years passed, he and his brothers would play for a local baseball team called the Bay Bears—an activity that would later help shape Schulte's military experience.

"I graduated from high school in Owensville in 1952 and went to work at a general store in nearby Mt. Sterling making thirty-five cents an hour," Schulte recalled. "After a few months of that, I went to work on a local dairy farm with the intention of eventually finding a way to go to college."

As Schulte explained, during a conversation with an older brother who had served during World War II and was awarded a Silver Star Medal, the suggestion was made to go to his local draft board and "volunteer" for the military draft. This, he explained, would move him to the top of the draft list and require that he serve two years in the military rather than four.

"It all worked out because after I volunteered for the draft, I soon got my letter for induction into the U.S. Army at Jefferson Barracks and I ended up getting in three months before the Korean War GI Bill expired," he said.

Following his induction, the twenty-year-old draftee was sent to Camp Chaffee, Arkansas, for eight weeks of basic training. He remained on the post for 12 weeks of communications training during which he learned Morse code. With his training completed, he was transferred to Europe in the early weeks of 1955 for his first and only overseas duty assignment.

The armistice agreement that brought about the cessation of hostilities during the Korean War was in effect, Schulte explained, and the U.S. Army did not need additional troops in Korea at the time. The newly trained soldier was assigned to a service company at the Chinon Engineer Depot, located approximately seventy-five miles Southwest of Paris, where he discovered his previous training would be of little benefit.

"I don't think there was a radio on the entire base," Schulte mirthfully recalled. "Instead, I ended up working in the office of the company clerk because I knew how to type."

Schulte explained that the base served as a major supply route to Berlin, Germany, during the Cold War and, as a NATO site, there were Polish soldiers serving as guards and French troops working in the kitchen. However, the logistical mission of the base became of little importance to the young soldier when he was informed of tryouts being held for a camp baseball team.

"My brothers and I had all played for a baseball team back home in our younger days, so I thought I would go ahead and give it a try," recalled Schulte. "I made the team and for the remainder of my two-year enlistment, I played baseball for the Chinon Red Devils."

According to an article appearing in the June 27, 1954 edition of the Asbury Park Press (Asbury Park, New Jersey), the baseball league for the armed forces stationed in France was a "big circuit (that was) divided into two divisions." The Western Division, of which the Chinon Red Devils was part, consisted of six teams while the Eastern Division had seven. In his first year playing for the Chinon team, Schulte was a substitute in left field and quickly gained the experience to progress. During his second year, he became a shortstop and played in that position for the remainder of his enlistment.

"We played from the first day of spring until fall," said the veteran. "During the week, we'd travel to whatever camp we would be playing at that week." He added, "Thursday was our day off, Friday we'd practice on the other team's field and then we'd play a double-header on Saturday and another on Sunday."

Although the Chinon Red Devils won their division title while playing throughout France, they occasionally played games against U.S. military teams in Germany—a match-up that often appeared less than equitable.

"We never won against the teams in Germany," Schulte said. "When soldiers transferred for duty in Europe, they would process through Germany. If it was found they had experience in the minor leagues, they would make sure the soldiers were stationed in Germany so they could play for one of their teams."

Finishing his enlistment in August 1956, Schulte was sent back to the United States and received his discharge at Ft. Sheridan, Illinois. Returning to Mid-Missouri, he married Mary Lou in 1957 and the couple has raised two daughters and a son. In the years after his military baseball experience, the former soldier used his GI Bill benefits to attend the University of Missouri, earning his bachelor's degree in civil engineering in 1960. He would go on to complete a lengthy career as a consulting engineer in addition to serving as a city engineer for a local community.

Reflecting on the timing of his military service, which came on the heels of the Korean War, Schulte affirmed that for many years he was unable to join his brothers in membership and support of their local American Legion post in the community of Bay.

"My father served in World War I and three of my brothers also served. They were all members of the American Legion 541 in our hometown," recalled Schulte. "It was formed after World War II and for many years I was unable to join because the VA did not recognize my dates of service as eligible since it was after the official ending date of the Korean War."

He added, "Twenty years or so later, the VA informed me that the eligibility dates were changed and I was able to sign up. It has been a wonderful opportunity to join my father and brothers in the American Legion because it is one big family—there is a camaraderie that tends to exist among everyone who has served." *(Photograph courtesy of Harold Schulte)*

Nick Monaco

Jefferson City

When Nicholas Monaco was a young boy growing up in the St. Louis area, his father was told that if he wanted his son to "grow up right," he should get him a military education. Consequently, young Monaco went on to attend Christian Brothers College High School, completing his high school education and discovering that he "took to the military structure" through the school's Junior Reserve Officers' Training Corps (ROTC) program. Following his graduation in 1948, he then went on to attend the University of Missouri-Columbia, where he continued both his studies and participation in the ROTC program.

"Upon graduation [in 1952]," said Monaco, "I was commissioned a second lieutenant and transferred to the 43rd Bomb Wing with the Strategic Air Command [SAC] at Lackland Air Force Base in Texas." He added, "From there, I was reassigned to Davis Monthan Air Force Base at Tucson, Arizona"

As noted in the book *Bigger Bombs for a Brighter Tomorrow* by John M. Curatola, the Cold War legacy of the SAC and its crews stretched forth more than fifty years following the close of World War II and "provided considerable deterrent power for the U.S. military and offset the Red Army's numerical superiority." Curatola added, "Sitting atop the most potent and powerful weapons ever devised," wrote Curatola, the men and women of the SAC stood as the bulwark against potential Communist expansion."[97]

---

[97] Curatola, *Bigger Bombs for a Brighter Tomorrow*, 1.

After completing advanced training as a personnel officer in Texas and Arizona, Monaco was given temporary duty assignments, resulting in his transfer to Brise Norton Air Base in England. It was here, Monaco explained, that he served under General Curtis Lemay—a World War II veteran who at the time commanded SAC and later went on to become the fifth chief of staff of the U.S. Air Force.

"Lemay was a very compassionate leader, but he was also very definite about what he wanted to accomplish," said Monaco. "He wanted to reach the enemy and he knew that enemy was Stalin."

For three-month periods, Monaco further explained, units would rotate in and out of Brise Air Base due to the "tedious nature" of their assignment in deterring the Soviet encroachment into Eastern Europe.

"A piece of serving as a deterrent was having aircraft in the sky 24/7," he said. "This required us to work with squadron commanders, wing commanders and so on, to have oversight of all of our personnel and equipment. He added, "We had to make sure there were appropriate personnel at all times to maintain and operate the aircraft."

While stationed in England, Monaco and several of his fellow airmen were temporarily assigned to help provide security for the coronation of Queen Elizabeth II on June 2, 1953, when she ascended to the throne of the United Kingdom following the death of her father, King George VI. Following completion of his overseas duty, Monaco was transferred to Tucson, Arizona in July 1953, where he met Mildred Pickett. The couple married later the following year and Monaco went on to finish out his active duty commitment with the 43rd Bomb Wing in September 1954.

"I eventually settled in Jefferson City and enrolled in law school at the University of Missouri," said Monaco. "I continued in my military service in a reserve capacity by joining the 9698th Air Reserve Squadron [Air Force Reserve] located at the airport in Jefferson City," said Monaco.

The veteran graduated from law school in 1958 and has since enjoyed a lengthy career as an attorney. However, throughout the years, his full-time civilian career continued to run parallel with his Air Force Reserve commitment.

"I was appointed as the Air Force Academy Liaison Officer and responsible for recruiting high school graduates from a territory in North Central Missouri," said the veteran. "My mission was to interest qualified high school students to become cadets at the Air Force Academy in Colorado."

During his early years as a liaison officer, Monaco noted, only men were allowed to become candidates for the academy. In 1975, women were authorized by Congress to attend the academy and General Stephan Allan, the Air Force Academy superintendent, was appointed by President Gerald Ford to make the announcement nationally.

"I requested that General Allan, who was the person I reported to as academy liaison, to make the announcement in Jefferson City," said Monaco. "They agreed to make the announcement at the Missouri Hotel [now the site of the Missouri Baptist Building] before an audience of nearly six hundred people."

During his twenty-eight years in the Air Force Reserve, Monaco was also afforded the opportunity to teach the Uniform Code of Military Justice to local high school students, introducing them to courtroom proceedings. In 1990, Monaco retired from the reserves, having risen to the rank of lieutenant colonel.

Many milestones exist in the military experience of the Jefferson City veteran, yet it was his time served with the Strategic Air Command during the early years of the Cold War that were some of the most memorable of his lengthy career.

"We had to work as a unit, think out solutions and everything we did was highly classified," Monaco said. "In fact, it was so classified that people did not know what we did...including my parents." He acknowledged, "During the service, you learned to do what you were told, when you were told to do it and in the manner in which you were expected to do it. And although I don't believe that I did anything spectacular, I certainly enjoyed my time in the Air Force." *(Photograph courtesy of Nick Monaco)*

Charlie Kuensting

Jefferson City

Jovial, witty and knowledgeable—adjectives serving as apt descriptions of one's first encounter with local Korean War veteran Charlie Kuensting. Like so many of his generation, Kuensting appeared initially hesitant when discussing his war experiences. However, as the conversation unfolded, memories erupted leading into a story possessing both intrigue and relevance. Raised on a farm in rural Marries County (near the community of Vienna), a young Kuensting attended Visitation Catholic School. But his formal education would draw to a close when, upon graduating the eighth grade in 1942, he made the decision to leave school.

"We lived on a five hundred acre farm and all of the boys were gone to the service [fighting during World War II]," Kuensting remarked. "I had to stay home to help my parents on the farm."

But a mobilization of the nation's youth similar to the one necessitating the young farmer's need to remain home to support the family farm would draw Kuensting into service of his own.

"In 1951, I received a draft notice in the mail," Kuensting recalled. "They didn't have any trouble finding me!" he joked.

On June 6, 1951, the soldier-to-be was married and, in September of the same year, reported for in-processing with the U.S. Army at Jefferson Barracks, Missouri. Following his induction into the service, Kuensting was sent to Camp Chaffee, Arkansas, where he completed basic combat and artillery training. Sometime near the Christmas holiday, he was sent to Ft. Lewis, Washington, in preparation for an overseas deployment in support of the Korean War. After about a week, he and his fellow soldiers departed "Pier 91" onboard a troopship destined for Japan.

Unfortunately, like so many of his rural counterparts who had never spent time onboard a ship, the young soldier succumbed to a common affliction—seasickness.

"We hit bad weather as soon as we left port and I couldn't even keep a square-inch soda cracker down," Kuensting said. "The storm ended, but we didn't even have enough time to clean up before we hit another storm. Thank God I had the top bunk," quipped the veteran.

After almost two weeks enroute, the troopship reached its first port at Yokohama, Japan. It is here that Kuensting and his counterparts received all of the necessary immunizations and in-processed for their approaching combat duty assignments. A week later they were back onboard the same ship that had brought them to Japan and enroute to Inchon, Korea, where the troop ship docked a few miles off the coast.

"They brought us into port on the LST's [landing ship tanks] from the Second World War," shared Kuensting.

The inexperienced young soldier from mid-Missouri was then taken to Seoul for a couple of days before joining up with the 69th Field Artillery Battalion, 25th Infantry Division near Chunchon, Korea. According to Kuensting, "We were fifty or sixty miles North of the 38th parallel [demarcation line between North and South Korea]. It was just mountain after mountain and very cold," he recalled.

As an artilleryman working near the front lines of combat, Kuensting worked with the "guns" for about two weeks before volunteering to work in the motor pool.

"The vehicles we were using were old World War II pieces shipped in from the Philippines," he stated. "They were mostly Ford, Willy's and Kaiser jeeps."

Due to the age of the equipment, the newly-assigned soldier was often performing such tasks as "sopping" water out of carburetors on equipment that had set for a long period of time.

"As part of our job in the motor pool, we had to haul ammo to the gun pits on the front lines, but we also had to do a little bit of everything, such as guard duty, since we were always kind of short-handed," Kuensting recalled.

Living in bunkers dug into the side of a mountain, the veteran clearly recalls the perpetual lack of heat.

"It was usually around twenty-two to twenty-three degrees below zero from December through March," he noted. "Since we were within a mile of the infantry on the front lines, we were not able to have fires because the smoke would draw attention."

Even dropping the tailgate on a vehicle was not allowed as the sound could carry for miles in the cold weather, potentially alerting enemy troops. Although the surroundings were austere and the service oftentimes difficult, Kuensting did experience some serene moments while in country.

"While I was over there [in Korea], some of the guys that I knew from Osage County looked me up and we were able to visit for a little while about things going on back home," said the veteran. "They read about my service in the local paper that had been mailed over by their families and found out they were serving in the same area that I was."

On a separate occasion, Kuensting and his fellow soldiers were treated to a USO show during which Marilyn Monroe made a brief appearance. After spending almost sixteen months overseas, Kuensting returned to the port at Inchon in April 1953, and boarded a troopship to return to Yokohama, Japan, where completed his out-processing.

"You basically had a week to ten days everywhere you went," related the veteran. "But we had to get out of port before the first of May because the Japanese were celebrating a holiday."

The seasoned soldier's return trip was slightly less abrasive than the trip over. "The sea was as calm as it could be on the way back," stated Kuensting. "There wasn't even a whitecap on it."

Arriving at San Francisco on May 12, 1953, Kuensting was released from Army after out-processing through Camp Carson, Colorado. Returning home, the veteran reunited with his wife and met for the first time the son that had been born during his absence. During the ensuing years, the veteran and his family moved to Jefferson City, where he worked as a mechanic for several area car dealerships until retiring in 1993.

"My main job now is doing nothing," he joked.

Although he remains eminently proud of his service, Kuensting realized when it his time for his military service to end.

"I was a staff sergeant when I was leaving," he noted. "They offered me another stripe if I would agree to stay." But the veteran clearly recalled his instantaneous response: "But I said, 'Heck no! I'm going home,'" he laughed.

Charles A. Kuensting passed away on September 21, 2016. He was laid to rest in Resurrection Cemetery in Jefferson City. *(Photograph courtesy of Brenda Kuensting)*

Don Wyss

Enon

A common theme that often emerges among veterans of the Korean War era is that their service was unexpected and often necessitated by their receipt of a draft notice. Such was the case for local veteran Don Wyss, who insisted that although unanticipated, his service in U.S Army provided him a key lesson in leadership that he later incorporated during his career in education. Raised in the small Moniteau County community of Enon, Wyss explained that following his graduation from Russellville High School in 1946, he began teaching class at a one-room schoolhouse while also attending college part-time during the summers.

"I learned more teaching in that small school than I ever did in college," Wyss grinned. "But in 1950, I resigned as a teacher and started attending college full-time to finish my degree."

The Korean War began while Wyss was approaching the completion of his degree and he soon realized the likelihood of being drafted. In an effort to acquire some control over his military career, he thought he would enlist in the Coast Guard.

"They tested me for color blindness and I failed the test," recalled Wyss. "So I thought I might be able to get my commission in the Navy and managed to pass the test." He added, "They told me they'd let me know if I was accepted into the program."

While awaiting a response from the Navy, he went on to graduate from college in Warrensburg in May 1952 with a degree in science and physical education. However, as Wyss explained with a hint of levity, the week after leaving college, he received his draft notice from the U.S. Army. Within days, he was sworn into the service at Kansas City and the sent to Camp Crowder (near Neosho, Missouri), to process into the Army as a private. He then boarded a train bound for Camp Roberts, California—a WWII post re-activated as a training site during the Korean War— and completed several weeks of basic infantry training.

"I remember when we pulled into Camp Roberts, they were shooting .50 caliber machine guns...with all that noise just blasting," Wyss said. "That's when I thought to myself, 'This is for real.'"

The newly minted soldier then received orders for Fort Ord, California—a former Army base situated on Monterey Bay along the Pacific coastline. It was here, Wyss said, that he completed eight weeks of supply school.

"I ended up back at Camp Roberts in late summer 1952 and worked as a supply sergeant in a basic infantry training company until receiving my orders for Korea in August of 1953," he said. "I had learned to take orders and decided that I would go to Korea and just do the best that I could do."

The soldier departed California aboard a troopship and, following a brief stop in Japan, arrived in the South Korean port city of Pusan, approximately a month following the signing of the armistice agreement. Upon arrival, recalled Wyss, he was assigned to a quartermaster company on an Army base in Pusan, essentially "living in the supply room" and issuing various types of provisions and equipment to his fellow soldiers.

"Pusan was really a mess at that time," recalled Wyss. "There were people living in cardboard shacks everywhere and there was a stench, it seemed, that hung over the entire city."

In late November 1953, the odor of filthy living conditions was overpowered by the stench of smoke when a Korean housewife "left a charcoal burner unattended for a few moments and it tipped over, igniting the straw-matted floor," reported *The Tipton Daily Tribune* (Indiana).

This sparked a blaze that was fueled by winds up to thirty miles an hour, destroying one-sixth of the city and resulting in an estimated 45,000 homeless. Many of these displaced persons were provided temporary shelters in U.S. Army warehouses.

"After the blaze started, I was ordered to issue live ammunition to the troops," said Wyss. "At that time, with the fire and all of the activity, they thought the Communists had started the war again."

Days later, as the fire subsided and the cause of the fire realized, the live ammunition returned to the supply sergeants and the rebuilding of the decimated city began. Wyss remained in Korean until March 1954, traveling to Ft. Carson, Colorado, where he received his discharge weeks later. The years following his discharge focused on both family and education as the veteran was married, raised three children and earned a master's and doctoral degree using the GI Bill benefits he earned in the Army. Throughout the years, the former soldier served in several leadership positions in education ranging from high school principal to vice-president of a university prior to his retirement in 1983.

Although he admits the ravages of age may have weakened his physical stamina in recent years, Wyss affirms that the value of the lessons he received in the Army has provided him unyielding inspiration throughout his entire life.

"I've drawn many lessons from my time in the service such as the importance of being of service to others...your family, your church and your country." He added, "A good soldier doesn't complain and a good soldier doesn't make excuses—you do your job to the best of your ability," Wyss said. "But most importantly, the Army demonstrated to me that you can't be a good leader until you learn first to be a follower." *(Photograph courtesy of Don Wyss)*

Richard Schroeder

California

In his rustic home situated on sixty-six acres of woodland in rural Moniteau County, Missouri, Richard Schroeder shared many chuckles while discussing the circumstances that led him into service with both the Navy and Marine Corps several decades earlier. A 1950 graduate of Jefferson City High School, Schroeder explained that serving in the military was never his ambition, especially while he was attending the Kansas City Art Institute.

"Back then, my future mother-in-law was the clerk for the draft board [in Jefferson City]," said Schroeder. "She said that if I was thinking of enlisting, I had better go ahead and do it."

Schroeder and a friend decided to visit their local recruiting office to avoid being drafted. At first, they intended to enlist in the Marine Corps, but when the line for the Navy began moving faster, they decided to switch lines. Enlisting in October 1951, Schroeder completed his boot camp at the Naval Training Center in San Diego with hopes of serving aboard submarines. Instead, the Navy decided that his services would be best utilized as a corpsman—enlisted medical specialists able to provide emergency care in a field environment.

"They sent me to Bainbridge [Maryland] Naval Training Center for hospital corpsman school," said Schroeder. "I had no desire to be a corpsman because all I could think about was [patients] puking and all of that stuff," he laughed. "So I tried to flunk out of the training by failing all of my tests."

After months of training, the former sailor humorously noted, he graduated second from the bottom of his class. Returning to Jefferson

City on leave, he married his fiancée, Carole Schreen, in July 1952. He and his wife then returned to Bainbridge, where Schroeder was assigned to an eye, ear, nose and throat clinic. Although he helped perform routine exams and assist with minor surgeries, one event demonstrated to him the dangers that existed with many types of medical treatment.

"I was assisting a doctor with a bronchoscopy and the doctor sprayed the patient with Pontocaine [topical anesthetic]," Schroeder recalled. "The guy's heart stopped and the doctor cut him open to massage his heart, but his hands were too big for the procedure. I had to stick my hands in and do it myself." Solemnly, he added, "The patient did not make it. That was a very traumatic experience for me."

The young corpsman soon discovered all sailors were required to perform sea duty or complete a tour in an overseas location, resulting in orders attaching him to the Fleet Marine Force—a landing force comprised of U.S. Marines and supported by elements of the Navy, including corpsman.

"I spent some time in training at Camp Pendleton [California] and attended what was basically a shortened Marine boot camp," he said. "Then I took field medical training, learning to deal with trauma injuries such as shock, head injuries and amputations. Also," he continued, "we were issued Marine uniforms."

He became a member of the Third Marine Division and traveled by troopship to Japan. Following his two-week journey across the ocean, Schroeder, as part of "Easy" (E) Medical Company, was attached to a headquarters unit stationed in an outpost near Nara, Japan, which, he described, was "in the middle of nowhere and surrounded by rice paddies." During the next year, he applied his medical training in a quite unexpected fashion.

"The job I was assigned was associated with venereal disease [VD]," he soberly remarked. "The [Marines] would come in with an issue and I would have to take a sample to be tested to determine if a VD or something else was causing their problems."

His duties, he noted, also required him to accompany a Japanese doctor and three Japanese police officers on weekly visits to local "establishments" to determine where the men were acquiring their ailments.

"In Japan, prostitution was legal and the government was very good at keeping everything clean," he said. "Each prostitute was given a government card with a number on it and each month they had to have a physical exam."

Also participating in regular military training maneuvers as a medic supporting amphibious landings and battle simulations, Schroeder completed his overseas tour in the summer of 1954, returning to the United States to reunite with his wife and to meet his nine-month-old son.

Schroeder completed his enlistment at a clinic on New Orleans Naval Station, receiving his discharge in September 1954. He then moved his family to Columbia, where he enrolled in the University of Missouri, using his GI Bill benefits to earn his bachelor's degree in education. In the years following his discharge, his family grew in size to three sons and a daughter. He was hired as an agent with the Missouri Department of Conservation in 1960 and went on to retire from the agency with thirty years of service.

Reflecting on his brief military career—one with many interesting and unexpected deviations—Schroeder said that he has since benefitted from the training he received, albeit in a specialty he initially viewed as objectionable.

"Although I first wanted to serve on submarines, because of the education that I received in first aid and healthcare, I was able to get a job while in college at the MU Medical Center—that really helped me support my family," he said. Had I been in the submarines, I would never have learned these skills," he added.

"But, looking back," he paused, "the best part of it all was the way it helped me grow up—I got away from my parents and all of those who regulated my activities as a young person and learned to make my own decisions." *(Photograph courtesy of Richard Schroeder)*

Virgil Koechner

Tipton

When Virgil Koechner turned seventeen years of age, he informed his father that he was tired of working on the farm, asserting it was an ideal time to strike it on his own and to "see the world." Leaving his Tipton, Missouri, area home, Koechner thought that he could fulfill his wanderlust by enlisting in the Navy—a decision that would soon carry him half a world away.

"My oldest brother had been drafted into the Army during World War II and was injured while serving with the Ninth Armored Division," said Koechner. "Since I knew I wanted to join the military and get away from home, I figured I would have a better chance of survival if I was in the Navy," he grinned.

Following his enlistment in April 1947, the aspiring sailor completed his boot camp at San Diego before traveling to Memphis, Tennessee, where he spent the next several weeks attending radio school and learning to send and receive messages through Morse code.

"They [the Navy] put me in the radio school," Koechner affirmed. "It's not something that I asked to do."

Finishing his training in late summer, Koechner's quest for excitement entered its first stages when he was assigned to the aircraft carrier *USS Princeton (CV-37)*, spending the next year repairing radios in the ship's "radio shack."

"That's where I was (aboard the *Princeton*) when Mao Zedong and Chiang Kai-shek were fighting it out in China," Koechner recalled. "They sent us over to Tsingtao, China in 1948, to basically serve as a show of force." (In 1949, Mao Zedong established the

People's Republic of China while Chiang Kai-shek and his followers formed a separate republic after fleeing to Taiwan.)

In 1949, he was transferred as a radioman to the aircraft carrier *USS Valley Forge (CV-45)*, completing only a single cruise with the ship before he was transferred to a seaplane squadron in San Diego.

"We had nine (sea)planes and about 125 sailors—ground crew, pilots and all," said Koechner. "The planes were called 'PBMs,' or 'Patrol Bomber, Martin,'" he added.

The members of the squadron were soon on their way to the Philippines, spending several months conducting patrol maneuvers and training while operating from the naval station at Sangley Point.

"On Sunday, June 25, 1950, I was sitting at a bar in the Philippines and was very happy that our squadron had just completed months of deployment and would be returning to the states soon," Koechner said. "That's when a crewman from my plane walked in and said that the Korean War had broken out and that we were leaving for Korea in the morning."

For the next several months, Koechner's seaplane squadron was assigned to clear Korean coastal areas of mines that had been placed by North Korea. The PBM was equipped with a .50 caliber machine gun that was used to fire on the floating mines, thus detonating the device and removing the threat to American ships. Though it is uncertain as to the total number of mines placed during the war, in the book *The Sea War in Korea*, authors Malcolm Cagle and Frank Manson describe a "massive field of more than 3,000 mines" that had been laid off of the North Korean port city of Wonson, all of which was done "under the direction of Soviet naval experts."[98]

"I was assigned to the radio position, relaying our position back to base and letting them know what was going on...what we were seeing," Koechner said.

Koechner and his fellow crewmembers received confirmation of the importance of their task on October 10, 1950, while operating with the *USS Pledge*—an American minesweeping vessel—near Wonsan Harbor.

---

[98] Cagle, *The Sea War in Korea*, 122.

"The *Pledge* struck a mine and was sinking," Koechner solemnly recalled. "A North Korean gun emplacement on the shore began firing on the survivors. Our PBM flew over and strafed the position with our machine gun and took out the gun," he added.

In late 1950, Koechner's squadron was called upon to fly into the Chosin Reservoir to help rescue Marines wounded in battle after they were surrounded by enemy forces. However, Koechner explained, "somebody forgot to tell the admiral that the reservoir was frozen over and we could not land on the ice."

Remaining available for the next two weeks, the reservoir never thawed enough for Koechner's squadron to make any landings, but the Marines were eventually able to fight their way through their encirclement.

After he was sent back to the United States in 1951, the sailor finished out his enlistment at Moffett Field, California, receiving his discharge in April 1952. He returned to Tipton and joined an Army Reserve unit for a few weeks, but after "sleeping on the ground" during a training exercise at Ft. Leonard Wood, decided that Army life was not for him. In 1956, the Korean War veteran married his fiancée, Mary Jane Hartman, and the couple raised six children together. Following his discharge from the Navy, Koechner was employed by Bell Telephone Company and remained with them for forty-four years.

Conceding his experiences in the Navy during the Korean War do not fit the mold cast by many of his fellow servicemembers, Koechner affirms that he recognizes the importance of the work of the seaplane squadrons during the conflict.

"In my judgment, we were successful in clearing the mines and preventing our ships from hitting them," he said. "And although it wasn't our bailiwick to take out the North Korean gun emplacement [when the USS Pledge struck a mine]—that was a job for the [fighter] jets—I'm sure our quick actions certainly saved the lives of many of those sailors." He added, "There's not many seventeen- or eighteen-year-olds that have these types of experiences happen to them...except in the military." *(Photograph courtesy of Virgil Koechner)*

Jack Gainer

California

According to a 2016 fact sheet published by the U.S. Department of Veterans Affairs, the United States suffered a staggering 33,739 "Battle Deaths" during the Korean War. Among those losses was a young man from Moniteau County, Missouri, who began his service as an enlisted soldier in the U.S. Army, but he later achieved his goal of becoming an officer in the infantry.

"Jack enlisted in 1948 after graduating from California High School," said Judy Campbell, the late veteran's sister and only sibling. "A couple of his buddies joined at the same time, so I believe that is why he chose to go in the Army."

As Campbell explained, her brother was seven years her elder and "treated her like a little princess." She added, "I remember that I didn't want him to leave for the service, but it wouldn't do me any good to argue about it—he had his mind made up."

The former Boy Scout began his military service by completing his basic training at Ft. Knox, Kentucky in late 1948. From there, he was assigned to a unit at Ft. Devens, Massachusetts, where he remained for most of 1949.

"While he was in the service, he was around a group of guys who decided to become officers and they provided the encouragement for Jack to do it as well," said Campbell.

According to the July 15, 1951 edition of the *Sedalia Democrat*, Gainer traveled to Ft. Riley, Kansas to attend officer candidate school and "received his commission as a second lieutenant" on October 5, 1950. He then traveled to Ft. Benning, Georgia for three months of training as an infantry officer. In March 1951, Lt. Gainer was able to return home for three weeks of leave before traveling to Kansas City to board a plane bound for Camp Stoneman in California. After a brief layover on the West Coast, he was aboard a ship sailing for Yokohama, Japan, from where he would soon embark upon his final military assignment.

In mid-April, Gainer arrived in Korea to command a platoon within the 32nd Infantry Regiment (IR) of the 7th Infantry Division. Elements of the regiment had been in Korea since September 1951, serving as "part of the 7th Infantry and 1st Marine Divisions (that) slammed ashore at Inchon and battered its way inland toward Seoul," noted a small book published by the first battalion of the 32nd IR during the war.

The division was already full of veterans of some of the most hellish episodes of the war—to include the bloody campaign in the Chosin Reservoir—by the time Lt. Gainer arrived in April 1951. However, that did not mean that the dangers to his personal safety had in any way diminished. The freshly trained infantry officer joined the regiment as they fought to push the North Korean and Chinese forces north of the 38th parallel. Battling on the front lines of the war, the 7th Infantry Division continued to incur heavy casualties, including the young infantry officer from Mid-Missouri.

"Jack was killed on June 6 [1951] when he was shot through the stomach by a sniper...he had only been overseas for a month," said Campbell. "It is our understanding that he was killed in the area of Chuncheon, Korea, based upon letters that our family received after this death," she added.

Though many years have passed since the death of her brother, Campbell still clearly recalls the dispiriting moment when their family first learned of his loss through the delivery of a Western Union telegram.

"On July 5 [1951]," said Campbell, while pointing at the original copy of the telegram," the local cab driver, Casey Jones, picked up the telegram at the local train depot and parked across the street from my grandmother's house, where we were living at the time." Pausing, she added, "I saw him coming and knew it was about Jack."

The body of the twenty-year-old Gainer was initially laid to rest in a cemetery in Korea, but his remains were exhumed several months later and returned to the United States in December 1951, along with the remains of twelve fellow Missourians killed during the war. During a memorial service held at the California Christian Church, reported the *Sedalia Democrat* on January 13, 1952, Gainer's mother was presented a Silver Star Medal posthumously awarded to her son. The presentation, the newspaper further explained, was made by Lt. Col. William Harvey—a former resident of California and friend of the family who was at the time assigned to Ft. Leavenworth, Kansas.

Gainer was the first of only a handful of Moniteau County residents to lose their lives in the Korean War, and was later reinterred in the California City Cemetery. Despite the many decades that have passed since her brother's death, Campbell continues to embrace the memories of Jack's mild-mannered and pleasant demeanor.

"We were really very close despite the seven-year difference in our ages," said Campbell. "He treated me wonderfully and I could do no wrong in his eyes. That's the kind of brother that he was." Pausing, she added, "Many years after the war, I believe it was in the mid-1990s, we were contacted by Kenneth Funke—who was one of Jack's sergeants and ended up earning a Bronze Star for going in to retrieve his body. I remember him talking about what a great guy Jack was and how everybody in the platoon really liked him, which was truly an honor to his memory." *(Photograph courtesy of Judy Campbell)*

Gus Fischer

Lohman

When Lohman area veteran Gus Fischer graduated from Russellville High School in late spring of 1956, he recalls a job market limited for young person's striking out on their own. During conversations he shared with older brothers who served in the military, Fischer decided an enlistment in the Navy might provide him not only an early footing in his post-high school career, but afford him the opportunity to see some of the world.

"The Navy had a program at that time called 'Kiddie Cruise,'" said Fischer. "It gave you the opportunity to sign up as soon as you turned eighteen years old and serve a three-year enlistment instead of four, getting out of the service when you turned twenty-one years old."

Enlisting on July 9, 1956, the day after he turned eighteen, Fischer traveled to the former U.S. Naval Training Station at Bainbridge, Maryland, where he completed several weeks of basic training. From there, he was sent to Newport, Rhode Island, for storekeeper school.

"My older brother who had been in the Navy told me that if I joined, I should become a storekeeper," Fischer explained. "The training basically introduced me to the organization and operation of the Navy's procurement system, including how to acquire, store and transfer various supplies."

He completed his initial training in December 1956 and returned to Lohman for a brief period of leave. In January 1957, he traveled to San Francisco to report to his first duty assignment aboard the *USS General A.E. Anderson*—a troop transport ship that had seen service during both World War II and the Korean War.

"The ship carried not only a complement of sailors, but we hauled troops and their dependents to different duty assignments in the Pacific," said Fischer. "I remember the ship going to places like Japan, Taiwan and Korea."

While assigned to the ship, Fischer's duties as a storekeeper placed him in charge of the bulk store room and, when the ship was in a U.S. Navy port, he would acquire items such as candy, cigarettes and toiletries that were later distributed to smaller retail stores on the ship.

"Since we were traveling with women and children aboard the ship, who were dependents of the troops traveling to various overseas duty assignments, we would also stock items that were suitable for them."

Finishing his one-year assignment aboard the *USS General A.E. Anderson* in January 1958, Fischer transferred to the U.S. Naval Air Base on the Kwajalein Atoll in the Marshall Islands in the west-central Pacific. It was here, he explained, that he spent the next year actively engaged in his continued duties as a storekeeper.

"The island was essentially a refueling stop for planes traveling across the Pacific," Fischer said. "My primary job was unloading ships coming into the harbor, placing the pallets in a warehouse and then later loading them aboard smaller landing craft."

As the veteran explained, he was often unaware as to the contents of the pallets he was unloading from the incoming vessels. However, he speculates it might have been materials used to support some historic testing that occurred in the vicinity of the Marshall Islands. Beginning in 1946, the United States conducted nuclear testing in the region under several operational titles and detonated atomic bombs to research the effects. While Fischer was assigned to the naval base at Kwajalein in 1958, a series of thirty-five nuclear tests were conducted under the title of "Operation Hardtack I."

Fischer said, "There was one time, I remember, being up at 5:00 a.m. and it was completely dark outside. This was during the time when the nuclear testing was going on and they detonated a bomb in the distance—the entire sky lit up for a little while as if it were daytime."

His duty on the island came to a close in January 1959, at which time he returned to the United States for this final assignment aboard another Word War II era troop transport—the *USS General W.A. Mann.*

"It was a sister ship to the previous transport I served aboard," said Fischer. "As was the case on the previous ship, I served as a store-keeper in the bulk store room and we delivered troops and their dependents to different overseas assignments. However, unlike my earlier assignment, we usually sailed out of Seattle rather than San Francisco."

A few months later, on July 7, 1959, Fischer completed his three-year enlistment and was discharged from the United States Navy. He returned to Lohman and, the following year, married Jeannette Knernschield, with whom he has raised two children. Despite the scarce employment opportunities characterizing the period prior to his enlistment, his post-Navy service included seven years as a state employee. Fischer then became a business partner with his brother when he bought into the Lohman Milling Corporation, which he managed until they sold the company in 1983. He concluded his career as a stock broker, retiring from AG Edwards in 2003.

Sitting at a table in the home that he built upon the same farm where he was raised decades ago, Fischer paused in reflection to con-sider the manner in which his service in the U.S. Navy during the late 1950s has remained an important feature in his collection of life experiences.

"It was certainly a way for me to see the world and kind of planted a seed with regard to traveling," he explained. "Since the service, my wife and I have traveled to different places overseas, such as Germany, Croatia , Slovenia and Africa." He added, "But I think most importantly, it was a way for me, as a young man, to get started in life. As I said before, I really didn't have a plan when I left high school and the Navy's 'Kiddie Cruise' program provided me the opportunity to experience the military for three years and prepare for my future." *(Courtesy of Gus Fischer)*

Donald Matthews

California

The "DEW" line—a distant early warning system designed to detect a Soviet missile attack during the Cold War—might appear to some an unremarkable section of a history book meant for reading by younger generations, but it was a tense reality lived for many months by veteran Donald Matthews.

"I guess I was just cut out for the military," said Matthews. "I had really become bored with high school and wanted to get out and see a little of the world."

Raised in the Centertown, Missouri, area, Matthews' military journey began in 1952 with his enlistment in the Missouri National Guard, but the following year, he chose to continue his military service...though along a slightly different path. Captivated by the technology-based educational opportunities offered by the Air Force, the young recruit was soon in a uniform and attending boot camp at Lackland Air Force Base (AFB), Texas.

From there, he traveled to Francis E. Warren AFB near Cheyenne, Wyoming, where he received communications training and graduated in July 1954 as an "installer cable man."

The adventure sought only months previous soon arrived when he was given orders for deployment to McAndrew AFB in New Foundland. As Matthews explained, he was provided training as a cable splicer and attached to the 22nd Communications Construction Squadron under the Northeastern Air Command, which, he noted, required temporary assignments at locations in both New Foundland and Greenland.

"At that time," he said, "the Air Force was extending the runways for the B-52s [a long-range bomber] and we were installing the communication networks for the towers and buildings around the runways." He added, "I also worked on the steel communication towers that helped transmit the information collected by the 'DEW' line, which was an imaginary line of radars that, if crossed by enemy aircraft, would provide an early warning."

Matthews also said that the B-52s were—at that time—"in the air nearly 24 hours a day" because of the perceived threat from the Soviet Union.

The young airman remained overseas for nearly two years, eventually returning to the United States in 1955. He finished the final two years of his enlistment installing communications at several stateside locations as a member of the 1st Communications Construction Squadron.

"They [Air Force] were cutting back at that time and I got the urge to finally settle down," he grinned.

Discharged in 1957, Matthews married his fiancée, Darlene Hofstetter, the following year. The couple went on to raise three children: Terry, David and Lisa. Unable to secure a civilian job in the communications industry after leaving the service, Matthews was hired as a pressman and printer with the California (Missouri) Democrat newspaper.

His life began to assume the mantle of many returning veterans—focusing his energies on a career and building a family—until a conversation with his son several years later awakened an interest in revisiting what he had previously begun.

"My oldest boy was in the [Missouri] National Guard and told me there were a lot of new benefits...and that I ought to get back in." With a grin, Matthews added, "He was kind of the instigator of it all."

In 1981, after nearly a quarter century since leaving the Air Force, Matthews enlisted in the National Guard at the age of forty-seven and went on to serve with several Mid-Missouri units. He retired from his career with the newspaper in 1986 and went to work for the state of Missouri. In 1995, he embraced "full retirement," leaving his state job and finishing his career in the National Guard with twenty years of military service.

"Now I enjoy rockin' in my rocking chair," Matthews joked.

Though he experienced a protracted break in service and enlistments spanning two branches of the military, Matthews asserts his memories of the Cold War remain the most poignant and believes the history surrounding the Soviet threat needs to be preserved.

"It was a very interesting and distressful time. We all had to wear detectors on our uniforms that would warn us of any fallout from a nuclear attack," Matthews said. "But you just went about doing whatever you were doing—making sure your job was done." In conclusion, he said, "It seems to me that a lot of the younger generation are no longer familiar with the events that I and others experienced during the Cold War and the threats that actually existed." *(Photograph courtesy of Donald Matthews)*

Blue Star Memorial Dedication

Jefferson City

On September 14, 1953 in a roadside park on Ten Mile Drive west of Jefferson City was the dedication of the area's first Blue Star Memorial marker. Pictured in the unveiling of the marker are Mrs. Frank Voss, left, Blue Star chairman of Hawthorn Garden Club and Mrs. Ernest Levy, president of Hawthorn Garden Club. Attendees at the event included Rex Whitton, who was then chief engineer of the Missouri State Highway Commission and Harris Rodgers, chairman of the commission.

During the construction of the Capital Mall in the late 1970s, the marker was moved to make room for expansion of the roads in the area and placed in the roadside park across from Steak 'n Shake on Missouri Boulevard. However, the marker has since been moved and placed at the entrance to Washington Park in Jefferson City.

Raymond Lister

Lohman

There are many reasons an individual chooses a path leading to military service—some are inspired by the service of a relative while others may seek assistance in financing a college education. In the case of Lohman veteran Raymond Lister, his motivation came from the lack of employment opportunities in his rural farm community, which, he added, led to an adventure that provided him the skills to later embark upon a successful career. Born in Bear County, Texas in 1937, Lister's family moved to Southeast Missouri in 1950. Following his graduation from a high school near Sikeston in 1955, he realized his prospects for making a living were bleak and, since he could not afford to attend college, enlisted in the United States Air Force.

"I don't know why I chose the Air Force rather than another branch of service," said Lister. "I guess it just happened to appeal to me the most."

Traveling to Lackland Air Force Base in San Antonio, Texas in February 1956, the young recruit underwent several weeks of basic training. From there, he was sent to Ft. Belvoir, Virginia, to attend a six-month refrigeration specialist course at the Army Engineer School, learning to maintain and repair different types of heating and air-conditioning units.

"I never asked to be a refrigeration specialist, that's where the Air Force sent me...probably because of my test scores when I enlisted and it was likely where there was a need at the time," Lister grinned. "Back then, the Air Force didn't offer that specific training so we had to go to an Army school to learn that type of trade."

When his training on the East Coast was finished in October 1956, Lister returned home for a brief period of leave before traveling to San Francisco to board a troop ship. He soon reported for his first official duty assignment with the 6029th Support Group at Chitose Air Base located on Hokkaido, the northernmost of Japan's four main islands. The airman spent the next year on the base working on larger, commercial style air-conditioning and heating units for service buildings such as those used for aircraft hangars and mess halls.

"While I was stationed at Chitose, I also did a little bit of traveling to the different radar sites in the area to work on some of that equipment," he recalled. "Radar units produced a lot of heat so we had to keep the air-conditioning units operational."

In November 1957, Lister was transferred to the 6143rd Air Base Group at Itazuke Air Base on Fukuoka, the southernmost of Japan's main islands. The month following his arrival at Itazuke, the United States returned the air base at Chitose to Japanese control.

"I seem to remember that the runway was right in the middle of a living area and there was a lot of rice farming that surrounded the base," the veteran explained. "There was plenty of air traffic going on there, mostly F-100s, which were very impressive aircraft." (The F-100 Super Sabre was a supersonic jet fighter.)

As Lister went on to explain, he worked out of a shop on the base and performed virtually the same activities he did while stationed at Chitose, maintaining the air-conditioning and heating equipment on many of the larger buildings including the base hospital.

"I was stationed at Itazuke for less than a year," Lister said. "When I was stationed up north, the weather was cold and dry, but when they moved me south it became cold and wet," he mirthfully recalled.

His overseas tour ended in August 1958, at which time he returned to the United States and became a member of the 312th Consolidated Aircraft Maintenance Squadron at Cannon Air Force Base in Clovis, New Mexico. He remained at Cannon until receiving his discharge from the Air Force on February 14, 1960.

"Although I learned a lot while I was in the service, I had reached a point where I didn't think the military was for me any longer," Lister said.

Two months following his return to Southeast Missouri, the veteran married Virginia, whom he met through his sister. In the years since, the couple has raised two children.

"After I got back home, I was looking for a job and went to Poplar Bluff to see if there was any work there," Lister said. "I was told by someone that there was a guy in Jefferson City looking for a person who could service air conditioners and I ended up getting that job," he added.

He worked for Harold Butzer Inc., in Jefferson City for nineteen years before moving his family to Lohman. Lister purchased the building that once housed the Lohman Milling Corporation and used the facility to operate his own heating and air-conditioning business until retiring in 2003.

Several decades have passed since Lister left the Air Force but he recognizes the role his brief experience in the military has played in providing the initial foundation upon which he built a successful career.

"The Air Force allowed me to learn a trade and it's still doing it for those of the younger generations who may be looking for a little experience because they don't want to or can't afford to go to college," the veteran explained. "Not counting the trade that I learned, the Air Force taught me how to work with people from different backgrounds and to accomplish many difficult tasks." In conclusion, he added, "I loved doing mechanical work and the service certainly gave me a challenge in learning how to accomplish my job." *(Photograph courtesy of Raymond Lister)*

James Lang

Tipton

As a young man growing up in Tipton, James Franklin Lang possessed a fascination with the skies—an interest that later led to his enlistment in the Air Force and eventual service during the Vietnam War. The conflict may have unexpectedly cost the young aviator his life. However, memories of his infectious personality and positivity still resound in the reflections of his siblings.

"He was smart and loved the stars and the sky...he could point out all of the constellations," recalled Paulette Fischer, the late veteran's younger sister. "He was also very funny and passionate about everything he did," she added.

Born November 22, 1941, Lang was the fourth of nine children. Following his graduation from Tipton High School in 1959, he spent a year attending college at the University of San Diego before transferring to the University of Missouri-Columbia. While in college, Lang began his journey toward an Air Force career while participating in the Reserve Officer Training Program (ROTC), eventually receiving a promotion "to cadet first lieutenant and assigned to the post of Squadron Administrative Officer," as noted in the February 14, 1962 edition of the *Jefferson City Post-Tribune*.

"He took pilot lessons while he was in ROTC and already had his pilot's license by the time he was commissioned," said Gene, one of Lang's younger brothers.

Upon graduation in 1963, Lang received his commission as a second lieutenant and traveled to Vance Air Force Base in Enid,

Oklahoma, where he completed his flight training and went on to earn his "wings" as an Air Force pilot the following year.

"Jim went to an Air Force base in Florida and flew fighter jets for a while," said Gene. "He then transferred to Biggs Air Force Base [now Biggs Army Air Field located on Ft. Bliss in El Paso]."

As his brother explained, while stationed in Texas, Lang met and married Alice Cordero on January 6, 1966 and the couple soon welcomed into the world their only child, Gregory.

"After his assignment in Texas, Jim was sent to Wurtsmith Air Force Base in Michigan," said his brother. "There he was flying B-52s when he got orders for Vietnam."

Beginning his overseas combat tour on February 5, 1968, Lang was stationed at Da Nang Air Base with the 20th Tactical Air Support Squadron, flying solo observation and reconnaissance missions in the cockpit of a Cessna O-2A Skymaster—a small, twin-engine aircraft designed to allow for clear ground observation. But on April 28, 1968, less than three months into his foreign service, Lang was killed in action when his unarmed aircraft was struck by enemy ground fire during a night mission, crashing in the Thua Thien Province of South Vietnam. The May 1, 1968 edition of *Sedalia Democrat* notes that Lang was initially "reported missing in action."

"I was sixteen at the time and it was a school day when they came and got us out of class and sent us home," said Paulette. "It seems that everybody in town was at our house—every minister and pastor, too—when they told us he was missing." She added, "I had the silly optimism from the time they told us he'd been shot down to the time his body was found that he was somehow still alive."

In the book *Leave No Man Behind: The Saga of Combat Search and Rescue*, the authors describe a mission into the A Shau Valley in early May 1968 to "investigate a recently detected crash site," which was confirmed to be Capt. Lang. However, they were unable to recover the body until a month later.[99]

"I remember it was on a Saturday when a blue Air Force car pulled up in front of our house with two men in uniform and a priest

---

[99] Galdorisi and Phillips, *Leave No Man Behind*, 347.

inside," said Paulette. "They asked if my parents were home and I told them that dad was at work and mom was at church." Somberly, she added, "That's when my optimism was over."

A memorial mass was held for the fallen airman on June 22, 1968 at St. Andrews Catholic Church in Tipton, after which Lang's family traveled to El Paso for burial of Lang's remains at Ft. Bliss National Cemetery. In the years since Lang's passing, his wife has remained living in Texas. Her son, who now has two sons of his own, has spent many years as a schoolteacher and administrator in Texas. In 1988, twenty years after his crash, the Veterans of Foreign Wars memorialized the fallen Air Force veteran by naming their post in Tipton in honor of the community's native son—the Capt. James F. Lang Post 5085. (The VFW post has since disbanded.)

Recently, the Lang family received a letter from an Air Force veteran from Florida who operated radios used to communicate with reconnaissance pilots during the Vietnam War. As noted in the letter, on the day Lang went missing, the radio operator "tried all day to contact [Lang] with no reply." It was not until years later, on Memorial Day of 2015, that the veteran found information regarding Lang's death through a Vietnam memorial website.

For his siblings, preservation of Lang's history of military service and legacy of giving to others has been the paramount motive behind sharing his story throughout the years following his passing.

"Telling his story keeps him alive...it preserves his memory and the history of all he was able to accomplish in such a short life," said his sister, Paulette.

With a momentary hesitation, his brother Gene concluded, "Talking about him makes me think about what he did with his life. He shared with so many people. He was thoughtful, helpful and truly happy. He brightened the lives of so many people and hopefully they have gone on to share his light with others."

In 2018, a monument was placed in the Tipton City Park as an enduring tribute to the service and sacrifice of James Franklin Lang. *(Photograph courtesy of the Lang family)*

George Kishmar

Chamois

The Cold War, for many, was a period in our nation's history filled with anxieties and fears as the United States and the Soviet Union were in a standoff with scores of missiles at their disposal—initiatives that placed each country on a heightened alert and resulted in billions of dollars being poured into various strategic programs. Chamois, Missouri, area veteran George Kishmar affirms that although he came of age during this threat-filled period of our nation's history, there was one missile program that seemed to resonate more with opportunity than concern.

"The Army recruiter came down and gave a presentation to our senior class," said Kishmar, a 1957 graduate of Chamois High School. "When he told us about the different schooling options [in the Army], I really became interested in the Nike missile program," he added.

According to a manual released April 6, 1970 by the Nuclear Training Directorate Field Command, the Nike-Ajax missiles "became operational in late 1953" and were the first generation of the Nike system, providing a weapon "whose range, altitude capabilities, and warhead lethality were far superior to the gun-type antiaircraft artillery."

Enlisting in the Army in June 1957, after he was guaranteed electronics training, Kishmar was sent to Ft. Polk, Louisiana, to complete his basic training. He then traveled to Ft. Bliss, Texas, for a forty-two-week electronics course that provided him the instruction and background necessary to serve as a maintenance person for the Nike-Ajax missile systems.

"We started out learning about basic electronics," said Kishmar, while describing his initial time at Ft. Bliss. "Back then, most of the equipment that we used still had the old vacuum tubes. We learned to troubleshoot problems with the Nike system, such as broken wires or blown fuses."

In describing the missile system, Kishmar noted that Nike "was a fairly new concept in electronic warfare—a surface-to-air missile designed to shoot down enemy aircraft." He added, "It was guided through target tracking radar and would explode near the target and send shrapnel through it, like a shotgun shell going off."

When his primary missile training was completed, the young soldier remained at Ft. Bliss for an additional twelve weeks of training on the newer Nike-Hercules missiles, which superseded the Ajax and had a surface-to-surface capability.[100] During the mid-1950s and early 1960s, nearly two hundred and fifty Nike missile sites were constructed throughout the United States to serve as protection against the threat posed by long-range Soviet bombers, and were situated in areas that would allow for defense of key strategic sites. As such, Kishmar believed that once his training was completed, he would be assigned to one of these locations.

"Instead," he said, "once I completed my training, I stayed on as an instructor at Ft. Bliss for the remainder of my enlistment."

For the next two years, the soldier helped provide classroom training for new recruits that immersed them in all aspects of maintenance and operation of the missile systems—each system, which, he noted, consisted of three radars, a computer, launcher and missiles.

"Following the classroom training, each of the four batteries in our battalion would be issued a complete [Nike missile] system to set up, operate and maintain," said Kishmar. "During the final phase of the training, we would move the equipment to (nearby) McGregor

---

[100] The deployment of the Nike Hercules occurred in 1958 and a total of one hundred and forty-five missile batteries were deployed. Deactivation of the Nike Hercules batteries was completed by 1975. The Nike Historical Society, *Hercules MIM-14*, http://nikemissile.org/IFC/nike_hercules.shtml.

Missile Range and let each battery fire three missiles at radio controlled aerial targets."[101] (The targets, he explained, were similar to propeller-driven model airplanes.)

Once the training for the aspiring missile personnel was finished, they and their equipment were sent to one of the many Nike missile sites located throughout the United States. While working as a trainer at Ft. Bliss, Kishmar recalls many humorous experiences that occurred, some of which were connected to their proximity to an Air Force base.

"Biggs Air Force Base bordered Ft. Bliss to the north, and at that time they were a Strategic Air Command and had B-36s, B-47s and B-52s stationed there," he said. "The south runway took them directly over our barracks during take-offs and the noise was deafening...especially the B-52s." He added, "If you happened to be lying in your bunk when they took off, it felt like you were going to be crushed into your mattress." With a grin, he concluded, "The local joke was [the soldiers] arguing about who would be assigned to clean the tire marks off the roof of our barracks the next morning."

Kishmar completed his enlistment and was honorably discharged on June 6, 1960, enrolling at the University of Missouri a few months later. The following year, he married his fiancée, Mary Lou Stieferman, and went on to earn his bachelor's degree in electrical engineering in 1965. The Army veteran went to work for the Boeing Corporation in Seattle, Washington, remaining with the company until his retirement in 1995 after twenty-nine years of employment. Two years later, Kishmar and his wife moved back to the Chamois area.

In addition to the experiences of working within a unique missile program during the heated period known as the Cold War,

---

[101] The McGregor Range is located in New Mexico and includes more than 606,000 acres that have been withdrawn public use and jointly operated by the Bureau of Land Management and the U.S. Army. Although the range is open year-round, it is closed to the public during Army training exercises. U.S. Department of the Interior, *McGregor Range*, https://www.blm.gov/nm/st/en/prog/recreation/las_cruces/mcgregor_range.html.

Kishmar affirms there were many valuable, less threatening lessons from his time spent in the Army.

"I had grown up in the rather isolated environment of a small town," he said, "and suddenly I was pushed into an environment of big cities from all kinds of backgrounds—it was a real eye-opener!" he exclaimed. "But the real take away from my time in the service was all of the electronics training I received in the Army because it really gave me a head start in college. And to be honest with you," he concluded, "I'd do it all again in a heartbeat since it really is an excellent way for young men and women to develop a skill and learn to work with others." *(Photo courtesy of George Kishmar)*

Bill Gerth

Jefferson City

Graduation from a Nashville area high school in 1956 was only the beginning of a technology-laden adventure for local veteran Bill Gerth. Accepted for a highly competitive Navy ROTC (Reserve Officer Training Corps) scholarship, the aspiring sailor relinquished his future to the promise of training with the newest of technologies.

"After high school, I went directly to Vanderbilt University on scholarship," he said. "I had the option to attend other universities, but I chose Vanderbilt because I knew I could live a lot cheaper if I were to remain at home."

Earning his bachelor's degree in engineering in 1960, Gerth was required to fulfill a term of service with the Navy. Enthralled by the opportunity, he requested assignment to their guided missile program.

"I always had an interest in aviation and rockets," he said, "and [the Navy] granted my wish."

Prior to departing for advanced military training, Gerth married his fiancée Erika, whom he had met in college, two days after his graduation. For the next four months, the young sailor attended the Naval Guided Missiles School at Dam Neck, Virginia, learning the fundamentals of rocket propulsion and the different types of guidance systems—specifically those related to the Talos missile (named for a figure from ancient Greek mythology).

"The Talos was a surface-to-air missile," explained Gerth. "When the missile got within certain range of its target, a proximity fuse was triggered and blew it apart," he added.

In the fall of 1960, the newly trained ensign received his first duty assignment aboard the *USS Galveston (CLG-3)*—a former light cruiser that underwent conversion into a guided missile cruiser. For the next year, Gerth remained aboard the vessel, preparing for future duty on a more technologically advanced ship.

"They trained me as the track radar officer [on the *Galveston*]," he said. "I was essentially in charge of two high-powered radars that would track targets and then send the information to missile computers which would indicate to the missile launchers how to target a potential threat."

Gerth transferred to his second and final duty assignment in late 1961, this time aboard the *USS Long Beach (CGN-9)*—a nuclear-powered guided missile cruiser undergoing construction at the Bethlehem Steel Corporation's shipyard in Quincy, Massachusetts.

"They gave me a scrap of the teak wood from the deck of the *Long Beach* since I was a plank owner," Gerth said. (A plank owner refers to a sailor of the Navy or Coast Guard who was a member of a ship's crew upon commissioning.) In his new assignment, Gerth drew upon previous experience while serving as the ship's weapons direction officer, overseeing "the computer system that tied together the tracking radar and the guidance radar."

In this capacity, he added, his duties also had him involved with the ship's Terrier missiles—surface-to-air missiles slightly smaller than the Talos. Additionally, Gerth remarked, the *Long Beach* was equipped with anti-submarine capabilities known as the ASROC, although he did not work with this system. The next two years consisted primarily of exercises throughout the Caribbean to test the ship's nuclear propulsion plant and to train crewmembers in their various specialties.

"We had exercises using drone targets, which were full-sized jet fighters controlled via remote control by another plane flying nearby," said Gerth. "When the remoted plane got close, our ship took control of it and it was then used to train us in targeting. Instead of explosives in the warheads, there was an electronics package that determined how close we got to the target after the missiles were launched."

Though most of his time aboard the ship was fairly uneventful and training-focused, Gerth notes that the Cuban Missile Crisis provided him and the crew with a brief period of unexpected excitement. Serving as the officer-in-charge of a small boat that floated a defensive perimeter around the *Long Beach* while it was anchored in Guantanamo Bay, Gerth heard an unidentified vessel approaching, which placed the handful of Marine Corps sharpshooters aboard Gerth's boat on alert.

"It was night and we could hear the boat continue to approach—and they didn't identify themselves," he said. "The Marines were ready to fire on the boat on my command, but [the boat] changed its course at the last second and it turned out to be a fishing boat." Pausing, he added, "It was really a tense moment, but I knew what I had to do to protect [the *Long Beach*]."

The sailor completed his active naval obligation in June 1963, returning to Vanderbilt University, and using his GI Bill benefits to earn a master's degree in electronics in 1964. In the years following his military service, Gerth worked in several technology-focused career fields, retiring in 2003 from an electronics security company he helped establish. The veteran maintains that although his service did not place him in harm's way—at least in a conventional sense—his time in uniform not only introduced him to new and innovative forms of technology, but also helped him to understand the threats that existed during the period known as the Cold War.

"We often tend to think of the larger conflicts—the World Wars, Korea and Vietnam—but many people don't realize that had the Cold War gone in another direction, we could have experienced a nuclear conflict that would have been catastrophic for the entire world." Firmly, he concluded, "And even if I was fortunate enough not to have been involved in any major altercations during my naval service, it imbued in me the feeling that I was dependant upon to accomplish my part of the mission. I needed to know my job—just as I relied upon others to know theirs—and that's teamwork, which was just as important as the technologies that I was exposed to." *(Photograph courtesy of Bill Gerth)*

Rick Price

Russellville

When Ronald "Rick" Price enlisted in the Army in the early 1960s, he predicted his military career might land him in an overseas assignment, such as the war beginning to unfold in Vietnam—instead, he remained stateside and became part of a secretive program, the details of which have only recently been declassified. Inducted into the Army in November 7, 1962, the Mendon, Missouri native began his basic training at Ft. Leonard Wood days later. As he neared the end of his initial training, the recruit learned of an opportunity that triggered his curiosity.

"We were told about a new program that was a 'real good deal,'" said Price. "We didn't know what it was, but they wanted people with farm experience, which I had from working on farms growing up."

The young soldier wondered if he had made the right choice in volunteering for the mysterious program, as he underwent a battery of psychological exams, including lie detector tests, to determine his fitness for the program.

"There was a group of us that began the process and it was the worst kind of thing I had ever been through," Price explained. "Especially the lie detector test...the questions they asked were very strange and they had us scared to death that we—and our families—would be thrown in jail if we didn't tell the truth."

Days before graduating basic training, Price and a group of program candidates boarded a plane bound for Denver, Colorado, reporting to Rocky Mountain Arsenal in mid-February 1963. While there, Price said, they underwent further testing which "really pared down the group." He continued, "They put us on these machines I had never seen before, something like a small combine with a hopper in front. For a week or so, all we did was drive those things up and down the road."

Days later, he traveled to Fort Dietrich, Maryland for training on how to respond when approached by individuals attempting to collect information, which Price summed up as being told "not to make friends" outside of his group. He returned to Colorado and was told to pack up his military uniforms because he would not see them again until he left the service. After a few days of training at Yuma Test Station in Arizona, he was sent to El Centro Naval Air Station in California, where he was assigned to a group of plain-clothed soldiers who had their own facilities, ID cards and work area.

"We were on TDY (temporary duty) and made sixteen dollars a day on top of our regular Army pay," he said. "Our job was to grow wheat with a very potent wheat rust on it— a mold-like substance that attacked the wheat stem."

Price also noted that he soon discovered the reason for the combine-like machines he had operated in Colorado, as he and his fellow soldiers began using the equipment to harvest the wheat rust, which was then placed in air-tight containers and shipped back to Rocky Mountain Arsenal for testing.

"The rust," Price said, "was primarily used as a very effective material that could be spread on the crops of a country, destroying them and essentially starving the population."

An article on a history website of Palm Beach County, Florida describes a similar operation that once existed on Boca Raton Air Force Auxiliary Field in the late 1950s. The Army Chemical Corps, the article states, "recruited men from the farm states of the Midwest" as part of a program to form spores from spraying wheat with a fungus that was later tested for use in biological warfare.[102]

"It was called 'Project TX,'" Price said. (A fact sheet printed by the Deployment Health Support Directorate under the Department

---

[102] Palm Beach County History Online, *U.S. Military on Boca Raton*, www.pbchistoryonline.com.

of Defense notes that "TX" is the "agent symbol for the 'fungus *Pucciniagraminis var. Tritici*,' commonly known as stem rust of wheat.")

Price spent the majority of his time at the El Centro facilities, but also performed temporary duty at locations such as Edwards Air Force Base in California, assisting in the training of soldiers new to the project.

"We were just pretty much ignored wherever we were stationed," he said. "The military people didn't know what we did—we just looked like farmers—and if questioned, we were told to say that we worked for a construction company."

During the latter part of his enlistment, Price returned to Colorado for a few weeks until receiving his discharge in November 1964, at which time he signed a fifty-year non-disclosure agreement regarding the duties he had performed. Returning to Mendon, Price enrolled in college and, in 1966, married his fiancée, Judy. He graduated with a bachelor's degree in history, education and psychology from Missouri Valley College in 1969, the same year moving to Russellville when hired as a teacher and counselor for the high school.

The following year, he left his teaching and began his employment with state government, with whom he remained until his retirement in 1991. Since then, he has kept busy while engaged in various construction pursuits. Although he believed his service would result in overseas duty, Price asserts he is proud of the unique contribution he was able to make to his country and the close friends he met along the way, despite the secretive nature of his job.

"Looking back, it really didn't seem like what we were doing was a big deal, but now I know what we were doing was an important part of preparing for national defense," Price said. "And one of the best parts of my job was the close friends I made with the few guys who worked in the project... and we still remain in contact." Mentioning an upcoming "project" reunion, Price added, "We all know each other's names and where everyone lives, and I think it is somewhat unique among military organizations that we have such a tight-knit group." *(Photograph courtesy of Rick Price)*

Melvin Stubinger

Lohman

The summer of 1961 should have been an enthusiastic period for Lohman area resident Melvin Stubinger as he had recently graduated from Russellville High School and prepared to embark upon establishing a career for himself. However, with the military draft a pervasive reality for men of his age, he realized there was an important decision he needed to make.

"It was one of those situations where you knew that Uncle Sam was going to get you sooner or later, so I decided to go ahead and enlist to get it out of the way," Stubinger explained. With a grin, he added frankly, "I decided to join the U.S. Army because I figured it was about the easiest branch of service to get into at that time."

Taking his oath of enlistment in St. Louis on July 29, 1961, the young recruit was soon aboard a bus and on his way to Ft. Leonard Wood for basic training. Several weeks later, he traveled to Ft. Sill, Oklahoma for advanced training in "artillery surveying."

"That was a situation where the Army decided they needed me in a specific job and that's where they put me. I didn't have any choice in the matter," he affirmed.

During his final two months at the Oklahoma post, Stubinger and his fellow soldiers spent many hours in both the classroom and participating in field training exercises to learn how to operate a theodolite—a device that helped them complete the calculations that were provided to the gunners directing the fire of large guns such as the 155mm howitzer. When his initial training was completed in December 1961, Stubinger was sent to San Diego and boarded a military transport bound for the Hawaiian island of Oahu.

Upon his arrival, he was assigned to Headquarters Battery, 3rd Battalion, 13th Artillery located at Schofield Barracks—a U.S. Army installation established in 1908 to provide for a mobile defense of Pearl Harbor and the island. Settling into the routines of Army life, Stubinger recalls that his battery soon began a cycle of training exercises and maneuvers to maintain their respective proficiencies of firing and supporting the howitzers.

"We would go out and practice firing the guns while set up in the middle of sugar cane and pineapple fields on Oahu," Stubinger said. "There were many times when they had to limit the amount of powder they could use in the projectiles because sometimes there just wasn't enough space to fire the guns at full capacity," he added.

Once a year, Stubinger further explained, the battery would conduct a month-long training exercise on the "Big Island" of Hawaii. They would load their equipment on LSTs (Landing Ship, Tank) and set up on lava fields, which was an open area that afforded them more space and fewer restrictions when firing the howitzers. While stationed on Oahu, Stubinger was also assigned to a funeral detail supporting the burial of veterans in the National Cemetery of the Pacific in the Punchbowl Crater in Honolulu. Some of these funerals, he explained, were not only for local veterans who passed away, but also for the internment of remains that were located of World War II veterans killed in Pacific battles.

"The way the sound carried in the Punchbowl whenever they played Taps at a funeral just made the hair stand up on the back of your neck," said Stubinger. "It was one of those experiences that you never forget."

During his tour in Hawaii, the young soldier also had the opportunity to visit Pearl Harbor and witnessed many remnants of the devastation that resulted from the Japanese attack in World War II.

"You could still see oil slicks in the harbor because of the liquids leaking from the sunken ships," he said. "There were a lot of buildings, including our barracks on Schofield Barracks, which still showed bullet damage from the strafing from Japanese airplanes."

In July 1964, Stubinger packed his few belongings and boarded a Navy LST bound for the West Coast. Upon his arrival back in the United States, he received his discharge papers from the Army and returned to Mid-Missouri. In the years that followed, Stubinger married, raised two children and completed a thirty-four-year career with a local telephone service company. He and his wife, Joan, visited Hawaii in the early 1990s. However, it had become virtually unrecognizable to the former soldier.

"The pineapple and sugar cane fields were all gone and even the parade fields we had at Schofield were covered with new housing complexes built for the military members stationed there," he said. "Even along the highways, rows and rows of houses had popped up and I could no longer tell when we went from one town to another... it all just ran together."

Time may now separate the veteran from his initial experience as a soldier in Hawaii, but as Stubinger explained, there remain many poignant memories of his youthful military experience that will not diminish despite the passage of years.

"The one thing I learned is that pineapples taste a lot better when they are ripe out of the field," he chuckled. "But seriously, my time in the Army was important because it really made me grow up since I was on my own and the decisions that I made were mine to own." He added, "And there was the prestige of being selected to serve on the funeral details in the Punchbowl. For me, there was nothing more important than making sure those who served received the appropriate final honors they had earned." *(Photograph courtesy of Melvin Stubinger)*

Glen Stubinger

Lohman

The Vietnam War was a pervasive reality for young men of the draft age, such as Glen Stubinger, who graduated from Russellville High School (Russellville, Missouri) in 1967. For a couple of years after finishing high school, he was able to continue in the exhausting work on his family's farm through a draft deferment. However, when his deferment expired in 1969, he chose to enlist in the United States Marine Corps.

"I didn't want to be drafted into the infantry and I was going to have to do two years [of military service] either way, so I enlisted because the recruiter said that he was sure that he could get me some type of schooling," Stubinger recalled.

He went on to complete his boot camp at the Marine Corps Recruit Depot in San Diego followed by several weeks of training as a teletype operator, the latter of which provided instruction on how to relay and receive encrypted messages.

"As part of the [teletype] training, I had to be able to type a certain number of characters in a minute," Stubinger explained. "I had never typed before in my life and had some difficulties at first, but I eventually was able to get by," he grinned.

After returning home for a couple weeks of leave in December 1969, he reported to his first duty assignment with the 2nd Reconnaissance Battalion located at Camp Lejeune—a Marine Corps base in Jacksonville, North Carolina, with several miles of beaches that can be used for amphibious assault training. As Stubinger bluntly explained, his first stint as a fully trained Marine was anything but glamorous, but was still full of moments he seemed to enjoy nonetheless.

"I walked a lot of guard duty there," he said. "They also put me in the mess hall making salads and such for a while, which I liked except for having to get up so early," Stubinger chuckled. "While I was there, there were never any teletype machines that worked and I never sent a teletype message the entire time I was in the service."

In the summer of 1970, Stubinger believed that his opportunity for Vietnam combat duty was quickly approaching since he received orders for overseas service. Traveling to Okinawa, he was assigned to a headquarters company with the 1st Marine Division at Camp Schwab. In the book *Not Your Ordinary Vietnam War Stories,* Jim Pepper wrote "During (President) Nixon's 1970-71 drawdown of American troop strength, getting an assignment overseas...ranged somewhere between difficult to nearly impossible—even more impossible to get specific orders directly into Vietnam."[103]

Stubinger said, "That was about the time they were bringing people out of Vietnam and not sending in replacements. They kept me at Camp Schwab and my job was working in an office typing weekly training schedules and to go around to the different companies in the battalion to check equipment statuses—what was working, what was broke, what needed repairs."

While stationed in Okinawa, Stubinger—who was accustomed to the Mid-Missouri threat of tornadoes—received his first and only exposure to the Pacific typhoon season and the intensity generated by hurricanes.

"We had to stay in the barracks for a couple of days and that was about the extent of things that I can remember," he said, adding, "other than there being lot of rain and wind."

When his two-year enlistment ended in April 1971, Stubinger boarded a troop ship and was sent to Treasure Island, San Francisco, where he received his discharge from the Marine Corps. From there, he returned to his family's farm near the historic community of Millbrook (south of Lohman, Missouri). In 1973, he was mar-

---

[103] Pepper, *Not Your Ordinary Vietnam War Stories,* 154.

ried to Donita Wolfe and the couple went on to raise five children. Following the death of his father, Stubinger made the decision to cut back on his farming operations and went to work full-time for WAVCO Construction, retiring from the company in 2016 after twenty-four years of employment.

A member of St. Paul's Lutheran Church in Lohman and the American Legion in Jefferson City, Stubinger mirthfully said of the time he spent in the service, "I'd never go through any of that again but I'm glad that I went through it in the first place."

Though the years of the Vietnam War were ones of great insecurity for many young men who did not know what experiences that draft might deliver them, Stubinger affirms that a brief stint in the military might prove to be of lasting benefit to the younger generations.

"It was a good experience and I got the opportunity to see parts of the world that I wouldn't have seen otherwise," he said. "The way they teach you discipline was quite a rude awakening for me," he wryly grinned, "but you sure do learn how to take orders quickly." He added, "Not only did the entire experience provide me with a lot of good lessons, it is really something that I think wouldn't hurt everyone to go through after they leave high school." (*Photograph courtesy of Glen Stubinger*)

Melvin Loesch

Lohman

Many idyllic images often come to mind when picturing Christmas as celebrated in France. The holiday, as celebrated in this European nation, might to some serve as the perfect backdrop for unspoiled festivity, but for Millbrook, Missouri, resident Melvin Loesch, it brought feelings of homesickness for a young man serving with the U.S. Army thousands of miles from home.

"It certainly wasn't home to me and it was the first time that I had been away from my family...and that's pretty much the kind of thoughts that go through your mind in such situations," said Loesch during a recent interview.

Growing up on a farm not far from Lohman, Loesch explained that his journey with the Army began shortly after his graduation from Russellville High School in 1961, when he realized the draft might soon draw him into the service.

"I remember that the Army recruiter came out to the farm and rode on the back of the tractor while I hauled corn out of the corn-field," grinned Loesch. "He guaranteed me that I could get training as a welder if I enlisted, which is what I wanted," he added.

Enlisting in October 1961, within weeks Loesch was undergoing his basic training at Ft. Leonard Wood. After his graduation, he traveled to Aberdeen Proving Grounds in Maryland, where he spent the next three months learning basic welding skills.

"I really went in the service for the welding training," said Loesch. "In Maryland, we learned to do some welding on armor plating and some aluminum wire welding, but we didn't do any of that kind of work when I got to my unit." He added, "We got to go into [Washington] D.C., a couple of nights while I was stationed in Maryland and for an eighteen-year-old coming straight off of the farm, that was quite an experience."

In mid-May 1962, the newly trained soldier traveled to Ft. Dix, New Jersey, and was soon aboard the *USNS General Maurice Rose*—a transport ship built during World War II—to make the seven-day journey to the port at Bremerhaven, Germany. Shortly after arriving overseas, Loesch was boarding a train and traveled to his first overseas duty assignment with Company B, 97th Engineer Battalion (Construction).

"I was stationed in Toul, France, in what was at one time the Joan of Arc Hospital [Jeanne d' Arc Hospital]," said Loesch. "It had been a hospital during World War II, I believe, but when I was there in the 1960s it had been converted into a military compound with barracks and offices."

The soldier soon became a participant in a number of construction endeavors, one of which included the erection of a 40' x 100' storage Quonsets along an airfield. The buildings, Loesch recalled, were disassembled in the United States and shipped to France to be rebuilt for use in storing NATO supplies.

"What I did on that project was to weld the framework used to lower the doors onto the Quonsets," he said. "I did a lot of temporary duty supporting construction projects in other locations." He added, "On one occasion, I welded the window frames for an addition being built onto a building that was used to rebuild engines for military equipment."

A substantial construction project that Loesch recalls was for a hangar to be used in "Exercise Big Lift,"—a major NATO military exercise in 1963 that was intended to demonstrate the United States' ability for rapid deployment of troops and equipment to Central Europe. The hangar was disassembled at Ft. Belvoir, Virginia, stored and later sent to France to be reassembled.

"We built this big hangar at the U.S. Army Field Maintenance and Avionics Center at the Brienne-le-Chateau Army Airfield [France]," said Loesch. "I ended up having to make a bunch of parts that were missing, such as drainage pieces for the sewers and other odds and ends."

The battalion later transferred to a depot at Nancy, France, where Loesch continued to use his welding skills to support a number of missions. Additionally, he noted, the frenetic nature of his duties were not enough to keep his mind off of home, especially during the two Christmas holidays he spent overseas.

"We didn't do much during the holidays other than hang around the base and relax," Loesch said. "That first Christmas I did get a little homesick but I remember that we went to a local orphanage and fixed all of the children there a nice Christmas dinner." He added, "I had almost forgotten about this until looking through some old photos recently."

The soldier returned to Ft. Dix, New Jersey in December 1964 and was discharged shortly thereafter. He married Marjorie Leithauser in 1966 and the couple raised two children. In the years after the war, Loesch worked forty years for the Jefferson City News Tribune, retiring as a foreman in the pressroom in 2006.

During the three years he spent in the Army, much of it in a foreign country far removed from the familiar surroundings of family and home, Loesch explains that it was a brief experience that provided him with opportunities he would have otherwise never encountered.

"It put a whole new perspective on life for me and gave me the chance to travel to several places in Europe and see and experience things I otherwise wouldn't have been able to as a boy coming off of the farm," he said. He concluded, "Also, I had the opportunity to see and experience all of these things in a non-hostile way that would not have been possible many years earlier, while World War II was taking place." *(Photograph courtesy of Melvin Loesch)*

Larry Fletcher

Lake Ozark

In the years following his service in the Vietnam War, local veteran Larry Fletcher fervently searched for books about the Air Force's special operations squadrons and the pilots and crews who operated the AC-119G "Shadow" gunships. When he discovered this was a historical niche largely overlooked, the Air Force veteran chose to fill the gap with a narrative based upon his personal experiences.

"There just didn't seem to be anything about [the special operations squadrons], so I decided to take it upon myself and write about it," said the Lake Ozark veteran.

A 1961 graduate of California (Missouri) High School, Fletcher pursued an education by attending Southwest Missouri State College (now Missouri State University), graduating with a bachelor's in education in 1965. The following year, he graduated from the University of Missouri-Columbia with a master's degree in education.

"My father fought the Japanese in the Pacific during World War II and then worked as a mechanic at the Ford garage [in California] much of his life," said Fletcher. "I remember him telling me I wasn't going to be a mechanic like him and that I was going to attend college," he added.

Initially, Fletcher's professional outlook did not gravitate toward a military career despite the war raging in Vietnam. Instead, he fulfilled his desire to become an educator by teaching at a high school in Illinois his first year out of college. In 1967, he transferred to St. Charles (Missouri) High School and began teaching several classes while also coaching sports.

"I remember the superintendents had to write letters to the Moniteau County draft board requesting a teacher deferment," said Fletcher. "But one day, during a current events class I was teaching, a student asked me how I kept from getting drafted." Fletcher continued, "When I told him I had a teacher's deferment, you should have seen the look on his face...like I was a big chicken or something of the sort."

During a "snow day" at the school, Fletcher decided to visit a local recruiting office and was soon signing the enlistment papers to become an Air Force pilot although he had never before set foot on an airplane. In June 1968, the young recruit arrived at Lackland Air Force Base, Texas, undergoing a ninety-day course designed to train officer candidates in the fundamentals of serving in the Air Force. Upon his graduation later that summer, the newly commissioned lieutenant moved to nearby Randolph AFB to begin fifty-three weeks of flight training.

"Pilot training consisted of three stages—the first was thirty hours of flying a T-41, which was basically a Cessna 172 used for initial pilot training. After that," he explained, "we moved on to sixty hours in a T-37, which was a twin-engine subsonic jet. The final phase was ninety flying hours in a T-38 Talon." For a number of years, the T-38 held the world record for climb rate."

Completing his initial flight training in October 1969, Fletcher received his Air Force "silver wings." Shortly thereafter, he learned that he would be assigned to fly the AC-119—a prop twin-engine, side-firing gunship. Survival and POW (prisoner of war) training in the states of Washington and Idaho were completed before the crew trained on AC-119 gunships in Ohio. In April 1970, Fletcher received orders for Vietnam, reporting to Tan Son Nut Air Base (near Saigon) as a member of the 17th Special Operations Squadron.

"We flew the AC-119Gs," he said, "which was the 'Shadow' model. It was a twin-engine gunship with four 7.62 mm miniguns—one gun would fire 6,000 rounds per minute." He continued, "Our mission was direct close air support of American and Allied ground forces. We could talk directly to the troops on the ground from the airplane and direct our fire as necessary."

As the former pilot explained, the plane was equipped with a night observation scope (NOS) that would assist in the detection of enemy troops, mortar positions and anti-aircraft guns. Information from the NOS was processed through an onboard computer and relayed to the aircraft commander pilot's gun sight. With a crew complement of four officers and four enlisted personnel, Fletcher affirms that their "Shadow "successfully operated on teamwork, completing one hundred and seventy-seven combat missions that carried them throughout Vietnam and Cambodia.

"It was like the Wild West with everything going on over there," he said, "but we were able to save a lot of friendly troops, villages, garrisons and convoys with our air support."

After leaving Vietnam in May 1971, the combat veteran remained in the Air Force until resigning his regular commission at the rank of captain on August 15, 1973 to return to his career in teaching. In later years, he earned his doctorate in education at the University of Missouri and served in several educational capacities to include superintendent of California R-1 School District.

Though retired since 1997, Fletcher has remained active in preserving the history of those who served in the special operations squadrons, dedicated to sharing stories from the Vietnam War that he believes have remained largely undocumented. He has written several novels based upon his experience in the Air Force, including *Shadows of Saigon*, *The Shadow Spirit* and *Charlie Chasers*.

"It was the war of our generation...and it was a bad war," Fletcher said. "When I came back from Vietnam, I had two more years to serve on my five-year obligation. When I separated from the Air Force, I hung up my uniforms and went back to teaching. For years, hardly anybody even knew that I had served in the military. But, I went on thinking that someday a scholar would write about the special operations gunships, but nobody ever did."

With a brief moment of reflection, he concluded, "These books, everything I have written, is stuff that I carried in my head for twenty-eight years. Much of what we did, especially the missions over Cambodia, were top secret and no one—not even those on the air base [Tan Son Nut]—knew what missions we had completed."
(Photograph courtesy of Larry Fletcher)

Donley Dan Amick

Jefferson City

Donley "Dan" Amick recognizes that although the Vietnam War is often viewed as an unpopular conflict, his personal decision to join the military during this tumultuous period was motivated by a desire to serve the nation he loves.

"I thought that we had a good thing going here [in America," said Amick, "and believed that I should be willing to fight for it...to give something back."

Amick's journey to the military did not commence immediately upon his graduation from Jefferson City (Missouri) High School in 1966. Instead, it waited until he completed two years of college in mid-Missouri. But after watching his older brother return from his own combat tour of duty with the Marine Corp in Vietnam, Amick soon decided, "Why not me, too?"

Graduating from Marine Corps boot camp in December 1968, Amick embarked for Camp Pendleton, California, where he completed six weeks training with an infantry training regiment, undergoing a rigorous introduction to a cycle of tactics and weapons instruction.

"I came home for about fifteen days of leave and then went to a training battalion for a month or so," Amick said, "where I was given fire direction control training with the artillery."

Weeks later, the untested recruit traveled to 29 Palms, California, a location he describes as "a huge artillery base situated in the middle of the Mojave Desert" and which is currently the home of the Marine Corps Air Ground Combat Center. It was here, Amick said, he was

451

first exposed to the notion that even when a recruit is trained to perform within a specific military occupational field, the needs of the Corps always takes precedence.

"They placed me in the intelligence section with the headquarters for the 5th Field Artillery Group," he grinned. "I was told they were short of intelligence personnel."

However, the pendulum would soon swing the other direction in the latter part of August 1969, as Amick received orders for Vietnam—a deployment that would return him to his previously trained specialty. Arriving in Da Nang the following month, the twenty-one-year-old Marine remained in a "replacement depot" for a few days before receiving assignment to 3rd Battalion, 11th Marines at a location known as "Hill 55/LZ [landing zone] Baldy."

As the veteran described, "I reverted back to a fire direction control MOS (military occupational specialty). We had six guns—105 (millimeter) Howitzers—and provided direct fire support to Marines operating in the field. Part of my job," Amick added, "was to convert coordinates on a map [called via radio by Marines operating in forward observational locations in the field] and determine such things as elevation, height of the gun, powder charge and type of explosive to be used."

The pace of warfare soon resulted in a fluctuation in duty assignment, moving Amick to other Marine Corps bases such as LZs Ross, Ryder and Bushwack, the latter which was located upon mountainous terrain along the Que Son Valley.

"All that was up there was our six 105s and all the people it took to support them...about a hundred of us," he said. "We spent eight hours on duty and eight hours off—and other intermittent duty—and that's all we knew for about six months."

Amick also noted that many of his duty locations, including Ryder and Bushwack, were so remote that supplies such as C-rations, water, explosives, personnel (and the bulky Howitzers) had to be brought in by helicopter. Though much of his time was with I Battery of 3rd Battalion, the combat veteran was transferred to H Battery during the latter part of his deployment, with whom he remained until leaving Vietnam in September 1970. After spending a few days in Okinawa for what he jokingly refers to as his "decompression" from combat, Amick flew back to San Diego and was mustered out of the service. In later years, the former Marine utilized his GI Bill benefits to become a union electrician, from which he retired in 2013 after dedicating more than four decades to the vocation.

While many of his experiences from Vietnam contain memories he would assume leave in a combat zone so many decades ago and thousands of miles from home, Amick remains proud of his role with the Marines and what he and his comrades did to help maintain the strength of the nation.

"This country is worth fighting for and you don't have to be a Marine, in the Coast Guard, Army or any military branch to defend it," he said. "Our nation is just too good to not be willing to give back in some capacity."

A declaration based upon experience, Amick added, "Much of Vietnam was a dirty war with one-on-one combat and a high level of unpopularity back here...at home. But there's a lot of people who don't realize that they are enjoying freedoms they never earned, but were paid for by men and women willing to give their lives to defend it." *(Photograph courtesy of Donley Dan Amick)*

John Bamvakais Jr.

Jefferson City

March 30 of each year has been designated in Missouri law as Vietnam Veterans Day, a brief moment in time "designed to encourage Missourians to observe the day with appropriate events, activities and remembrances of those who served during the Vietnam conflict," as noted in a press release from former Missouri Gov. Jay Nixon. Most profound of these efforts, however, are instances spent in reflection of the more than 1,400 Missourians who lost their lives during the war, as families and friends strive to ensure the sacrifices of their loved ones never fade from public awareness.

"We grew up in a family of ten kids—five boys and five girls," recalled Tony Bamvakais, while discussing the life of his older brother, John Bamvakais Jr. "Our father had served during World War II and John [Jr.] wanted to follow in his footsteps," he added.

The Bamvakais family moved to Jefferson City from St. Louis in 1963, where their father served as a staff officer with the Missouri National Guard's 35th Command Headquarters.

"My brother [John Bamvakais Jr.] attended Jefferson City High School and enlisted in the Army after he graduated in 1965," said Tony. "What's interesting is that for the brief time he was in the service, he actually followed in our father's footsteps because he went on to serve in the same unit that our father had served in during World War II."

Completing his basic training at nearby Ft. Leonard Wood in early 1966, Bamvakais then traveled to Ft. Benning, Georgia for his advanced and airborne training. Assigned to 4th Battalion, 503rd

Infantry, 173rd Airborne Brigade, Bamvakais soon received the opportunity to apply in combat the skills he had acquired during his training. He deployed to Vietnam in July 1966 and joined the paratroopers of the 173rd Airborne Brigade who had earned the distinction as the first U.S. Army ground combat unit committed to the war upon their arrival the previous year.

Bamvakais and his fellow soldiers would make history once again when participating in an offensive known at Operation Cedar Falls, which has since been recognized as one of the largest American ground operations of the war. During the operation, nearly 16,000 U.S. soldiers from the 1st and 25th Infantry Divisions, 173rd Airborne Brigade and 11th Armored Cavalry Regiment, joined 14,000 South Vietnamese troops in an effort to disrupt insurgent operations in the area of Thanh Dien Forest Preserve and the Iron Triangle—a sixty-square-mile area of jungle believed to contain communist base camps and supply dumps in the vicinity of Saigon.

Beginning January 8, 1967, the operation lasted for eighteen days and led to the wounding of Bamvakais on January 12 when he was "hit in the right foot by hostile arms fire while on a combat operation," as noted in the January 14, 1967 edition of *The Daily Capital News*. The injury resulted in his treatment at a forward medical area and receipt of his first Purple Heart. Later that summer, after finishing his one-year tour, Bamvakais briefly returned to Jefferson City to visit his family. However, demonstrating the zeal of determination forged in fellowship of combat, he volunteered to serve an additional six months in the Southeast Asian country he had just recently departed.

Shortly after his return overseas, the September 29, 1967 edition of the *Jefferson City Post-Tribune* reported that the twenty-year-old soldier went "missing in action Thursday after a search and destroy mission...." His father, then a lieutenant colonel with the National Guard, received the disheartening news in a report from a senior Army advisor at Ft. Leonard Wood.

His brother explained, "[On September 28] he was on patrol with his unit. They were crossing over a river on a rope bridge when he was shot, fell down into the river and disappeared," Tony Bamvakais solemnly noted.

Days later, the fallen soldier's remains were recovered and returned to Jefferson City. Following the funeral service held at St. Joseph's Catholic Church on October 10, 1967, he was laid to rest at Resurrection Cemetery with military honors provided by the Missouri National Guard. In 1968, Bamvakais' parents returned to their hometown of St. Louis, at which time they had their son reinterred at Jefferson Barracks National Cemetery.

"I still have those memories of us growing up in St. Louis when me and John played Army in some alley and would use 2x4s for bazookas," Tony laughed. "It just seemed as if he was just meant to be a soldier someday."

Tony explained that although his older brother's dedication to his country resulted in the forfeiture of his life, one of the most enduring tributes was the support that poured forth from their Mid-Missouri community.

"The funeral was packed," he said. "I remember that it was so busy that people were still leaving the church even after the funeral service at the cemetery had already ended. But what was most profound," he paused, "was that even at a time when so many Vietnam vets returned home only to be unfairly judged and called horrible names like 'baby killers,' that never happened in Jefferson City. Everyone in the community was wonderful. They were very supportive and recognized that he had made the ultimate sacrifice."

Bamvakais was awarded posthumously a second Purple Heart, Army Commendation Medal and Armed Forces Honor Medal, and is recognized on Panel 27E/Line 23 of the Vietnam Memorial in Washington, D.C. *(Photograph courtesy of Tony Bamvakais)*

James Wood

Eldon

Sifting through documents on his kitchen table, Eldon resident Mike Wood paused to grab the telegram his parents received more than fifty years ago regarding the death of their oldest son in Vietnam. Then, grasping a small piece of paper with handwritten notes on it, Wood stated, "These are the names of the other Eldon men killed in Vietnam—Richard Claxton, Jimmy Lester and Arthur Wood." He added, "There were more than 58,000 killed in the Vietnam War and each one of them has a story."

Jim Wood was born in Eldon on September 2, 1947, the oldest of four brothers. His father, Joe Wood, had served with the U.S. Navy in World War II and was well known in the community for repairing electronics and operating Woods Radio and TV for more than fifty years. Graduating from Eldon High School in 1965, Jim Wood was a tour guide at Stark Caverns (known for many years as Fantasy Caverns) near Eldon and later began a management trainee program with the local Mattingly Brothers Store—a company that ran five-and-dime stores in several small towns.

"In terms of age, I was two years younger than Jim so we were close," said Mike Wood. "I can remember that in the summer of 1966, when Jim had been drafted, but was not yet inducted into the Army, we took a trip to the Southwest [United States] in his 1960 Chevy that he had bought for nine hundred dollars." Wood added, "He was proud of that car and during the trip, the muffler and the tail pipe fell off and we had to wire it up for the trip back home.

When that happened," he chuckled, "I think some of Jim's pride in that car diminished."

Entering active military service in the U.S. Army on October 19, 1966, Jim Wood was sent to Ft. Leonard Wood to complete his basic training. From there, he received orders for Vietnam and assigned to the 19th Engineer Battalion of the 45th Engineer Command.

"I remember taking Jim to the airport in Kansas City to leave for his service in Vietnam," said Mike Wood. "I can still see that plane taking off...and that Jim was not at all bitter about having to go. He saw it as his duty. Before he got on the plane, he said, 'I'll see you in a year.'"

A brief history on the website of Ft. Knox, Kentucky notes that in March 1965, the 19th Engineer Battalion "deployed to Vietnam in an amphibious landing on the beaches of Qui Nhon"—a coastal city in central Vietnam. The battalion's primary mission became to "upgrade highway QL-1 from virtually a dirt trail to an all-weather road from Qui Nhon to Bong Son."[104]

When he arrived in Vietnam on March 22, 1967—two years after the 19th Engineer Battalion first landed in country—Jim Wood was appointed to run the Post Exchange at the base camp at Qui Nhon because of the managerial retail experience he had acquired prior to entering the military.

"It is my understanding that it wasn't a major retail operation like one you would have seen at a major Army base," said Mike Wood. "It was a small camp out away from things and Jim said they often had problems getting supplies to stock the store."

While Wood ran the camp exchange, the soldiers of the battalion continued forward with construction projects designed to improve roads in the region. As the young soldier from Eldon neared the end of his one-year deployment to Vietnam, he trained up his replacement to run the exchange and then spent his final few days in country as security for the battalion's construction equipment. On February 15, 1968, while acting as security for a bucket loader operator traveling to a fill site along National Highway QL-1 south of

---

[104] 19th Engineer Battalion, *History*, www.knox.army.mil.

Sa Huynh, Vietnam, Wood became the first casualty of the Vietnam War from Eldon, Missouri.

"As they neared the site they were suddenly fired upon by hidden Viet Cong riflemen," wrote Capt. Larry S. Bonine in a letter addressed to Wood's parents dated March 17, 1968. Bonine added, "His comrades rallied around him and medical aid was summoned immediately, but to no avail."

The commander's letter was accompanied by communication from the battalion's chaplain, Capt. James T. Jackson. He noted that two memorial services were held for Wood on February 17, 1968— the first for the company to which he was assigned in the final days of his Vietnam service and a second at the base camp where he had run the camp exchange, "at the request of his many friends that knew him there." The chaplain added, "I met Jim shortly after my arrival in the unit, nearly eight months ago, and came to know him very well. He was liked and respected by everyone who knew him and we all feel his loss very deeply."

As Mike Wood explained, "When they returned his body a couple of weeks later, his funeral service was held at First Baptist Church here in Eldon and I think so many people showed up to it that they couldn't all get in. Since he was the first local Vietnam casualty, it was really a shock to the community."

Time has done little to erase Mike Wood's memories of his older brother—a young man adored by his family who looked forward to coming home from the war. However, despite the loss of a "typical rural boy that loved sports, hunting and fishing," he recognizes that his brother and others who died in Vietnam will always be more than a statistic.

"Jim had a story, just like all the other citizens who were killed in Vietnam," said Mike Wood. "When he had to go overseas, even in the midst of an unpopular war, Jim never questioned the politics of the situation but rather saw it as his duty. Even after fifty years," he added, "it's still tough to think about his loss." *(Photograph courtesy of Mike Wood)*

John Knaup

California

The period of the Vietnam War was filled with many fears and uncertainties, leaving many to wonder of the outcome of the war raging in Southeast Asia. Yet one promise seemed to remain in the forefront of every young man's thoughts: the potential of being caught in the military draft. Upon his graduation from Jefferson City High School in 1964, local resident John Knaup knew that he might one day end up in a military uniform, but chose to first pursue his education at Lincoln University.

"Let's just say that I wasn't really focused on my studies back then and ended up leaving school," Knaup humorously explained. "I knew at that point they were going to draft me, so I decided to join the Navy and hopefully not have to go to Vietnam." Smiling, he added, "Instead, I ended up going to Vietnam twice because that's where [the Navy] liked to send us, it seemed."

The recruit attended his basic training at Great Lakes, Illinois in April 1966 and then transferred to Port Hueneme, California, beginning several weeks of training to become a light vehicle mechanic for the "Seabees"—a group of sailors possessing both construction knowledge and fighting abilities.

"I told them that my first choice was to serve on submarines and my second choice was to be a Seabee, but I didn't pass the depth perception test," Knaup said. "That's at least what they told me...but maybe they were just in need of Seabees really bad," he grinned.

Completing his training, Knaup was assigned to the 31st Naval Construction Regiment on Port Hueneme, which he describes as "little more than a holding company" where he performed "horribly mundane duties" such as sweeping and painting barracks. In May 1967, he was assigned as a light vehicle mechanic with Mobile Construction Battalion 3 (MCB3) and deployed to Vietnam, where his newly acquired skills were modified for a lube rack, changing oil and performing maintenance on bulldozers and other heavy equipment.

"We arrived at Phu Bai [an Army and Marine airbase that now serves as an international airport] and the battalion started building a brand new base about ten or twelve miles from the A Shau Valley," he said.

For several months, Knaup explained, the Seabees operated forward of the rest of the troops assigned to the area while they built a new base, with a battery of 155mm howitzers positioned to the rear to provide any necessary artillery support.

"Six months or so into our deployment," Knaup shared, "we came under attack. The artillery began firing rounds that were supposed to be forward of us, but they hadn't properly plotted our location," he added.

By the time the episode ended, two of his fellow Seabees were killed and seventeen wounded because of outgoing American artillery rounds falling short of their intended targets.

"You got as close to the ground as your body would let you," he said. After that incident," he glumly noted, "we built ourselves much better bunkers."

Knaup recalls leaving Vietnam in late January 1968, days before the eruption of the famed Tet Offensive. He remained in Port Hueneme for five months of stateside training, returning with MCB3 to Vietnam in July 1968.

"This time they sent us to Da Nang and we relieved another Seabee Battalion," he said. "I was placed in charge of a tire shop and had another soldier working for me and two older Vietnamese men that had worked for the French Army."

With a battalion of seven hundred sailors, Knaup said, he and his crew remained busy repairing damaged tires for all of their assigned equipment. By March 1969, the battalion's tour ended and they returned stateside, where Knaup received an early discharge after completing two tours in Vietnam. The following year, he married his fiancée, Linda, and the couple soon welcomed their only son, John. The veteran went on to spend several years working for a local supply company and retired in 2007.

"There was no fanfare when I came home. I wasn't treated any better or worse than I was before I went [to Vietnam]...it was like it never happened," Knaup said, when reflecting on overseas service nearly five decades past.

Though he has since faced medical concerns that were a result of his exposure to chemicals in Vietnam and has faced the realization that many of his fellow Vietnam veterans did not receive the homecoming they deserved, Knaup affirms that his experience in the Navy was, overall, an enlightening experience.

"It's a brotherhood—a mentality that you develop which proves that you are part of a group...not an individual," he stated. "Whether what we did helped change the world, I'll never know, but you quickly learn to watch out for each other because what you're doing might just save yours or someone else's life." *(Photograph courtesy of John Knaup)*

Richard Heidbreder

Lohman

Shortly before his graduation from Russellville High School in 1965, Richard Heidbreder recalls the Air Force recruiter visiting the school, full of promises of service that sounded much more palatable than those offered by the other military branches.

"Back in those days, we all kind of knew we were going to have to leave and go serve," said Heidbreder, when describing the Vietnam era draft. "When I talked to the recruiter, he told me that in the Air Force I wouldn't be involved in hand-to-hand combat, and the food and facilities would be much better than they were in the Marines and the Army," he grinned.

Enlisting in August 1965, the recruit traveled to Lackland Air Force Base (AFB) in San Antonio, Texas, spending the next several weeks in basic training. He was then assigned to Lowry AFB in Denver, Colorado, where he trained as a munitions handler.

"During the training," Heidbreder explained, "we learned to identify all of the munitions used by the Air Force including bombs and flares. Anything explosive," he added, "we would basically store and handle."

The airman then received orders for his first duty assignment at Richards-Gebaur AFB (closed in 1994) located south of Kansas City, Missouri—a small base used to train fighter and transport pilots. While there, Heidbreder said, his duties included "handling of inert missiles that were used in training by the pilots." After only a few months in his initial assignment, Heidbreder was transferred to Clark Air Base located on Luzon Island in the Philippines in June 1966.

"Once again, we were storing and transporting munitions used in training, but we also handled some live stuff that was used during air patrols while we were there," he said, including the 2.75-inch rockets on which they would test the fuses and then "attach to the wings of the planes."

The following year, Heidbreder received a three-month assignment to Uda Pao, Thailand, to help establish a new air base from which the United States could launch bombing campaigns against targets in Vietnam—missions that were previously flown from the island of Guam.

"The base was basically built on a swamp and they had to haul in several feet of rock to fill it all in," he said. "While we were there, they poured pads and built revetments to store the munitions," adding, "and then they began shipping in bombs to be used in Vietnam."

When his three-month tour ended, Heidbreder returned to Clark Air Base until November 1967, at which time he was transferred to McConnell AFB in Wichita, Kansas. He remained in his stateside duty location until receiving orders for Vietnam, returning overseas in July 1968. Assigned to the 303rd Munitions Maintenance Squadron on Bien Hoa Air Base near the city of Saigon, Heidbreder says that much like his earlier duty in Thailand, he was working with "the hard and heavy stuff," like the 750-pound bombs, which he describes as the "bread and butter" of their bombing missions.

"Mainly I got into breaking down the pallets, loading the bombs [and components] on a truck, and taking them to the flight line where they were installed on the planes for the big drop," he said.

While stationed in Vietnam, he discovered that much of what he had been told by his recruiter three years earlier resonated with a level of truth regarding their living conditions and work environment, and providing him with a renewed appreciation for his decision to join the Air Force.

"You'd see the Army guys coming onto base without having had a shower for days, who had been eating C-Rations and involved in heavy combat...those guys really had a struggle." He added, "The base was pretty secure except for the occasional rockets the NVA [North

Vietnamese Army] would lob in. When that happened, they'd sound the alarm and you would head for the bunker."

On one occasion, the veteran recalled, an enemy rocket struck a revetment filled with bombs stored for upcoming missions, setting off an explosion that shook the base and left a crater in the ground nearly one hundred feet deep.

"Somehow, I don't think anyone was killed on that one," he said.

In April 1969, Heidbreder was sent home to the United States and discharged from the military, with the three months he had previously served in Thailand reducing his one-year deployment in Vietnam to nine months. Shortly after returning to Lohman, he purchased a set of concrete forms and started Heidbreder Foundation Service. He married his fiancée, Rosemary, on June 12, 1976 and the couple has raised one son, Ryan, who now serves as Heidbreder's partner in the foundation business. Since his return from Vietnam, the Air Force veteran has pursued his hobby of collecting original, unrestored muscle cars and has more than thirty such vehicles in his collection.

Though stories abound of many veterans coming home from the Vietnam War only to be greeted with disdain, Heidbreder affirms that he received nothing but support from his Mid-Missouri community and was even able to extract a valuable lesson from his time in the service—primarily, that of a quicker transition into adulthood.

"Looking back now, at that time [when we enlisted], you were young and inexperienced enough that you didn't really know what you were going to do with your life...or what life was going to give you," Heidbreder remarked. "But going off to the military was just something you took in stride. It was part of your duty to serve and became tremendous maturing period for me and a lot of other guys."
(Photo courtesy of Richard Heidbreder)

Ron Bandelier

St. Martins

The stories of veterans can often vary among the different branches of services and the types of military duties for which one trained. As local veteran Ron Bandelier notes, his combat tour in South Vietnam was, in his opinion, an ideal example of such a unique experience and one witnessed with a group of American-trained Vietnamese Rangers. A 1965 graduate of Jefferson City High School, Bandelier of St. Martins, Missouri, received his draft notice in September 1967, while working for the state highway department.

"I know you've probably heard it before, but all of us just kind of knew [the draft] was coming," he said.

By late October, he was in Ft. Bliss, Texas, attending U.S. Army basic training with six other draftees from the Jefferson City area. Finishing their initial training in mid-December, the men returned home on leave, not to meet again until after the war.

"During the induction process, they put us through some tests and discovered that I was color blind," Bandelier explained. "They said it was a good thing because that meant I couldn't go in the infantry."

In early January 1968, the young soldier reported to Fort Huachuca, Arizona for training as a radio teletype operator, spending the next three months learning to operate military radio systems, including the AN/PRC 25—a short-range radio that would later become vital to his survival under combat conditions. Graduating in April 1968, the untested soldier received orders for deployment and traveled by commercial aircraft to Cam Rahn Bay, Vietnam,

471

arriving in country toward the end of the Tet Offensive—one of the largest military campaigns launched against South Vietnamese and American forces during the war. Within days, Bandelier was assigned to a U.S. Army Ranger group called MAC-V (Military Assistance Command) attached to the 21st Vietnamese Ranger Battalion, which he describes as a "highly mobile advisory team" comprised of four American soldiers and more than four hundred Vietnamese Rangers.

"The Vietnamese Rangers were very well trained," Bandelier said. "Our base camp was located in Phu Loc, northwest of Da Nang," he added, "and we were usually out on operations with one of us advisors cycling in to Da Nang for about three days of rest, usually once every two weeks or as combat conditions allowed."

As the veteran explained, the MAC-V was one of several military elements operating under a rather unique set of circumstances, separated from resupply and support, with the radio Bandelier carried serving as their lifeline to the outside world.

"Our primary purpose was reconnaissance of an area called Dodge City," he explained. "It was known to be a major infiltration route for attacks against Da Nang. When we would make contact with Viet Cong or NVA [North Vietnamese Army], I would use the radio to call in artillery or air strikes." He continued, "I can even remember times that we used naval artillery from the ships operating off of the coast."

As the lone radioman among only four Americans in their operational group, Bandelier said that with the tall antenna connected to the radio, it was easier to identify him as a target since enemy forces knew he was the connection between the Vietnamese Rangers and artillery support.

"I never used the long-range 'whip' antenna," he said, "unless it was really necessary for communication. Snipers always waited and aimed at the guys with antennas in the air, so I used the shorter three-foot tape antenna that I could run down the front of my backpack and pull it up for transmission."

In addition to the threat posed by snipers and enemy forces, Bandelier stated that the Rangers also had to contend with other deadly threats such as booby traps and land mines during their missions. After spending nearly a year performing operations in a "hot spot" of Vietnam, where "no place was safe," the combat veteran completed his tour and returned to the United States, receiving his discharge in May 1969.

Once back in Mid-Missouri, he returned to work with the state highway department and remained there until his retirement in 2002. The year following his discharge from the Army, Bandelier married his fiancée, Dorothy, and the couple has raised two sons. The veteran now enjoys spending his free time restoring and driving classic cars and has volunteered to drive a hospital van for the Disabled American Veterans. Despite however active he remains in his retirement, Bandelier's thoughts frequently return to friends he left behind decades ago and thousands of miles away.

"We essentially lived among the Vietnamese Rangers the entire time we were over there...they were our friends, they were our people," Bandelier affirmed. "When we left [Vietnam] and communist government seized control, most of them fought to end and never surrendered. For that," he paused, "they were placed in reeducation camps or killed." He added, "When our time was up, we got to come home, but they had to stay over there and deal with the consequences of defending their country." *(Courtesy of Ron Bandelier)*

Lynden Steele

Jefferson City

Graduating from Jefferson City High School in 1960, more than two years crawled by at the University of Missouri before Lynden "Lynn" Steele realized he was not prepared to excel in his academic endeavors—a perception that would inspire a break from his educational journey and eventually lead to his membership in an elite component of the armed forces.

"While I was in school at Columbia," said Steele, "my grades started to slip, so I decided to leave and go to work for the highway department. But then I cooked up this idea that it would be cool to become part of the Special Forces," he laughed.

Enlisting on August 30, 1963, the young recruit was soon on his way to Ft. Polk, Louisiana to complete his basic and advanced infantry training. From there, he transferred to Ft. Benning, Georgia for his "jump school" and then received assignment to the Special Forces Training Group at Ft. Bragg, North Carolina, spending the next year at the post undergoing the strenuous process of becoming one of the famed "Green Berets."

"It was a very difficult training program and you could flunk out at any point along the way," said Steele. "During that year, a recruit was cross-trained in several different areas that might be used during a mission, such as demolitions, engineering, language and medical," he explained.

Graduating in early 1965, Steele received his Green Beret and assignment to the Seventh Special Forces Group at Ft. Bragg, where he soon discovered the swiftness of operational tasking when he deployed to the Dominican Republic with seventy of his fellow "berets" during the Dominican Civil War.

"We kind of snuck into the country because we hadn't been invited," he grinned, "and camped out on the runway for about a week or so. We spent the next month pulling security on a mountaintop near Santo Domingo." He added, "It was jungle terrain, so we used demolitions to blow away the canopy to create an area for a helicopter landing pad."

A month later, as the conflict on the small island nation began to subside, Steele returned to Ft. Bragg, but weeks later received orders for his next operational assignment—this time in the beleaguered country of Vietnam. Arriving at Bu Dop on September 25, 1965—a small border surveillance outpost on the Cambodian border approximately sixty miles north of Saigon—Steele recalls the Special Forces camp protected by a mixture of World War II weaponry ranging from 4.2-inch mortars to smaller weapons such as the M-1 Garand and the Browning Automatic Rifle (BAR).

As a "demolitions man," Steele explained, he was "knowledgeable of field construction techniques" and "skilled in the preparation of camp perimeter defense systems," all useful skills that he employed when helping rebuild Bu Dop shortly after his arrival. (The camp was one of several nearly destroyed during attacks from Viet Cong regiments in the weeks preceding his arrival.)

In addition to carefully disposing of unexploded ordnance left in the area, Steele participated in patrols with soldiers from two companies of Montagnards (a "Bronze Age" people indigenous to Vietnam) and a company of Cambodians also residing at the camp. While participating in patrols, Steele discovered the dangers posed by an enemy that was oftentimes greater in threat than one armed with a rifle and, which culminated in an incident leaving the unsuspecting soldier in the hospital.

"It was summertime and raining...and I thought about wearing a poncho but believed it would be like sitting in a sauna in the hot weather," he explained. "I got wet and stayed wet, and the patrol lasted all day. Within a week after returning from the patrol, I had a fever and was sent to a field hospital with what ended up being pneumonia."

Steele returned to Ft. Bragg in September 1966 after spending a year in Vietnam and went on to serve as a demolitions instructor for Special Forces recruits and, in 1969, attended training to become an infantry officer. However, he left the Army during a reduction in force in 1971 while serving with the 24th Infantry Division in Germany.

Following eight years of active duty service, he remained with reserve units for the next twenty-five years, retiring in the late 1990s at the rank of lieutenant colonel. In the years after his return from Vietnam, he earned both a bachelor's and master's degree and retired in 2006 from his full-time employment with the U.S. Department of Labor. For the past several years, Steele and his wife have resided in Florida, but he has remained active with organizations such as the American Legion, VFW, and Special Forces Association Chapter 85, leveraging his experience from thirty-three years in military uniform to share with others the lessons he has learned while in the military.

"When I was growing up, I remember watching Audie Murphy in the movie *To Hell and Back*, and there was a scene of him and his unit digging in for a nighttime defensive position somewhere in the French countryside...and it was raining and they were getting wet. I remember wondering, 'How did they get warm and dry?'" Grinning, he added, "Years later on patrol while it rained in Vietnam, I wondered the same thing—and never did figure it out! But I also learned that there is nothing the Army will ask of you that you cannot do. It will help you learn to recognize and control life's lessons and experience the joy of sell-fulfillment." *(Courtesy of Lynn Steele)*

Nancy Maxwell

Freeburg

Growing up the second oldest of seven children in the Osage County community of Freeburg, Nancy Maxwell often felt she was living in the shadow of her older sister or younger brother. She went on to explain that years later, when making the decision to enlist in the U.S. Navy, she finally had the opportunity to step outside of the shadow and establish herself in a fulfilling career field. A 1967 graduate of Fatima High School, Maxwell began working at a bank in Jefferson City before making the decision to enlist in the military during the height of the Vietnam War.

"I just had a calling that I wanted to serve my country, to get an education and travel," she said. "When I enlisted in the Navy, I was sworn in on the local television station because I was one of the first females from the area to enlist during the Vietnam War."

Signing her enlistment papers in March 1969, Maxwell traveled to Bainbridge, Maryland to complete several weeks of basic training. Although it was an experience now several decades in hindsight, memories from the period remain quite vivid.

"It was cold—the wind was very frigid blowing in off the Chesapeake Bay," she recalled. "One thing that I quickly discovered was they were trying to weed out those who couldn't do what they were told to do. If someone didn't follow the orders they were given in basic training, they were soon gone," she added.

In the latter days of her training, Maxwell explained, the recruits filled out forms to identify three career fields in which they wished to receive training and an eventual assignment. For the young sailor, her annotated desire to serve in a medical field soon became a reality.

"I have always enjoyed helping people and wanted to serve in some type of medical profession," said Maxwell. "The Navy sent me to the (Naval) Hospital Corps School at Great Lakes, Illinois, which certainly became a blessing to me since it provided the initial training for the career I would enjoy years later."

Throughout the next several weeks, she and her fellow trainees learned many of the direct patient care tasks performed by a licensed practical nurse—administering IVs and catheters, giving enemas, treating infections, learning the medications prescribed by physicians, medical record keeping and changing of bed linens.

Graduating from the class on September 18, 1969, Maxwell and her fellow recruits filled out a "dream sheet," upon which they noted the three top locations where they wished to receive assignment. What she soon discovered, however, was that this list was secondary to the personnel needs of the U.S. Navy.

"We jokingly said that you're dreaming if you think they're going to send you to wherever you listed on your dream sheet," she grinned. "I think I put down somewhere warm like Hawaii and Florida, but I ended up on the East Coast."

She was provided two weeks of leave to return home to Missouri, after which she traveled to her first official duty assignment with the Naval Hospital in Philadelphia. Constructed in the mid-1930s, the hospital remained in operation until 1993, at which point it was closed as part of the Base Realignment and Closure Act of 1988 (BRAC).

"The Naval Hospital in Philadelphia was at the time the largest amputee center on the East Coast," she said. "The main building was twelve stories tall. Working there was quite an eye-opening experience for this little ol' country girl."

Early in her assignment, she worked on the medical intensive care unit floor as the senior corpsman, "making the rounds with doctors and training other corpsman." Much of her time, she sullenly explained, was spent treating eighteen- and nineteen-year-old servicemembers who had been severely wounded in the Vietnam War and who were oftentimes missing eyes and limbs.

"Treating the Vietnam veterans was so special to me because they were so young...my age or even younger," she recalled. "They were scared and confused since being wounded was very trying for them." She added, "We did the best we could to provide comfort and help them through it."

On one occasion, she remained the entire night with a young patient who had leukemia and needed the blood vacuumed from his throat to prevent him from choking. Despite the medical care and attention he was given, she solemnly explained, the veteran passed away the next morning.

"No veteran died alone on our watch," she softly noted. "We did the best that we could to ease their pain both physically and emotionally."

A year-and-a-half into her assignment, she transferred to the hospital's nuclear medicine department, where she remained until her discharge in 1972. In the years following her service, she married, raised two children and retired from Capital Region Medical Center in Jefferson City after more than two decades as a registered nuclear medicine technologist.

The Navy veteran has remained busy in retirement by volunteering as the adjutant of her local American Legion post, her church parish and its associated school, and serving as a guardian on a number of trips with the Central Missouri Honor Flight. She recognizes, however, that her appreciation for her fellow veterans was forged through her experiences of providing care for the wounded.

"There were many difficult times in the Navy, such as when I watched several of the male corpsman with whom I served deploy to Vietnam, knowing they would face the deadly threats they had helped treat back home," she said. "Also, it wasn't easy for the dependents of the wounded because they didn't know if their loved ones would live or what to expect when they returned home.

"But all things considered, I always enjoyed helping people –it was a fulfilling profession that allowed me the opportunity to witness someone improve and move on with their lives." *(Photograph courtesy of Nancy Maxwell)*

Don Schmoeger

Russellville

During the period of the Vietnam War (1964-1975, as recognized by the Department of Veterans Affairs), an estimated 3.4 million men and women deployed to Southeast Asia as part of the war effort. But what these numbers often conceal is that of the 8.7 million men and women who donned a military uniform during this same period, more than 5.3 million remained stateside or served in locations outside of the war zone, performing integral support roles and functions.

"When my class graduated [from Ft. Sam Houston, Texas], we were the first class that sent no medics to Vietnam," said Army veteran Donn Schmoeger, when discussing his time in military training during the late 1960s.

Raised near Russellville, Schmoeger spent a year working on his parents' farm after graduating high school in 1967, but the following year, shifted his focus toward a different career path.

"I got into a carpenter apprenticeship with Local 945 in Jefferson City," Schmoeger said, "and was working with them when I got my draft notice."

Since he was enrolled in an educational program, Schmoeger was approved for a one-year deferment while he continued his training to become a carpenter. However, the following year, he chose to "go ahead and get it over with" and finish his military obligation while he still possessed the advantage of youthful endurance. Leaving his apprenticeship, Schmoeger was inducted into the U.S. Army in June 1969, traveling to Ft. Leonard Wood to complete his basic training. While there, the young recruit volunteered to complete training for a military driver's license, an action that would later influence the course of his military career.

Several weeks later, as he prepared to graduate from his basic training, the young soldier was informed that he would be transferred to Ft. Sam Houston, Texas to expand upon his military driving experience by undergoing instruction to become an ambulance driver.

"They flew a plane load of us down [to Ft. Sam Houston] and once we got there, they divided us into two groups—those who would be ambulance drivers and those who would become medics," he said.

But, as the veteran explained, his ambulance training paralleled much of what the medics received since he learned more advanced procedures such as administering injections.

"Not only did we learn how to patch somebody up and prepare them to go to the hospital," Schmoeger said, "during the training we learned to give each other shots. We basically learned how to be medics," he added.

During their medical instruction, Schmoeger said that he and his fellow soldiers were advised that ninety-nine percent of those who received medical training would deploy to Vietnam, which led him to believe that would be his next duty assignment. However, he soon learned that his training class would become the first not to go to Vietnam.

"Admittedly, I was relieved," he said. "We all heard what was going on over there and I thought for sure we would be in the middle of a war zone...getting shot at."

When his class graduated in early 1970, Schmoeger was transferred to the 2nd Armored Division at Ft. Hood, Texas, spending a majority of his time as an ambulance driver supporting soldiers participating in field maneuvers while also delivering food and other provisions. The following year, in March 1971, his military career came to a close when he received an early discharge under a "seasonable work" authority, returning to Russellville to assist his father on the farm. Months later, he returned to the carpenters union to finish his apprenticeship and in 1972 married his fiancée, Sheryl Miles.

The veteran went on to work as a carpenter for several decades, retiring earlier this year.

Though subject to a draft that compelled him into military service nearly a half-century ago, Schmoeger affirms that the time he spent in olive drab fatigues is an experience that was sprinkled with a little good fortune and one he views through the lens of positive hindsight.

"Like I said before, we all thought we were going to Vietnam and it's something we would have done if we were sent," he paused, adding, "but we were also relieved when we didn't have to go...and I've always said that God must have been looking out for me." With a grin, he continued, "But it was still a very positive moment in my life and it taught me there's always something to learn. It's always good for a young person to get away from home and see what the rest of the world is like, and the Army can certainly do that for you!" *(Photograph courtesy of Don Schmoeger)*

Stan Putthoff

Fulton

Before graduating from Tonganoxie High School in Kansas, Stan Putthoff realized he wanted to become a sailor and made the decision to enlist in the Navy's delayed entry program. In 1970, just weeks following his graduation, he attended boot camp at the Naval Training Center in San Diego, beginning a period of service he believed would find him bobbing on the waves of the high seas rather than silently slicing through the ocean depths aboard a nuclear submarine.

"My dad and his brother had served in the Army in World War II and they talked about being in the mud and eating K-rations," Putthoff recalled. "I decided that if I were going to serve in the military, I would go where there was three 'hots and a cot' [hot meals and a bed]," he chuckled.

Upon graduation from boot camp, he traveled to Great Lakes, Illinois to attend advanced training as a machinist mate, spending the next four months learning system design and the operation of the turbines that propelled ships—what he referred to as "non-nuclear propulsion systems." He added, "When I graduated from the training in June of 1971, they gave me temporary active duty on the *USS Wasp*, which was an old World War II era aircraft carrier." It was this initial two-month assignment aboard his first ship, he noted, that resulted in his decision to request duty aboard a submarine.

"One day while I was standing on the pier looking at the ship when I realized the engine room—where I worked—was below the water line," he said. "Most of the other sailors on the ship worked in assignments above the water line." Pausing, he added, "That's when

487

I decided that if I'm going to be working underwater, I want everybody that I serve with to be underwater as well so that we all have the same desire to make it back above the water."

His request for submarine duty was approved and the young sailor was sent to Bainbridge, Maryland, for six months of nuclear power school, during which "two years of mechanical and nuclear engineering was crammed into six months," he said. He then traveled to Saratoga Springs, New York, where he completed the nuclear power prototype school.

"We worked on a mock-up of a nuclear destroyer," explained Putthoff, when describing the training he received in New York. "It was twelve-hour days—part of it spent in a classroom the other learning to operate the nuclear power plants used aboard ships."

Since he did well in the training, he remained in New York for three months of engineering laboratory technician school and received additional instruction in such areas as fission byproducts, boiler water chemistry and nuclear effects on water. A little more than two years after he entered the service, in December 1972, Putthoff finally received his first submarine assignment and traveled to Rota, Spain, to report to the USS Thomas Jefferson—a nuclear-powered submarine that was launched ten years earlier.

While working in the engine room, Putthoff completed a two-month patrol in the Mediterranean aboard the submarine observing Soviet activity and engaged in other classified activities. After the submarine returned to Spain, it was turned over to their counterparts, while Putthoff and the sailors of the "Gold" crew traveled to New London, Connecticut, for three months of off-crew time consisting of leave and training schools. The Gold Crew then traveled back to Spain and took the submarine on a North Atlantic Cruise, during which, Putthoff, recalled, they remained submerged for a period of sixty-eight days.

In the summer of 1973, the submarine remained at New London to perform diving exercises and introduced cadets attending the U.S. Naval Academy to the daily rigors of submarine duty. That fall, the USS Thomas Jefferson traveled to Mare Island, California, where it resided in dry dock for an overhaul for the next 17 months. The Gold Crew would then spend seven months in Pearl Harbor before flying to Charleston, South Carolina to relieve the Blue Crew and take the submarine to the Bermuda Triangle for "sound trials"—testing the sub "to see if it was leaking sound into the water."

Putthoff said, "After traveling [to the West Coast] to load torpedoes and test equipment, we went to Bremerton, Washington, to test fire torpedoes on a test firing range. After that, we went back to Pearl Harbor and I was transferred to the *USS Sea Dragon* to finish out my last two months of service." He added, "I was discharged in October 1976."

In addition to earning a bachelor's degree following his discharge from the Navy, Putthoff married, raised a family and enjoyed a lengthy career at the Callaway Nuclear Plant, retiring in 2008 as a training supervisor. He remained employed as a consultant at the plant for seven years following his retirement. The Fulton, Missouri, resident explained that his time in the submarine service may not resonate with the glamour and notoriety of others who have served their nation in uniform, but it was an experience bursting with stories of heroic service that have never been shared with the public.

"I view it as important to remember the time that Cold War sailors spent away from their families, missing important events so we as a nation could maintain the nuclear deterrent that kept our Cold War enemies in check," Putthoff said. Although it is important to remember the overt actions by members of our military that have received recognition from the media, there are still many people out there whose deeds go unrecognized because of reasons of national security." He affirmed, "We are the silent service [submarine service] and our job is to remain undetected—and we are very good at it." *(Photograph courtesy of Stan Putthoff)*

Jack Boswell

Jefferson City

When words such as "underground" are used to describe the Vietnam War era, what often comes to mind is the elaborate network of tunnels from which Viet Cong launched attacks against U.S. troops. During this same period, however, the United States was also embroiled in a Cold War standoff with the Soviets, while Air Force personnel operated from underground silos to maintain missiles that could be launched against targets at a moment's notice.

In late 1971, Jack Boswell was living in Alton, Illinois, and his life appeared to be moving in a positive direction—he had graduated from high school, was married and had a good job with General Motors. But he soon received an alarming notice that led to an unexpected stint in the military with service below ground.

"I had attended a few months at a local college and then went to work, so I lost my [draft] deferment," Boswell said. "But when I heard my draft number called [during a radio program], I was devastated. It was the furthest thing from my mind."

Rather than wait to be summoned for service in the U.S. Army, Boswell chose to pursue his interest in working with electronics and visited a local Air Force recruiter. Scoring high on the aptitude tests related to electronics, Boswell decided to enlist in the Air Force in October 1971. (Boswell noted it was fortunate he did not procrastinate in his decision to join the Air Force because two days following his enlistment, he received an induction notice for the U.S. Army.)

"I took my basic training at Lackland Air Force Base [Texas] in February of 1972," Boswell said. "Toward the end of basic, I was told that I would be going to missile school, which surprised the instructor because not many recruits were assigned to that type of program."

Traveling to Sheppard Air Force Base in Wichita Falls, Texas, the young recruit embarked upon twenty-six weeks of detailed training for the Titan II missile system. During the training, he was introduced to basic electronics, learned to work with the missile guidance computers and the processes used to target the missile. As he explained, the Titan II missile was the most powerful weapon in the U.S. Air Force inventory—a two-stage, liquid filled intercontinental ballistic missile (ICBM) with a nine megaton nuclear warhead. (The 150 Minuteman II missiles once buried in silos across western Missouri had 1.2 megaton warheads.) Despite the deterrence they provided against the Soviet threat that emerged during the height of the Cold War, the Titan II missiles were also modified to serve as the launch system in NASA's Gemini space flight program.

When his initial missile training was completed in October 1972, Boswell transferred to Vandenburg Air Force Base in California, spending the next five weeks participating in detailed and intense exercises to ensure he and the other members of a missile team could quickly troubleshoot any problems that might arise during a launch sequence.

"They were very tedious in making sure we were ready to take care of the missiles," Boswell affirmed.

From there, he reported to McConnell Air Force Base in Wichita, Kansas, his first and only duty assignment. While there, he and his wife were able to live off base in a small apartment in Wichita.

"At first, I was assigned to a crew and we did some more preparatory training for a few weeks," he said. "Then, after Christmas [1972], I began working with the Titan II missiles and pulling eight, twenty-four-hour alerts each month with one standby."

During his shift, the Cold War veteran explained, he and three other missile personnel lived and worked in an underground facility attached to the silo that housed a Titan II missile. The crew would go through checklists and maintenance procedures to make sure the missile was prepared to launch in under sixty seconds.

For the next three years, Boswell continued to work as part of a missile team. He was also able to enjoy time off from his military duties and continued to sharpen his technology skills by working at shops in the Wichita area repairing televisions and other electronic devices. While in the Air Force, he noted, his wife gave birth to their two daughters. On December 31, 1975, Boswell finished his enlistment and returned to Illinois, where he and his wife soon welcomed their only son. The Air Force veteran went on to use his GI Bill benefits to earn an associate's degree in electronics and retired from IBM in 2007 after thirty years of service—employment that brought him to his current home of Jefferson City, Missouri.

Though nearly three decades have passed since the last Titan II missile was decommissioned, Boswell asserts that the time he spent working on one of the most powerful weapons in the country's arsenal was a moment of paradox—feelings of safety that surfaced in the presence of deadly possibilities.

"We were always taught that these missiles were made to never shoot. They were created to serve as a deterrent," he said. "Russia knew the retaliatory abilities that we as a country had at our disposal and although the missiles were dangerous to work around, I always felt like we were safer for having them." He added, "And even if we now possess technologies that are just as deadly as those that we had back in the 1970s, when I learned that the [Titan IIs] had been decommissioned, it was like closing a door to my past." *(Photo courtesy of Jack Boswell)*

Dale Lee Clark

Jefferson City

Growing up on the east side of town, Jefferson City, Missouri resident Mark Schreiber recalls the days when he and Dale Clark, a close neighborhood friend, would dress up in military gear and "play Army" as kids. Many years later, as they grew older and graduated from high school, Clark would no longer have to pretend he was in the military when he made the decision to fulfill a dream by enlisting in the Marine Corps.

"I lived on Hobbs Terrace and Dale lived up on Ewing Drive," said Schreiber. "Sometimes, while we were playing, we ventured into the [Jefferson City] National Cemetery and we would walk through there...looking at the headstones and talking about the Civil War and those types of things," he added.[105]

A 1964 graduate of Jefferson City High School, Clark's younger brother, Dan, said that although his brother was several years older, he recalls that he attended one year of college at Lincoln University after finishing high school before finally making his decision to join the military.

"My parents were horribly against [his decision to enlist]," said Dan Clark, "because my father was a World War II veteran and I

---

[105] The Jefferson City National Cemetery is maintained by the Jefferson Barracks National Cemetery and is now closed to new interments. According to the Department of Veterans Affairs, the first burials in the cemetery date to the summer of 1861. Department of Veterans Affairs, *Jefferson City National Cemetery*, www.cem.va.gov.

don't think that he wanted Dale to go through what he had experienced during the war."

Undeterred by his father's concerns, on June 15, 1965, Clark signed his enlistment papers and went on to complete his basic training at the Marine Corps Recruit Depot in San Diego, California, in late August 1965. Several weeks later (November 27, 1965), he was sent to Vietnam, where he became a rifleman with Company K, 3rd Battalion, 9th Regiment of the 3rd Marine Division.

Schreiber noted it was not surprising that Clark's path eventually led to his military service, since he had "showed an interest in the Marines while we were in high school and even made several comments about it."

The young Marine remained in Vietnam for several months, conducting patrols and other military operations until a fateful event that occurred on August 19, 1966, which would secure for him the unfortunate distinction of being the first Cole County resident killed during the war. In a letter sent to Clark's parents by one of the lieutenants in his company, Dan Clark learned of the puzzling and ill-fated circumstances regarding the death of his older brother.

"I was thirteen years old at the time, but I remember being told that he had just returned from a patrol [in the area of Da Nang], was debriefed and was resting," said Dan Clark. "What happened next...I'm not really sure, but it is my understanding that a grenade that was attached to his equipment somehow went off and killed him," he added.

The body of nineteen-year-old Lance Corporal Clark was returned Mid-Missouri and laid to rest at the Jefferson City National Cemetery on August 26, 1966, following funeral services held at First Baptist Church where he had been a member.

"No, Dale didn't enjoy his duty in Vietnam," stated Rev. G. Nelson Duke, while officiating the funeral for Clark. "He had written his pastor and others about those weeks on C-rations, the filth and heat of the country, the uncertainty about the enemy." He added, "But he had sworn allegiance to duty for his nation, and he was performing it."

On the day of the funeral, John G. Christy, who was Jefferson City mayor at the time of Clark's passing, requested citizens of the community fly their flags at half-staff in recognition of the sacrifice made by Clark. The following month, the city council passed a resolution in memory of the fallen Marine.

These days, when Schreiber visits the National Cemetery, he can clearly recall the moments from many decades previous when he and his friend first visited the area that would eventually serve as Clark's final resting place.

"I close my eyes and can still see that tall, skinny, freckle-faced boy with his broad smile," Schreiber said. "It is still a very emotional experience for me, thinking of those times long ago, of all the glorious events that we foresaw in our minds." Somberly, he added, "When you come up together in school for all of those years, you arrive at the mentality that you'll see each other again tomorrow, but for Dale, there wasn't that tomorrow. I believe that his service is symbolic of so many local people that we have lost in past conflicts, who laid down their lives so that we might live to remember them."

Clark was posthumously awarded the Purple Heart and Vietnam Service medals and is recognized on Panel 10E/Line 19 of the Vietnam Memorial in Washington, D.C. *(Photo courtesy of Dan Clark)*

Robert Lee Cliburn

California

The narrative often shared by Vietnam veterans is that when they graduated from high school in the mid-to-late 1960s, they either enlisted in the military because they believed they would be drafted or they went to work, simply biding time until their draft letter arrived. California area veteran Robert Cliburn chose the latter and began working at a plant in Jefferson City after his graduation from Russellville High School in 1965.

"I had two older brothers who had joined the Navy," said Cliburn. "After I finished [high] school, my father asked me what I was going to do and I said, 'I think I'll take my chances and go to work,' but I was really just waiting to be drafted."

Whether foresight or simply an educated guess, Cliburn received "a big brown envelope" in September 1966, which contained his draft letter—an abrupt welcome to the world of the United States Army. In less than two weeks, the nineteen-year-old draftee processed through Jefferson Barracks and spent a few days at Ft. Leonard Wood, Missouri. He and a large group of trainees were then loaded on Greyhound buses and transferred to Ft. Hood, Texas, where they were attached to the First Armored Division for their basic and advanced training.

"At some point, they conducted interviews with [the trainees]," Cliburn explained. "I told them that I was a farmer and could run a tractor, and that my father was in the bulldozer business and that I could operate a dozer as well." With a grin, he added, "So, they made me a tank driver."

Weeks later, he finished his training and remained at the fort, participating in training exercises as the driver for an M48A2

Patton—a medium tank with a 90mm main gun and a gasoline-powered engine. Later in the war, many of the M48A2s were replaced with the newer M48A3s, which converted the tank to the longer-range diesel powered engines.

During his cycle of training, Cliburn witnessed "allocations that came down," identifying soldiers scheduled for service in Vietnam. However, he seemed to somehow sidestep the selection process until reaching the eleventh month of his two-year enlistment.

"They finally got me," he said, "and before I knew it, I was landing in Tan Son Nhut Air Force Base [Vietnam] as a replacement."

In August of 1967, he transferred to Camp Bearcat—a U.S. Army base near the city of Biên Hòa in southern Vietnam. It was here he was attached to Troop B, 3rd Squadron, 5th Cavalry.[106]

"The first six months or so we operated on missions around Bearcat," Cliburn said. "B Troop consisted of nine tanks and twenty-seven personnel carriers and we could kick some butt with that arrangement," he smiled. "But the monsoons were going on and we were getting stuck in the jungles down there—a heavy tank doesn't work well in that type of environment."

While participating in southern operations, Cliburn and his fellow tankers were often engaged in guerrilla warfare against small groups of enemy forces, which he described as "we'd fight and push them back, and then we'd get pushed back a little...and so on." He continued, "Then they loaded us on LST's [landing ship, tank] and sent us north of Da Nang," he recalled. "We were on more solid ground and they seemed to be having more trouble up there, too. In the south, we fought smaller groups, but up north we started fighting battalion size elements of NVA [North Vietnamese Army]."

In addition to dismounting their tanks and securing a network of underground tunnels that housed a significant cache of enemy weapons, Cliburn received a harsh introduction to the dangers of armored warfare when he assisted in the rescue of a stranded tank.

---

[106] Camp Bearcat was abandoned during the latter part of the Vietnam War and has essentially been converted back into farmland.

"We thought a tank was dead after it had been hit by an enemy rocket," Cliburn said. "I went in there to help retrieve it and when I jumped off our tank to hook up the tow cable to drag it out of there, I could hear it idling. It had been idling all night," he said.

With bullets from NVA soldiers "pinging" around him, he climbed into the tank, shifted it into reverse and drove to safety. Though he avoided injury, he later would spend more than a month on a hospital ship after receiving serious burns when a flare accidentally ignited in his tank. Regardless, none of these previous experiences served as the central reflection of his time spent in Vietnam.

Well into his tour, Cliburn was "pulled from the jungle" and given "several days of R & R (rest and relaxation) in Hong Kong.

"I had four hundred dollars to take with me and I knew that wouldn't be enough, so I borrowed one hundred dollars from my friend, Jack Monturi," he said. "I told Jack I would pay him back the following month.

When Cliburn returned, he learned that Monturi was medically evacuated after receiving serious wounds during a mission.

"I never saw him again," he said.

Cliburn's tour ended in late July 1968, at which time he returned to Mid-Missouri, married his fiancé, Timmie Hume, and went on to raise a son and daughter. Now retired from a lengthy career in construction, Cliburn notes he was recently able to repay the debt he incurred in Vietnam nearly a half-century ago.

"Last year I bought my wife a new laptop and I asked her if she could find the contact information for Jack [Monturi]—and she did," Cliburn explained. "When I called him and I told him who I was, he said, 'You owe me one hundred dollars.' We talked for a while and I got his home address and went and visited him [recently] and gave him five hundred to cover the loan with interest."

In closing, Cliburn added, "You really don't know what we went through [in Vietnam] and we really didn't know what we were there for...we just knew that we had to be there. But meeting people like Jack and being able to connect after all those years to share our stories...well, you can't put a price on that." *(Photo courtesy of Robert Lee Cliburn)*

Bob Verslues

Jefferson City

Raised in the Taos area, Bob Verslues began his freshman year at Fatima High School in the late 1950s, but he soon postponed his education to assist his father on the family farm. This decision, he explained, did not delay the inevitability of the Vietnam era draft as he and scores of young men from the community received the call to serve their nation.

"My draft notice came in early 1965 and they sent me to Ft. Leonard Wood for basic training," said Verslues. "Somewhere along the line they gave us aptitude tests and I guess they decided I would be a good fit for armored training."

During the summer of 1965, the young soldier attended the U.S. Army Armor School at Ft. Knox, Kentucky, where he learned to serve as an armor crewmember on the M60A1—a medium tank weighing nearly fifty tons and armed with a 105mm gun.

"You basically learned anything and everything to do with the operation of the tank," Verslues recalled. "I started out as a tank driver and later worked my way up to different crew positions."

During the latter part of his armor training, Verslues and his fellow soldiers received orders for their initial duty assignments. As their names were read off a list, many of the soldiers with whom he trained received assignments for service in Vietnam.

"They told me that my orders were for duty in Germany," he said, "and I guess I let out a sigh of relief. It was one of those situations that since I was drafted, I had no idea where I would be sent," he added."

Assigned to the 14th Armored Cavalry located in the small Bavarian community of Bad Kissingen, Verslues recalls being engaged in an assortment of duties that included mobilization drills to prepare them for rapid deployment in a crisis. On other occasions, the veteran explained, they traveled to nearby training areas at Wildflecken to conduct maneuvers and maintain proficiency with their tanks. While in Germany, Verslues said, he rose to the position of acting tank commander.

"I remember that while we were on one of these exercises, we threw one of the tracks off of our tank," he said. "We had to basically camp with the tank for two or three days, eating rations and all of that kind of thing, before they could get someone out there to get the track back on the tank."

Although far removed from the war in Vietnam, Verslues and his fellow soldiers were on the front lines of another war that raged for more than four decades and brought the Soviet Union and United States to the brink of a nuclear exchange—the Cold War. In 1961, the communist-controlled German Democratic Republic (East Germany) began construction on what was known as the "Berlin Wall," which consisted of a concrete barrier separating East and West Berlin in addition to miles of barbed wire fencing interspersed with fortifications and guard towers.

According to an article retrieved from the History Channel website, the primary purpose of the barrier was to prevent the exodus of "skilled laborers, professionals, and intellectuals" from escaping East Germany and entering into the democratic West Germany.[107]

"My platoon began a cycle of going to a border camp near the Czechoslovakian border for thirty days at a time," Verslues explained. "We brought all our rations and supplies with us and would spend our time there patrolling the border between East and West Germany."

He continued, "I drove a lieutenant in a Jeep around the perimeter of the fences in the rural areas to observe what the East German guards were doing on their towers. There were times it snowed so

---

[107] History Channel, *Berlin Wall Built*, www.history.com.

504

much while we were up there that it was fence-post deep, and you could hardly get around."

When their thirty-day tour was finished, Verslues said, his platoon would return to their regular duty station in Bad Kissingen for a period of three to four months before returning to the border camp to relieve another platoon and again conduct border patrols. While in Germany, Verslues took night classes and earned his high school diploma, rose to the rank of Specialist Five and won a trophy for being the top tank gunner. In April 1967, he returned to the U.S. and received his discharge from the military. He remained in contact with his girlfriend, Rosie Hoelscher, during his overseas duty and the couple married on July 20, 1968.

In the years following his discharge, he and his wife raised two children and he went on to complete a lengthy career in law enforcement. The Army veteran has also gained a reputation in the community for the quality of the honey he once harvested and sold from the beehives on the hills surrounding his Jefferson City home.

When reflecting on the two years he spent in the U.S. Army during the mid-1960s, Verslues affirmed that this brief period of his life not only strengthened his affections for the woman who later became his wife, but also provided him with the foundation for the career he chose to pursue.

"Being in the Army, even for such a short time, really set my mind on public service and I knew that I wanted to carry on with that when I left the military," said Verslues. "That's probably the biggest reason I became a police officer."

He added, "But honestly, it was kind of scary to leave the states and my girlfriend, knowing that I wouldn't be home for nearly two years. But Rosie and I wrote to each other whenever we had a chance and she kept all of our letters from back when I was in the Army. In fact," he smiled, "she still has them in an old shoebox upstairs."
(Photo courtesy of Rosie Verslues)

Larry Strobel

Russellville

When Larry Strobel (picture above, left) graduated from Russellville High School in 1963, the focus of his pursuits was to attend college and become an engineer. These plans, he admits, essentially proceeded in an undeterred manner until the beckoning of the war Vietnam dictated his service as a platoon leader and officer in the U.S. Army.

"I did two and a half years at Lincoln University and then went to college in Rolla," Strobel said. "I graduated with my engineering degree in 1968 and, after a couple of interview trips, I figured out that I didn't really want to do that kind of work."

The recent college graduate then made the decision to enroll at the University of Missouri-Columbia and began working on his graduate degree.

"When I was at Lincoln, I participated in the ROTC [Reserve Officers' Training Corps] program because it was mandatory at the time," he said. "I went ahead and finished the remainder of my ROTC commitment while at MU because I had friends who had been in the service and they told me not to come in unless I was an officer." He added, "Also, at that time, I just knew that I would be drafted once I finished school."

Graduating in early 1970 with a master's degree in business administration, Strobel received his commission as a second lieutenant and traveled to Ft. Belvoir, Virginia to complete the Engineer Officer Basic Course. The newly commissioned lieutenant spent the next several weeks acquiring both the technical and tactical knowledge to serve as a platoon leader in a military engineer company. He then transferred to Ft. Benning, Georgia, where, for the next few weeks, he was assigned as platoon leader for a float bridge company. However, he received little hands-on military experience since the untested officer soon received orders to report to Vietnam in late 1970.

Reflecting on his overseas orders, he noted, "Going to Vietnam wasn't any big surprise...we all knew it was coming. It just seemed as though all of my friends had been there so now it was my turn."

Departing from Travis Air Force Base in California, Strobel arrived at the air base in Biên Hòa, Vietnam in December 1970 and became a platoon leader with the 31st Engineer Battalion. His first assignment, the veteran explained, was in a remote location north of Biên Hòa known as Phước Vĩnh Base Camp.

"I flew in on a Chinook [helicopter], met my platoon sergeant and then got in my hooch [living quarters], which was pretty much a big culvert covered with sandbags. The next day," he continued, "our platoon went out and did a five-mile mine sweep."

As Strobel recounted, he led a platoon whose duty was to conduct mine sweeps to identify any deviations in the composition of the roadways that might indicate the presence of a buried mine. If a suspected mine was located, a C-4 (plastic explosive) charge was placed near the suspicious area and detonated, which neutralized the potential threat.

"When we first got there, we used metal detectors, but the VC [Viet Cong] got wise to that and began placing explosives in plastic. Soon after that, they sent us German Shepherds to smell for the explosive material. If one of those dogs stopped and sat down during a mission, you stopped and checked out the area."

In addition to their minesweeping missions, Strobel's platoon engaged in goodwill initiatives to assist the local populace by helping build large culverts along roadsides near their area of operations. These culverts, he stated, provided for better drainage and prevented erosion from making the roadways impassable during the rainy season. During the latter part of his one-year deployment, Strobel's platoon was sent to a small airstrip near An Lộc, where they repaired the pads that held eight-inch guns used in defense of the small military base.

"If you didn't have concrete pads during the rainy season, the tracks of the guns would sink into the ground and not allow for accurate targeting," Strobel explained. "While we were there, we also helped repair the airfield."

Upon arrival, recalled Strobel, he held the false impression that his new duty location would be a "nice assignment" and provide for "quiet" surroundings.

"The afternoon we first arrived, the artillery guys came out and started firing. You couldn't sleep through that because the concussion would just about knock you out of your cot. Later," he added, "you eventually got to where you could sleep through the artillery fire but would wake up when small arms fire went off."

In October 1971, Strobel returned briefly to the airbase at Biên Hòa before traveling to Travis Air Force Base and receiving his discharge from the Army. Awarded a Bronze Star for meritorious service, the combat veteran moved to Columbia, Missouri following his discharge and began working for Mutual of Omaha. As the years passed, Strobel married, raised three daughters and worked many years in Phoenix, Arizona. In 1995, he and his wife, Fran, returned to Russellville, where he continues to work in the insurance business.

Though decades now separate him from his service in Vietnam, Strobel maintains that despite the hardships he and others may have experienced while overseas, many Vietnam veterans have derived from their time in uniform a certain "resolve" that has proven beneficial later in their lives.

"Back in those days, you came from the middle of the jungle and eighteen hours later you were back home—it's a lot to ask of your mind to make such a transition in such a short period," he said. "But those of us who came back and weren't wounded, it made us stronger. It gave us strength to face challenges and helped us put everything in perspective." He added, "It's all relative, you discover, because regardless of how bad your experiences might have been, there's always someone that had it much worse than you. In the end, you just learn to play the hand that you're dealt." *(Photo courtesy of Larry Strobel)*

Kelley Shoemaker

California

Graduating from Eldon High School in 1962, Kelley Shoemaker went on to spend the next three years working for a local automotive parts company, eventually reaching the mistaken conclusion that the U.S. Army would not need his services during the developing Vietnam War. However, unexpected events would lead to his service in the military and solidify his adoration for the country he calls home.

"A lot of my friends who were eighteen and nineteen years old had gotten their draft notices and had already been sent off to the war [in Vietnam]," said the California area veteran. "But in 1965, when I was twenty-one years old, I was drafted into the Army and sent to Ft. Leonard Wood for basic training," he added.

While he was in training during the early summer of 1965, Shoemaker's younger brother also received a draft notice and went on to serve with the Army in Germany.

"During my boot camp, they told me that they wanted me to go to clerk school and I told them that I wanted to something else," Shoemaker recalled. "Then they said that's what I was going to do. I didn't have any choice in the matter."

Remaining at the Mid-Missouri Army post, the recruit completed eight weeks of clerk training. Upon graduating, he received orders for Korea—a country he believed would be much too frigid for his taste.

"I hate cold weather," he laughed. "But someone told me if I signed up for Airborne School, it would waive any orders that I had already been issued and I would also make an extra fifty dollars a month."

Shoemaker was soon on his way to Ft. Benning, Georgia, where he spent the next few weeks completing his airborne training and making five successful parachute jumps. He was then assigned to 82nd Airborne Division at Ft. Bragg, North Carolina.

"We got to run five miles every day before breakfast [at Ft. Bragg]," Shoemaker chuckled. "For about five months or so, I was stuck behind a desk typing reports, but sometimes in the afternoon, my sergeant would let me go down and help work on vehicles in the motor pool."

In late spring of 1966, the paratrooper volunteered for duty in the Dominican Republic to get away from desk duty, but jokingly remarked that since he demonstrated his willingness to serve overseas, the Army instead decided to issue him orders for Vietnam. Flying into Tan Son Nhut Air Base near Saigon, Vietnam, in mid-May 1966, Shoemaker was assigned to the administration section of Company A, 173rd Airborne Brigade located on Bien Hoa Air Base, several miles northeast of Saigon.

"I pulled a lot of guard duty on the thirty-four-foot towers," Shoemaker said. "I also did some typing [of reports] there, but I kept asking if there was any way I could get out from behind the desk," said Shoemaker. "I was going nuts after only being there for a few weeks."

His wish was soon fulfilled when he was assigned to a support group operating near the Cambodian border in which Shoemaker was "used where necessary," often performing such tasks as filling sandbags for the protection of bunkers, driving in convoys or transporting supplies.

"There were times where I drove our sergeant to Saigon to deliver photographs and information for the Star and Stripes [military-focused newspaper]," Shoemaker said.[108] "Other times we delivered intelligence reports or other important information," he added.

---

[108] The *Stars and Stripes* is a newspaper that operates from within the Department of Defense yet is editorially separate from it. The paper can trace its roots back

Toward the latter part of February 1967, Shoemaker recalled, the 173rd Airborne Brigade participated in Operation Junction City—a major military operation involving more than 25,000 troops and intended to batter Viet Cong strongholds along the Cambodian border. The only major airborne operation of the war, Shoemaker did not get to make the combat parachute jump with his fellow paratroopers. Instead, he explained, he drove a Jeep with a trailer onto a Chinook helicopter carrying thirty "field-dressed soldiers," who were then dropped off in support of the eighty-two-day military operation.

"I continued to serve in a support role, doing whatever was needed," he said. "We did have two combat photographers in our group and one of them, Douglas Carl Holland, was a good friend of mine."[109] Sullenly, he added, "Doug was killed by enemy rifle fire twenty-one days before he was supposed to come home...and that just kind of jerked the rug out from under me."

Shoemaker was picking up supplies at Bien Hoa in May 1967 and, while at the air base, heard his name called over the loudspeaker. When he reported to the administrative offices, he was told if he could be ready in forty-five minutes, he could process out of the Army and go home.

"I ran down to and grabbed everything I could out of my hut and ran back to the office," he said. "Then I got on a plane and flew out of Vietnam six days early."

After returning home from the war, Shoemaker married his fiancée, Mary Lehman, and the couple raised two children. The Army veteran went on to enjoy and extensive career working for several local car dealerships before retiring from the former Mike Kehoe Ford in Jefferson City in 2007.

Reflecting on his time spent along the Cambodian border during the Vietnam War, Shoemaker affirms that there are both

---

to the Civil War and has remained a viable news source through all wars (and periods of peace) since its establishment.

[109] A native of Iowa, Douglas Carl Holland was killed on April 9 1967 and is honored on Panel 18E, Row 4 of the Vietnam Veterans Memorial in Washington, D.C.

memories and lessons that have never diminished despite the passage of several decades.

"I can remember flying on a helicopter to Saigon and there was a body bag lying at my feet with blood running out of it," he solemnly recalled. "That's something you can never forget, something that never leaves your thoughts." He continued, "Before I got to Vietnam, I don't think that I ever saw anyone starving, but over there you saw all of those orphans...those kids...that were truly hungry. They would beg you for stuff we thought was garbage but all they wanted was something to eat." Pausing, he added, "It made you realize just how lucky you are to be in America, to reside in this great nation." *(Photo courtesy of Kelley Shoemaker)*

Charles Jobe

Russellville

The years following Charles Jobe's 1961 graduation from Eldon High School were characterized by independence—he was making a good salary as parts manager at a local car dealership and, in 1964, married his fiancée, Kathleen Bradshaw. But as the mid-1960s arrived and the country's involvement in the Vietnam War began to scale upward, he soon realized the likelihood of being drafted.

"I received my draft notice for the Army in 1966 and took a bus from Tuscumbia to Jefferson Barracks [St. Louis] for my physical," Jobe recalled. "They then sent me back home and I got a letter a few weeks later to report to Tuscumbia and we got on a bus for Ft. Leonard Wood."

While the twenty-four-year-old draftee was completing his basic training at the Missouri post in late 1966, he recalls being asked what type of specialty training he would like to attend. When he responded that he would like to work in vehicle parts management since that was his civilian job, he did not know what kind of assignment to expect.

"That's what they sent me to do," he grinned. "I ended up going to Ft. Lee, Virginia for several weeks and attended a school where we learned how to read vehicle schematics and identify various [military] vehicle parts." According to his discharge papers, the Army identified his military specialty as "Stock Control Specialist."

With the arrival of spring, in 1967, came Jobe's transfer to the 2nd Armored Division at Ft. Hood, Texas. For nearly six months, he was assigned to a supply office and assisted in ordering repair parts for the division's equipment. He was then transferred to 5th Battalion, 46th Infantry—a newly activated battalion that was building up personnel and equipment for service in Vietnam. While stationed at Ft. Hood, his wife moved to the area and was able to find employment. However, when Jobe's unit deployed to Vietnam in March 1968, his wife returned to Missouri to be closer to family.

"It took us about six months to get the unit ready to go," Jobe recalled. "The entire time I was working to get my parts section to one hundred percent-plus." He added, "The plus was to have more parts and equipment on hand than we were authorized because the more experienced guys said that we would need it when we got overseas."

The battalion set up at a location called LZ Gator (LZ is a military acronym for "landing zone") that was two or three miles south of Chu Lai and about the same distance from the South China Sea, Jobe said. "It was on a hill that had been stripped of all vegetation and I got very little sleep the first week because of small arms and artillery firing all night."

In Vietnam, they were assigned to the 198th Infantry (part of the "America Division") and Jobe worked for a motor sergeant named Sergeant Grant, operating a parts section out of a wooden frame building with a tin roof. However, ordering parts was often a wasted effort since vehicle parts were in short supply, thus requiring the soldiers to locate any needed items through alternative means.

"It got to the point where you couldn't get some of the parts to keep the Jeeps and other vehicles running and the Army would just salvage them," said Jobe. "We eventually found where the salvage yard was located and we'd take a mechanic with us to sneak in and remove the part we needed to get one of our Jeeps running."

Oftentimes, he had the additional duty of delivering weapons such as rifles, machine guns and grenade launchers to the 198th Infantry in Chu Lai for repairs, explaining that even if their vehicles did not work, their weapons needed to.

"There were many times when the soldiers from Companies A through E would leave the area for seek and destroy missions," he explained. "When that happened, I would get pulled to perform guard duty not only along our perimeter, but also along the perimeter of the artillery unit on the hill next to us."

In October 1968, Jobe received notice that he was approaching his discharge date and was to be sent home. Since it was the height of the monsoon season and the roadway leading into LZ Gator was nearly flooded, he was sent to Chu Lai a day early to begin the discharge process. From there, he traveled to Cam Ranh Bay, Vietnam, for additional processing and boarded a military plane bound for Guam. The final leg of his journey was to Fort Lewis, Washington, where he received his discharge from the Army.

"When he got to Ft. Lewis, they found out that we had not been given water or food for about forty-eight hours," Jobe said. "So the guys in the mess hall were nice enough to fix us a steak dinner at around 8:00 p.m. that evening to welcome us home."

After returning from the war, the veteran reunited with his wife and the couple went on to raise a daughter. Jobe briefly returned to his job with the dealership in Eldon, but then went to work for the former McKay Buick in Jefferson City, retiring after a thirty-one-year career as their parts manager.

The Vietnam veteran recognizes his service to the country occurred during a tumultuous period in the nation's history. However, he explained, it was service that was mandated by the Army and the reception he received upon returning from Vietnam was anything but appreciative.

"A lot of people thought you were wrong for even going over there, but I didn't have a choice—I was drafted," he affirmed. "I guess I could have ran off to Canada, but I wasn't going to do that to my country." Somberly, he added, "My motor sergeant, Sgt. Grant, was scheduled to come back home the March after I came home, but he was killed when our hill was overrun a few weeks before his scheduled return."

With sober reflection, he concluded, "I was quiet about my service for many decades and a lot of people didn't even know that I had been in Vietnam. But after I visited the Vietnam Wall in the early '90s and saw the names of some of the men that I served with, I guess that's kind of when I began sharing my story." *(Photograph courtesy of Charles Jobe)*

Walter Foster

Sedalia

One thing that many young people search for after graduating from high school is a little direction in their lives, seeking out answers as to what might be their calling. For Mid-Missouri veteran Walter Foster, the way he found resolution to this ageless concern came from his decision to enlist in the United States Air Force. A native of Mississippi, Foster graduated from high school in 1969 and began taking classes at a local junior college.

"After a semester, I decided I wasn't ready to be back in school," Foster chuckled. "That's when I decided to join the Air Force because a lady with the draft board had told me that I would probably be drafted once I left school." Foster added, "Shortly after I enlisted, I received my draft notice and probably would have been sent to the Army had I not already joined the Air Force."

The young recruit's journey began in March 1970 when he traveled to Lackland Air Force Base (AFB), Texas, for eight weeks of basic training, followed by several weeks of specialized training at Ft. Lee, Virginia, where he learned to become a cook.

"Let's just say that becoming a cook was one of those situations that I did not choose—the Air Force knew that's where people were needed at that time so that is where they sent me," he laughed.

When he finished his cook school in early summer, he returned to Mississippi on a thirty-day leave before beginning his first overseas duty assignment with a service squadron on the air base in Osan, Korea. For the next thirteen months he was in Korea, Foster explained, he provided meals to the airmen stationed on "Site 91"—a radar surveillance post located more than sixty miles from Osan.

"Although I was assigned to Osan, I worked three days on and three days off at the radar site," Foster said. "It was a small station that maybe had three buildings and ten personnel assigned, and myself and another cook would prepare the meals."

When his tour ended in October 1971, he and a friend stationed at Osan received orders back to the states, which were assignments they viewed as less than favorable. Instead, Foster said, he and his friend volunteered for an opportunity that seemed to offer a little more excitement and the chance to "see more of the world."

"They were looking for cooks to volunteer for Vietnam, so we did," he said. "They sent me to a service squadron in Saigon and I began working as a cook in one of the mess halls—I believe it was the biggest dining facility over there," he added. Shortly after his arrival, Foster volunteered to work in the "in-flight kitchen," preparing box lunches for pilots and flight personnel, a job requiring him to work six—and sometimes seven—days a week to help keep up with the frenetic mission schedules.

"About twelve months into my tour, I was sent home on leave, and when I came back [to Vietnam], I was sent to work in the mess hall on Bien Hoa [an air base located fourteen miles northeast of Saigon that was used by the United States during the war]," Foster recalled.

For the remaining six months of his overseas tour, Foster continued to prepare meals in the base's mess hall, all the while enduring frequent rocket attacks. One of these attacks, Foster explained, pointing out a newspaper clipping he saved, resulted in the death of twelve South Vietnamese and the destruction of two American jet bombers in late August 1972—after a barrage of fifty-one Soviet-made 122mm rockets slammed the base.

The Vietnam veteran returned to the United States in January 1973 after receiving orders to report to 351st Combat Support Group at Whiteman AFB in Knob Noster, Missouri. While there, he spent the next several months working three-day alert tours as a rations cook at the various Minuteman II missile launch control facilities scattered across western Missouri.[110]

"While I was stationed at Whiteman, there was a dance on base and that's where I met Joyce," Foster recalled. "We fell in love and were married several weeks later."

In September 1973, Foster was discharged from active duty under "Palace Chase"—a program that allows active duty airmen with a remaining obligation to transfer to a reserve component to finish their enlistment. Foster returned to Mississippi and completed the next two years of his obligation with the Air National Guard. Following his discharge in 1975, he and his wife came back to Missouri and he continued his service in the Missouri Air Guard from 1976 to 1978. Full time, he spent a couple of years as a dining facility supervisor at Whiteman and then went to work for Waterloo Industrial in Sedalia, Missouri, eventually retiring in 2012 after thirty-four years of employment.

"Many years ago I was called into the ministry," Foster said. "I always had an inkling that I someday wanted to be a pastor," he added.

In addition to raising four children with his wife, the Air Force veteran served many years as associate pastor with Ward Memorial Baptist Church in Sedalia and was ordained in the ministry in 2000. Since 2003, he has served as pastor of Prairie Grove Baptist Church in Tipton, Missouri.

A man of many remarkable experiences, Foster insists that although his service in the military added direction and meaning to his life, his return from service in Vietnam has remained a very personal event forever ingrained in his memories.

"When I arrived in California on my way back from Vietnam, many of the people I encountered hated us—they hated anyone that was in a military uniform," Foster said. "It was actually so bad that

---

[110] According to the Missouri Department of Natural Resources, The State of Missouri was host to 165 Minuteman II missile sites managed by the U.S. Air Force (USAF) from 1964 until 1997.Missouri Department of Natural Resources, *Minuteman II Missile Sites*, www.dnr.mo.gov.

you removed your uniform and put on civilian clothes because they would just as soon spit on you as look at you."

With momentary reflection, he added, "It made me angry the way we were treated because we were just doing our job, but in more recent years, with the wars in Iraq and Afghanistan, there's been more support for those in the military and even us Vietnam veterans have finally begun receiving the welcome home we never had before. For some, it might seem a little late, but it's a good thing." *(Photo courtesy of Walter Foster)*

Gary Elliott

Lohman

For twenty-two years, Gary Elliott wore the uniform of a United States sailor, making the trip "around the world one and a half times." When reflecting on his experiences in exotic and interesting locations, Elliott affirms that regardless of either the hardships or pleasant memories from his naval past, it was an adventure that will never be forgotten and made possible by the support of his wife.

"I became a sailor in 1965 and I'm still a sailor to this day," said Elliott of Lohman, Missouri. "It's just a mindset that never leaves you."

Enlisting in August 1965, Elliott dreamed about joining the Navy as early as eight years old. However, receipt of his notice to take his physical during the era of the Vietnam War draft motivated his decision to join of his own accord. The young enlistee traveled to Great Lakes, Illinois in late August 1965, where he completed his basic training and was immediately assigned to the *USS America*—a supercarrier commissioned only months prior to his arrival.

"When I stepped aboard the ship at Pier 12 in Norfolk [Virginia]," Elliott explained, "it was the day that I turned nineteen years old."

Aboard the ship for its maiden voyage, the young sailor from rural Missouri received his first exposure to foreign lands, visiting countries such as France , Italy, Spain and Lebanon. However, Elliott said, since he was lacking in rank, he was relegated to duties that progressed from working as a mess cook to the maintenance and operation of large forklifts.

"I really just felt like I wasn't getting anywhere," he said.

Eventually, he was able to attend aviation ordnance school and traveled to Jacksonville, Florida for a year of training. From there, he began a lengthy assignment in aviation when he was sent to Moffett Field, California and was attached to a P-3 Orion Squadron. The Orion, Elliott said, was a Naval aircraft used to patrol the coasts for such clandestine threats as Soviet submarines.

"After I was at Moffett for a few months, I discovered that we would soon deploy and that sped up some of my plans," he smiled.

This news, he explained, served as his inspiration to return to Missouri on September 10, 1967 and marry his fiancée, Carol Fischer, who would in later years accompany him on many of his duty assignments.

Throughout the next several years, Elliott's duties primarily included service aboard an Orion airplane engaged in several six-month overseas deployments to locations such as Iwakuni, Japan, during which, he added, they would drop "sonobouys"—an expendable sonar system—in the ocean to help detect the presence submarines.

When his enlistment ended in 1970, the sailor made the decision to leave the service, but reenlisted in early 1972 after finding out that his wife was pregnant.

"I had been attending Lincoln University full-time on the GI Bill and didn't have insurance [for his child's birth]," Elliott said. "No insurance...no job—I just thought that it was time to go back in."

Elliott completed maintenance training for the F-4J—a twin-engine jet fighter/bomber—followed by nearly ten months of service on the USS Saratoga, which deployed to the Gulf of Tonkin during the Vietnam War and served as a platform to launch aircraft for bombing missions. While aboard the ship, he learned that he had become father to his first and only child, a son named Michael. The next few years were just as frenetic as the previous as he returned to flying with a Navy patrol squadron after attending training to became an anti-submarine warfare technician.

"This time I was not only loading and dropping the sonobouys, but I was also analyzing the information they were transmitting," he said.

He later deployed to the Naval Air Station at Kelflavik, Iceland, spending two years helping to train the Icelandic Defense Force and assisting with the storage and maintenance of weapons. He then returned to a P-3 Orion Squadron and was assigned to Barber's Point in Hawaii. However, after the Navy transitioned to a new patrol aircraft, he discovered his "ordnance" position had been phased out.

The final assignment of his career began in 1984 when he traveled to the Naval Air Station at Oceana, Virginia, where, for the next three years, he worked on weapons systems for various aircraft. Following his retirement from the Navy in 1987, Elliott and his family returned to Lohman. He went on to earn his certification in HVAC and refrigeration and worked many years in the industry, permanently retiring from the industry in 2010. The former sailor has continued his legacy of public service with the church council at St. Paul's Lutheran Church, as an alderman for the community of Lohman and by participating in many events to support veterans.

When considering all of the moves and uncertainties associated with this military career, Elliott asserts it was the support of his family that has been the foundation of his career.

"I'm glad I got to see the things we got to see and visit the places that we did," said his wife, Carol. "But I must admit, the deployments were very difficult...especially when they were back to back because it seemed like every time he was gone something happened—the car would break down, our child was born," she smiled.

Despite any hardships, she concluded, it was an experience that helped to create many wonderful and enduring memories for the family.

"Whatever obstacles came our way, you just went through it because you had to," Carol said. "I can say that it was all certainly worth it and that I am very proud of everything that my husband accomplished in his military career." *(Photo courtesy of Gary Elliott)*

REYNOLDS, LARRY W. CAPT, USAF

Larry Reynolds

Jamestown

When graduating from Jamestown High School in 1964, Larry Reynolds recognized an opportunity to continue his education through the University of Missouri-Columbia, participating in the schools' Air Force ROTC program. It was a decision that would later find him working around missiles with a nuclear yield of 1.2 megatons, which helped serve as a deterrent in a Cold War with the Soviet Union.

"I knew that I wanted an education and the ROTC program helped pay for that education," Reynolds said. "While I was in college, I married my sweetheart, Sue, and I went on to finish my bachelor's degree in accounting in January 1969," he added.

Commissioned a second lieutenant with the United States Air Force upon graduation, Reynolds was assigned to the former Kincheloe Air Force Base in the Upper Peninsula of Michigan. The young officer was soon greeted with the weight of responsibility in his first duty assignment. As he explained, the base had crews assigned from the Strategic Air Command who used the airstrip for the Boeing B-52 Stratofortess, a strategic bomber, and an aerial refueling aircraft known as the KC-135 Stratotanker.

"I was a twenty-two-year-old second lieutenant with no active duty military experience when I got there," he explained. "I reported on a Monday, inventoried and then signed for a million dollars' worth of equipment." He added, "The next day, the officer I was sent to replace left for another duty assignment."

Assigned as a data processing officer for the 4609th Support Group, Reynolds had responsibility for twenty-five enlisted airmen and thirty-five different computer systems ranging from aircraft maintenance networks to those used by a civil engineering squadron to track base housing.

"I had to support the commissary, personnel systems, maintenance, inventory of nuclear weapons and supply systems...just to name a few," he affirmed.

Accompanied by his wife on the tour, the first three years of his Air Force experience passed quickly because of his responsibilities on base. However, in 1972, now a first lieutenant, he received orders for Whiteman Air Force Base near Knob Noster, Missouri, where he began a new mission that bequeathed him an entirely new level of accountability. Selected for "missile duty," he departed Whiteman for four months of training at Vandenberg Air Force Base in California. While there, he learned the missile operations to include the equipment used, security protocols and the launch control facility. This included simulated training scenarios that not only prepared the officers to launch missiles in a time of war, but also demonstrated how to respond in emergencies such as fires or losses of power.

"Everything is done by a very detailed checklist," he said.

With his training complete, Reynolds returned to Whiteman and became a certified crewmember for the Minuteman II—an intercontinental ballistic missile with a 1.2 megaton nuclear warhead. During the height of the Cold War, Whiteman Air Force Base had oversight of the 150 Minuteman II missiles concealed in underground silos throughout western Missouri.

"I began to go on alerts in launch control center," Reynolds said. "There were fifteen launch control centers in Missouri and each center had operational control of ten missile locations."

The alerts, he explained, generally extended for two days. A commander and deputy commander worked in an underground "capsule" behind a ten-ton blast door at the launch control facility, monitoring missile activities during a twelve-hour shift. A second crew came to relieve the first crew, who would then go to an upper level of the facility for twelve hours of rest, later returning for another twelve-hour shift.

"In all, I pulled alert at most of the fifteen different launch control facilities," he said. Discussing the characteristics of the weapons with which he worked, Reynolds added, "The missiles were said to have been so accurate, the warhead could be dropped onto a soccer field in Moscow."

Achieving the rank of captain, Reynolds earned his MBA while stationed at Whiteman and remained in the missile program for three years. The officer was discharged in March 1975 after completing a little more than six years of service.

"I could have stayed in, but Vietnam was ending and I had a lot of friends who were pilots and held the rank of captain, but they were discharged because they didn't make major," he recalled. "Since I didn't have my [pilot] wings, I figured it was just a matter of time before I was downsized, too."

He and his wife returned to the Jamestown area and raised a son and daughter. In the years following his Air Force service, the veteran completed a career with the state of Missouri, worked fourteen years for an insurance group and, though he has since retired, continues to operate his own accounting business.

Acknowledging that his time in the Air Force may not be considered as the front lines of combat, Reynolds maintains that he and his fellow missile crewmembers—in addition to support staff—provided a level of defense that helped deter an attack on the United States.

"We knew the level of destruction the missiles could deliver," he said. "While we were in the first two days of our initial missile training, we were shown the destructive capabilities of nuclear armament through films of Hiroshima and Nagasaki in World War II. After that training, they sent us back to our homes and told us to come back the next morning after deciding if we could do the job, which meant they needed airmen who would launch the missiles if ordered to do so."

With momentary hesitation, he concluded, "You had to be able to resolve that issue with yourself. Fortunately, the missiles were available but never had to be used." *(Photograph courtesy of Larry Reynolds)*

Silver Star Families of America Commendation Award

A non-profit based out of Clever, Missouri, primary mission of the Silver Star Families of America is to support and recognize veterans who are wounded, injured, or have acquired an illness related to their service in a combat zone—regardless of service branch or military conflict. In keeping with this mission, the founders, president and board of the SSFOA conduct an election process to select the winner for the organization's premier honor—the SSFOA Commendation Award. The annual commendation may be awarded to military or civilian personnel, and departments or organizations that have positively affected the lives of wounded and ill veterans.

In 2016, the band *3 Doors Down* was selected for the distinguished honor for their unwavering support of the military community through USO shows and Armed Forces Entertainment events, visiting wounded warriors at military and veteran medical facilities, active support of charitable organizations which support the nation's veterans and military members, and their dedication to recruitment efforts of the National Guard through their song *Citizen/Soldier*. The commendation was presented backstage during a concert the band played in St. Louis during the summer of 2016. *(Photo courtesy of Tina Amick)*

Works Cited

Newspapers

Asbury Park Press (Asbury Park, New Jersey)
California Democrat (California, Missouri)
Daily Capital News (Jefferson City, Missouri)
Daily Oklahoman (Oklahoma City, Oklahoma)
Democrat and Chronicle (Rochester, New York)
Evening Missourian (Columbia, Missouri)
Folsom Telegraph (Folsom, California)
Franklin County Tribune (Union, Missouri)
Honolulu Star-Bulletin (Honolulu, Hawaii)
Houston Herald (Houston, Missouri)
Jefferson City Post-Tribune
Macon Republican (Macon, Missouri)
Macon Times-Democrat (Macon, Missouri)
Miami Daily News (Miami, Oklahoma)
Morning Chronicle (Manhattan, Kansas)
Nashua Reporter (Nashua, Iowa)
New Castle News (New Castle, Pennsylvania)
Portsmouth Herald (Portsmouth, New Hampshire)
Reading Times (Reading, Pennsylvania)
Scott County Kicker (Benton, Missouri)
Sedalia Democrat (Sedalia, Missouri)
Sedalia Weekly Democrat (Sedalia, Missouri)
Signal Enterprise (Wabuansee County, Kansas)
St. Louis Post-Dispatch
St. Louis Star and Times
Tipton Daily Tribune (Tipton, Indiana)

Tipton Times (Tipton, Missouri)
Washington Herald (Washington, D.C.)
Waterloo Press (Waterloo, Indiana)

Books and Articles

Arnold, Mark (ed.). *The Best of Harveyville Fun Times!* (Saratoga, CA: Fun Ideas Productions, 2006).

Berleson, Dr. Arthur. *War Dogs: The Birth of the K-9 Corps.* (U.S. Army Military History Institute). Accessed December 4, 2018. https://www.army.mil/article/7463/war_dogs_the_birth_of_the_k_9_corps.

Berlin, Ira; Reidy, Joseph; and, Leslie Rowland. *Freedom: A Documentary History of Emancipation, 1861-1867.* (New York, NY: Cambridge University Press, 1982).

Bushnell, Col. George E. *Tuberculosis. (U.S. Army Medical Department: Office of Medical History).* Accessed April 18, 2017. http://history.amedd.army.mil/booksdocs/wwi/communicablediseases/preface.html

Cagle, Malcolm & Manson, Frank. *The Sea War in Korea.* (Annapolis, MD: Naval Institute Press, 2000).

Company "M," 356th Infantry Regiment: Camp Funston, Kansas to Schweich, Germany. *Organization and Training.* (Trier, Germany: Gebr. Koch,1919).

Crowder, Enoch H. *The Spirit of the Selective Service.* (New York: The Century Company, 1920).

Curatola, John M. *Bigger Bombs for a Brighter Tomorrow: The Strategic Air Command and American War Plans at the Dawn of the Atomic Age, 1945-1950.* (Jefferson, NC: McFarland & Company, Inc., 2016).

Edwards, Evan A. *From Doniphan to Verdun: The Official History of the 140th Infantry.* (Lawrence, KS: The World Company, 1920).

Ford, James E. *A History of Jefferson City and of Cole County.* (Jefferson City, MO: The New Day Press, 1938).

Foss, Kenneth. "6th Field Artillery Regiment makes Ft. Drum its home." *The Mountaineer Online,* June 19, 2014. http://www. drum.army.mil/mountaineer/Article.aspx?ID=8477 (accessed May 27, 2017).

Gansser, Emil B. *History of the 126th Infantry in the War with Germany.* (Grand Rapids, MI: 126th A.E.F. Association, 1920).

Gillen, Michael. *Merchant Marine Survivors of World War II: Oral Histories of Cargo Carrying Under Fire.* (Jefferson, NC: McFarland and Company, Inc., 2015).

Gordosi, George & Thomas Phillips. *Leave No Man Behind: The Saga of Combat Search and Rescue.* (Minneapolis, MN: Zenith Press, 2008).

Gossman, D. Charles. *Occupying Force: A Sailor's Journey Following World War II.* (Lincoln, NE: iUniverse, Inc., 2003).

Grothoff, Ray. *Man of Two Worlds: A German Family Confronts the American Dream.* (Morrisville, NC: Lulu Press, Inc., 2009).

Greeley, Horace. *The American Conflict: A History of the Great Rebellion.* (Hartford, CT: O.D. Case & Company, 1865).

Heefner, Gretchen. *The Missile Next Door: The Minuteman in the American Heartland.* (Cambridge, MA: Harvard University Press, 2012).

History of the Missouri National Guard. *The 140th A.E.F.* (Published by Authority of the Military Council, Missouri National Guard, November 1934).

Hitch, Lt. Col. A.M. *Will Rogers, Cadet: A Record of His Two Years as a Cadet at the Kemper Military School.* (Boonville, MO: Kemper Military School, 1935).

Hougen, Lt. Col. John H. *The Story of the 34th Infantry Division.* (Literary Licensing, LLC, 2012.)

Hudnall, Ken & Sharon. *Spirits of the Border IV: The History and Mystery of New Mexico.* (El Paso, TX: Omega Press, 2005).

Hudson, James J. *Hostile Skies: A Combat History of American Air Service in World War I.* (Syracuse, NY: Syracuse University Press, 1968).

Jaroszyńska-Kirchmann, Anna D. *The Exile Mission: The Polish Political Diaspora and Polish Americans, 1939-1956.* (Athens, OH: Ohio State University Press, 2004).

Johns, Maj. E.B. *Camp Travis and Its Part in the World War.* (New York, NY: Wynkoop Hallenbeck Crawford Co., 1919).

Kamphoefner, Walter & Wofgang Helbich. *Germans in the Civil War: The Letters They Wrote Home.* (Chapel Hill, NC: University of North Carolina Press, 2006).

Kemper Military School 1923-1924 Catalog. *The School.* (Boonville, MO, 1923).

Lee, Van. *Vin Rouge, Vin Blanc, Beaucoup Vin, the American Expeditionary Force in WWI.* (Hattiesburg, MS: Realms of Mertox Productions, 2004).

McManus, John C. *The Americans at Normandy: The Summer of 1944—The American War from the Normandy Beaches to Falaise.* (Forge Books, 2005).

McMaster, James S. *McMaster's Commercial Cases for the Banker, Treasurer and Credit Man: Current Business Law from the Decision of the Highest Courts of the Several States, Volume 20, October 1916 to October 1917.* (Wall Street, NY: The McMaster Co., 1917).

Missouri State Board of Agriculture. *Wartime Farming in Missouri.* (Monthly Bulletin, Volume XV, Number VIII, April 1917).

Moniteau County Historical Society. *Moniteau County Missouri History 2000.* (Marceline, MO: Walsworth Publishing Company, Inc., 2000).

National Historical Annual of Missouri. *Fourth Missouri Infantry.* (Baton Rouge, LA: Army and Navy Publishing Company, 1939).

Newman, John J. *Uncle, We are Ready! Registering America's Men 1917-1918.* (North Salt Lake, UT: Heritage Quest, 2001).

Order of Battle (Volume 3, Part 1). *Air Service.* (Washington, D.C.: Center of Military History United States Army, 1988).

Page, James M. & M.J. Haley. *The True Story of Andersonville Prison: A Defense of Major Henry Wirz.* (New York, NY: The Neale Publishing Company, 1908).

Pepper, Jim. *Not Your Ordinary Vietnam War Stories.* (Bloomington, IN: AuthorHouse, 2013).

Report of the Adjutant-General and A.Q.M.G. of the State of Iowa to Hon. Horace Boies. *General Orders No. 21.* (Des Moines, IA: G.H. Ragsdale, State Printer, 1891).

Report of the Quartermaster General, U.S. Army, to the Secretary of War (1919). *Remount Depot.* (Washington, D.C.: Government Printing Office, 1920).

Romanelli, Otto C. *Blue Ghost Memoirs: USS Lexington CV-16, 1943-1945.* (Paducah, KY: Turner Publishing Company, 2002).

Sharpe, Henry G. *The Quartermaster Corps in the Year 1917 in the World War.* (New York: NY: The Century Co., 1921).

Shipley, David. *Neither Black nor White: The Whole Church for a Broken World.* (Word Books, 1971).

Soli, Tatjana. *The Lotus Eaters.* (New York, NY: St Martin's Press, 2010).

Statler, Gregory. *The Insurrectos Attack. (U.S. Army Heritage and Education Center, November 15, 2007).* Accessed April 18, 2017. *https://www.army.mil/article/6134/the-insurrectos-attack.*

Treadwell, Mattie E. *United States Army in World War II: Special Studies: The Women's Army Corps.* (Office of the Chief of Military History, Department of the Army; First Edition, 1954).

United Spanish War Veterans. *Souvenir Book of the Forty-Ninth Annual National Encampment.* (Kansas City, MO: August 24-28, 1947).

United Spanish War Veterans. *Proceedings of the Stated Convention of the 49th National Encampment United Spanish War Veterans: Kansas City, Missouri (August 24-28, 1947).* (G.P.O., 1948).

Online Resources

26th Infantry Division. *Unit History of the 26th Infantry Division: Prelude to Combat.* Accessed October 8, 2018. http://www.yankee-division.com/history.html.

34th Infantry Division Association. *Division History.* Accessed October 9, 2018. http://www.34ida.org/history/.

506th Parachute Infantry Regiment. *Unit History.* Accessed November 2, 2018. https://www.ww2-airborne.us/units/506/506.html.

Atomic Heritage Foundation. *Operation Crossroads.* Accessed November 12, 2018. https://www.atomicheritage.org/history/operation-crossroads.

Brundage, John F. & G. Dennis Shanks. *Deaths from Bacterial Pneumonia during 1918-19 Influenza Pandemic.* (Emerging Infectious Diseases 14.8 (2008): 1193–1199). Accessed May 10, 2017. https://www.ncbi.nlm.nih.gov/pmc/articles/PMC2600384/citedby/.

Camp Roberts Historical Museum. *The History of Camp Roberts.* Accessed December 2, 2018. http://www.camprobertshistoricalmuseum.com/Mission.html.

Cooper County Genealogical Society. *Strickfadden Cemetery.* Accessed February 2, 2017. http://cooper.mogenweb.org/.

Department of Veterans Affairs. *Jefferson City National Cemetery.* Accessed April 22, 2017. https://www.cem.va.gov/cems/nchp/jeffersoncity.asp.

First Cavalry Division. *WWII, Pacific Theater.* Accessed May 2, 2017. *http://www.first-team.us/assigned/subunits/7th_cr/7crndx02.html.*

Fort Jackson, South Carolina. *History of Fort Jackson.* Accessed April 21, 2017. http://jackson.armylive.dodlive.mil/post/museum/history-post-wwii/.

History.com. *Cu Chi Tunnels.* Accessed April 20, 2015. http://www.history.com/topics/vietnam-war/cu-chi-tunnels.

History.com. *Berlin Wall Built.* Accessed April 28, 2017. http://www.history.com/this-day-in-history/berlin-wall-built.

Idaho Military Museum. *Farragut, Idaho: Where Fightin' Blue Jackets Were Made!* Accessed December 1, 2018. https://museum.mil.idaho.gov/farragut.html.

Kansas Historical Society. *Camp Funston.* Accessed December 1, 2018. https://www.kshs.org/kansapedia/camp-funston/16692.

Library of Congress. *Fitzhugh Lee.* Accessed April 4, 2017. https://www.loc.gov/rr/hispanic/1898/lee.html.

Library of Congress. World War I: Conscription Laws. Accessed December 1, 2018. https://blogs.loc.gov/loc/2016/09/world-war-i-conscription-laws/.

Missouri Department of Natural Resources. *Minuteman II Missile Sites.* Accessed April 21, 2017. https://dnr.mo.gov/env/hwp/fedfac/MinutemanII.htm.

Missouri Digital Heritage. *Soldier's Records: War of 1812 – World War I.* Accessed April 29, 2017. https://s1.sos.mo.gov/records/archives/archivesdb/soldiers/#soldiersearch.

Moniteau County Cemetery Book. *Tipton Colored Cemetery.* Accessed February 10, 2017. www.moniteau.net.

National Archives and Records Administration. *World War I Draft Registration Cards.* Accessed April 15, 2018. https://www.archives.gov/research/military/ww1/draft-registration.

National Association of the 6th Infantry Division. *A Brief History of the U.S. Army 6th Infantry Division, by Thomas E. Price, on Behalf of the National Association of the 6th Infantry Division, Inc.* Accessed December 2, 2018. *https://www.6thinfantry.com/a-brief-history-of-the-us-army-6th-infantry-division-by-thomas-e-price-on-behalf-of-the-national-association-of-the-6th-infantry-division-inc/.*

National Park Service. *Andersonville.* Accessed March 2, 2017. https://www.nps.gov/ande/learn/historyculture/camp_sumter.htm

The Nike Historical Society. *Hercules MIM-14, MIM-14A, MIM-14B.* Accessed February 28, 2017. http://nikemissile.org/IFC/nike_hercules.shtml.

Nineteenth Engineer Battalion. *History.* Accessed December 19, 2018. https://www.knox.army.mil/partners/19eng/history.aspx.

NS Great Lakes. *History.* Accessed August 1, 2017. http://www.mybaseguide.com/navy/21-584.

Palm Beach County History Online. *U.S. Military in Boca Raton.* Accessed December 18, 2018. http://www.pbchistoryonline.org/page/us-military-in-boca-raton.

The Patriot Files. *7th Infantry Division, "Bayonet!"* Accessed December 30, 2018. http://www.patriotfiles.com/index.php?name=Sections&req=viewarticle&artid=2885&page=1

Sawyer, Amanda. *Camp MacArthur*. Accessed May 10, 2017. http://wacohistory.org/items/show/48.

Texas State Historical Society. *Camp John Dick*. Accessed May 10, 2017. *https://tshaonline.org/handbook/online/articles/qccwv*.

The Spanish-American War Centennial Website. *6th Missouri Volunteer Infantry*. Accessed April 19, 2017. http://www.span-amwar.com.

United States Artillery. *Coast Artillery Journal (November-December 1946)*. Accessed December 18, 2018. http://sill-www.army.mil/ada-online/coast-artillery-journal/_docs/1946/11-12/Nov-Dec%201946.pdf.

United States Department of the Interior: Bureau of Land Management. *McGregor Range*. Accessed February 28, 2017. https://www.blm.gov/nm/st/en/prog/recreation/las_cruces/mcgregor_range.html.

United States Department of the Interior: National Register of Historic Places Inventory. *Blees Military Academy*. Accessed April 2, 2017. https://dnr.mo.gov/shpo/nps-nr/79001380.pdf.

USS Hassayampa (AO-145) Veteran's Association. *Ship's History*. Accessed April 14, 2015. http://www.usshassayampa.com/Ship's%20History.htm.

Western Front Association. *Brothers in Arms*. Accessed May 10, 2017. http://www.westernfrontassociation.com/great-war-people/brothers-arms/81-going-down-of-the-sun.html#sthash.CNfQ1ETY.dpbs.

Widener, Chuck. *The Big Guns: Armed with .50 Caliber Weapons and the Knowledge They Can Die in Their Next Mission, Aerial Gunners Stand up to the Best the Enemy Can Muster*. Accessed May 10, 2017. https://www.thefreelibrary.com/The+big+guns%3A+armed+with+.50-caliber+weapons+and+the+knowledge+they...-a0110619958.

Yockelson, Mitchell. *They Answered the Call: Military Service in the United States Army During World War I, 1917-1919*. Accessed April 26, 2017. https://www.archives.gov/publications/prologue/1998/fall/military-service-in-world-war-one.html.

Index

CPSIA information can be obtained
at www.ICGtesting.com
Printed in the USA
FFHW012345060319
50862902-56261FF

9 781950 034239